A Guide to English Educational Terms

A Guide to English Educational Terms

Peter Gordon &
Denis Lawton

Batsford Academic and Educational Ltd *London*

Typeset by Deltatype, Ellesmere Port
and printed in Great Britain by
Billing & Sons
London & Worcester

for the publishers
Batsford Academic and Educational Ltd
4 Fitzhardinge Street
London W1H 0AH

British Library Cataloguing in
Publication Data

Gordon, Peter, 1927–
  A guide to English educational
  terms.
  1. Education—Dictionaries
  I. Title   II. Lawton, Denis
  370'.3'21   LB15

ISBN 0–7134–4375–8
ISBN 0–7134–4376–6 Pbk

Contents

Acknowledgements

We would like to thank a number of friends and colleagues who have been kind enough to comment on many of the entries in the Guide and to suggest items for inclusion: Richard Aldrich, Edwin Cox, Alan Crispin, Vincent Curnow, Harvey Goldstein, Janet Harland, John Honey, Alan Hornsey and Elizabeth and Neville Jones. The staffs of the University of London Institute of Education Library and the Department of Education and Science Library were unfailingly helpful in tracking down several obscure references and we are especially indebted to Michael Humby and Mark Staunton for making their bibliographical knowledge available to us. Our thanks are due to David and Tessa Gordon and Joan Lawton for their help at the proof-reading stage. We are also grateful to the many organizations which have supplied us with information. Finally, we are pleased to acknowledge the help of Joyce Broomhall and Suzie Gibbons in preparing the typescript for publication.

Introduction

Our purpose in writing this Guide is a fairly modest one: for many years we have been involved in trying to make the English educational system – in so far as it exists – more comprehensible to students, some from overseas, all of whom have found some difficulty in identifying the meaning of some words in educational usage as well as in knowing the exact functions of some educational institutions. This Guide is an attempt to clarify this area, to enable newcomers to the field to find their way a little more easily, and even to give specific guidance to those who are reasonably familiar with the world of education, but cannot be expected to know the whole field equally well.

In an effort to keep the Guide to a reasonable size, we have decided not to attempt to make the book a comprehensive coverage, but to concentrate on educational terms commonly used in connection with England and Wales. Only a few examples from the Scottish system are included, usually for obvious reasons. Similarly, we have made no attempt to include words which may be common in the educational systems in the United States of America, but which have not found a place in England.

We have, however, deliberately included a number of terms which might be labelled 'historical' rather than 'contemporary'. We have done this partly because many historical terms still have a certain currency, but also because we feel that anyone seriously interested in the English educational system cannot get very far in understanding that system without a certain historical background. Nevertheless, our 'historical' entries are intended more for the general reader than the professional historian.

Only in one sense have we attempted to make the book a little more than a glossary: where we felt it appropriate we have included one or two books which would help the reader to penetrate more deeply either into a fuller explanation or into some of the controversies which inevitably exist in a field as complex as education. Although the book is not intended as a guide to educational literature, we did feel that in some cases, rather than attempting to lead the reader through a good deal of detail, it would be more economical to include one or two key references which would provide reasonably up-to-date coverage.

Finally, we have made no attempt to convert this Guide into anything like an encyclopaedia of education. Readers will not find entries for individuals, however famous, but named reports such as Plowden are included.

We hope to bring the Guide up to date from time to time, and we would be glad to hear from any readers about inaccuracies or items which they feel should have been included.

Peter Gordon and Denis Lawton

May 1983

How to use the book

Those readers who are completely new to the English education system may find it helpful to begin by reading the outline of it which starts on p. ix. For those particularly concerned with the historical development of the system we have included a chronological list of 'Landmarks' in that development (p. xii). Readers already familiar with education in England will tend to use the main section – the Alphabetical Guide – as a dictionary, looking up individual terms in it; it should be noted that some words in the text are printed in bold type to indicate that separate entries will be found elsewhere in the Guide under corresponding headings. To look up an acronym (such as DES, EIS, etc.) the reader should first consult the 'Educational acronyms' section (p. 211) to establish what it signifies; the relevant entry may then be located in the Alphabetical Guide.

An outline of the education system in England and Wales

The compulsory school age in England and Wales begins at the start of the term in which a child is 5 years old. The minimum leaving age is 16.

There are two types of schools within the publicly maintained system – *county schools*, which are directly under the LEA, and *voluntary schools*, which are established by religious denominations, but are financially maintained by LEAs.

The following outline does not claim to list the large range of educational institutions which exist in the system, but is intended merely as a guide. Many of the institutions mentioned appear under the appropriate heading in the Guide.

Nursery

For children between 3 and 5 years, LEAs may provide, without charge to parents, *nursery schools* or *nursery classes* attached to primary schools. There are also *private nursery schools* and *pre-school playgroups* which are locally organized and privately run.

Primary

At the age of 5 a child enters a primary school. This may be either an *infant department* of a primary school or a separate *infant school*. At 7, the child moves to either the *junior department* of a primary school or a separate *junior school*, and remains there until 11 years of age.

An alternative pattern is found in LEAs where a three-tier system of schooling exists. Following the Plowden Report, Circular 10/65 suggested a variety of types of reorganization in order to provide comprehensive schools. *First schools* may cater for pupils between 5 and 8 or 9. The child then moves on to a *middle school* which can be 8–12, 9–13 or 9–14 schools. It is only the 8–12 range which is classified as primary.

In the private sector, there are *preparatory schools* which cater for children between 5 and 11 or 7 and 13.

Secondary

There is a variety of types of secondary schools. Where *grammar schools* still exist, the age range is 11–18 years: this applies also to many *comprehensive schools*. *Secondary modern schools* tend to provide an 11–16 education, but many pupils stay on beyond this age. As explained earlier, *middle schools* of the 9–13 or 9–14 age range are classified as secondary. Pupils from middle schools may go on to comprehensive schools which start their intake at 13 or 14 years.

In some areas, pupils may either remain at their school after compulsory leaving age and enter the sixth form, elect to join a *sixth form college*, or attend a *further education college*. Where LEAs have decided to provide post-16 further education courses as well as sixth form courses, pupils in that age range will attend a *tertiary college*.

Outside the State system, there are independent secondary schools, the best known of which are the so-called *public schools*. The age range is 11 or 13 to 18. Unlike most State schools, many of them have boarding facilities.

Note At both primary and secondary levels, special education is provided for physically and mentally handicapped children. This may take the form of *special schools* or special classes within ordinary schools.

Further and higher education

'Further education' refers to all forms of non–university post-school education, but it can be divided into advanced and non–advanced education, according to the level of courses offered. 'Higher education' is, for most purposes, coterminous with advanced further education. From 1966, there has existed a 'binary system' of higher education in England: it consists of universities and the 'public' sector colleges, the latter being for the most part more tightly controlled.

The public sector includes *adult education centres, tertiary colleges, colleges of further education, technical colleges, colleges of commerce* and *colleges of technology*. In this sector, *polytechnics*, university-level institutions, are responsible for the bulk of advanced work. Their courses, up to and including degrees, are validated by the Council for National Academic Awards. Smaller than the polytechnics but at a similar level are the *colleges* or *institutes of higher education*. Many were formerly *colleges of education*, some of which still exist. The colleges of higher education were created by a merger of two or more institutions. The training of teachers still forms part of their commitment.

On the other side of the binary line are the *universities*, which grant degrees to students who have as a rule successfully followed a three- or four-year course of study. Postgraduate studies form an important aspect of university work. These may take the form of either a higher degree course, or a diploma course.

One-year teacher training courses are available at most universities as well as polytechnics.

The control of education

It is often been claimed that education in England and Wales is a national system which is locally administered: that is, major policy is the responsibility of the central authority (the DES), but local education authorities (LEAs) have some latitude in the interpretation and implementation of central policies and recommendations. Thus there is no uniform pattern of primary/secondary schools, and LEAs varied considerably in the way they responded to central policy on comprehensive schools.

Traditionally the DES has been reluctant to exert too much pressure on LEAs, but since the bulk of the finance for educational expenditure comes from central government, control can sometimes be exerted by a threat to withhold funds. Only a small proportion of educational finance is raised locally from the rates.

About half the money spent on education by LEAs comes from central government. The balance of expenditure is met from local rates and from additional miscellaneous income, e.g. fees from evening classes and school-meal charges. The DES is concerned with basic educational standards and educational objectives, but does not exercise direct control over either the content of education or teaching method.

Landmarks in the development of English education since 1800

1802 *Health and Morals of Apprentices Act*. Apprentices to receive some instruction in the three Rs.

1816–18 *Select Committee on the Lower Orders* (Brougham). Inquiry into the educational provision for the poor.

1833 First government grant for education: £20,000 for elementary education.

Factory Act. Children at work between 9 and 13 to attend school 2 hours per day.

1839 *Committee of the Privy Council on Education* established. The beginning of a national education policy and the appointment of the first two HMIs.

1840 *Grammar Schools Act*. Allowed grammar schools to teach subjects other than Greek and Latin.

1853 *Science and Art Department* formed at South Kensington to encourage scientific and technical instruction for the industrial classes.

1856 *The Education Department*, with a Minister responsible for education, superseded the Committee of the Privy Council on Education.

1861 *Report of Royal Commission into the State of Popular Education in England* (Newcastle). Advocated cheap and sound elementary education for the poor.

1862 *Revised Code*. Introduction of 'payment by results'.

1864 *Report of the Royal Commission on the Public Schools* (Clarendon). An investigation into the endowments, finances, methods, subjects and teaching of nine leading schools.

1868 *Report of the Schools Inquiry Commission* (Taunton). An examination of some 800 endowed grammar schools. The Commission recommended that they should be divided into three grades according to social class.

1870 *Elementary Education Act.* Introduced by W. E. Forster, its intention was to provide efficient elementary schools in England and Wales. Elected school boards provided accommodation together with denominational bodies and marked the beginning of the dual system.

1872–5 *Report of Royal Commission on Scientific Instruction and the Advancement of Science* (Devonshire). Urged the development of science teaching at university and school levels.

1880 *Education Act.* The work of A. J. Mundella, it made education obligatory for the majority of children until the age of 10.

1882–4 *Report of Royal Commission on Technical Instruction* (Samuelson). Promoted technical education in elementary and secondary schools and highlighted the need for technical colleges.

1888 *Report of Royal Commission on Elementary Education Acts* (Cross). Commissioners were divided in their views, but all aspects of elementary education considered.

1889 *Technical Instruction Act.* Allowed county and county borough councils to levy a penny rate for technical education.

1891 *Elementary Education Act.* Made the great majority of public elementary schools free.

1895 Ending of 'payment by results'.

Report of Royal Commission on Secondary Education (Bryce). Called for well-organized system of secondary education in England with one central authority.

1899 *Board of Education Act.* A central body, the Board of Education, was set up in the following year with three branches, elementary, secondary and technological and headed by a President.

1902 *Education Act.* Known as the Balfour Act, after the Prime Minister, A. J. Balfour, it created local education authorities (LEAs) to promote all forms of education. Many county secondary schools and training colleges were established.

1905 *Handbook of Suggestions for Teachers.* Centralized control of the curriculum by regulations supplemented by *Handbook* suggesting approaches to teaching.

1907 *Free Places in Secondary Schools.* Regulations allowed free places for 25 per cent of secondary school population.

1911 *Report of Consultative Committee on Examinations in Secondary Schools.* Supported a system of public examinations at sixteen.

1917 *Secondary School Examinations Council* set up, an advisory body to co-ordinate the standards and methods of examinations. School Certificate examination introduced.

1918 *Education Act,* the work of H. A. L. Fisher, President of the Board of Education. The Act proposed raising the school leaving age to fifteen and providing compulsory part-time education up to eighteen.

1923 *Report of Consultative Committee on Differentiation of Curriculum for Boys and Girls.* Exposed the differences in opportunities available to boys and girls in secondary education.

1926 *Report of Consultative Committee on the Education of the Adolescent* (Hadow). Recommended the separation of primary and secondary education at the age of 11. Suggested two types of secondary school, the grammar and modern, for different types of child.

1931 *Report of Consultative Committee on the Primary School* (Hadow). Proposed a progressive curriculum for the junior part of the primary school, based on psychological research. Beginnings of the modern primary school curriculum.

1933 *Report of Consultative Committee on Infant and Nursery Schools* (Hadow). Recommended separate infant schools and the provision of a national system of nursery schools.

1938 *Report of Consultative Committee on Grammar and Technical High Schools* (Spens). Recommended a tripartite system of secondary schools – grammar, technical and modern – each with appropriate curriculum.

1943 *Report of Consultative Committee on the Secondary School Examinations Council* (Norwood). Reinforced views of Spens Report on tripartitism: also suggested the replacement of School Certificate.

1944 *Report of Committee on Supply, Recruitment and Training of Teachers and Youth Leaders* (McNair). To raise the status of teachers, suggested increasing teachers' salaries and proposed three years' training.

Education Act. R. A. Butler, President of the Board, was responsible for the Act. Reforms included provision for raising the school leaving age to fifteen and education was to be organized in three progressive stages – primary, secondary and further. Religious instruction was to be a compulsory element in the curriculum.

1945 *Report of Special Committee on Higher Technological Education* (Percy). Recommended the upgrading of some technical colleges to Colleges of Advanced Technology with new high level awards in technology.

Ministry of Education, with a Minister as head, replaced the Board of Education.

1951 Introduction of the *General Certificate of Education* examination.

1959 *Report of Central Advisory Council, 15 to 18* (Crowther). Recommended raising the school leaving age to 16 and condemned overspecialization in sixth forms.

1960 *Report of Departmental Committee on the Youth Service* (Albemarle). Called for an extension of age range covered by the Service and an expansion of its work.

Report of Committee on Secondary School Examinations (Beloe). Recommended the Certificate of Secondary Education for pupils of lesser ability.

1963 *Report of Central Advisory Council, Half Our Future* (Newsom). Considered the appropriate education of average or less than average ability children between 13 and 16 years.

Report of Committee on Higher Education (Robbins). Recommended the expansion of higher education in the 1970s.

1964 *DES Report of Working Party on Schools' Curricula and Examinations* (Lockwood). Led to setting up of Schools Council for the Curriculum and Examinations in the same year. It took over the work of the Secondary School Examinations Council.

The Department of Education and Science created, headed by a Secretary of State, in place of the Ministry of Education.

1965 *DES Circular 10/65. The Organization of Secondary Education.* Outlined six ways in which LEAs could reorganize schools for comprehensive education.

1967 *Report of Central Advisory Council, Children and their Primary Schools* (Plowden). Recommended positive discrimination in education, the expansion of nursery education and strengthening the links between home and school.

1968 *Report of Committee of Enquiry into Flow of Candidates in Science and Technology into Higher Education* (Dainton). Confirmed the belief that numbers of sixth form pupils in science not increasing. Recommended mathematics throughout school life and delay of decisions concerning science until as late as possible.

1970 *DES Circular 10/70. The Organization of Secondary Education.* The Conservative Government cancelled Circular 10/65 and allowed LEAs discretion in submitting comprehensive reorganization schemes.

1972 *Report of Committee of Enquiry into Teacher Education and Training* (James). Recommended reorganization of teacher training into three cycles and stated the need for in-service training for teachers. A new qualification, the Diploma in Higher Education, was to be introduced.

DES White Paper, A Framework for Expansion. Colleges of education to move away from being monotechnic institutions. Validation from CNAA was encouraged. The White Paper warned that fewer teachers would be needed in future.

1974 Assessment of Performance Unit set up by DES for assessing and monitoring pupils' achievement.

1975 *Report of Committee of Inquiry, A Language for Life* (Bullock). The Committee examined the role of language in education. Primary school teachers should devise a language policy: secondary schools were to develop a policy for language across the curriculum.

Sex Discrimination Act. The Equal Opportunities Commission set up to ensure fairness to girls and women in education.

1976 *Education Act.* Labour Government required LEAs to send in schemes for comprehensive education. Direct grant schools either joined the maintained system or became independent.

'*Great Debate*' on education launched by the Prime Minister, James Callaghan, at Oxford.

1977 *Report of Committee of Enquiry. A New Partnership for Our Schools* (Taylor). Recommended a widening of the powers and representation of interests on governing bodies.

Green Paper: Education in Schools. A Consultative Document. Summarized the discussion of the 'Great Debate' on aspects of curriculum, standards and assessment, teachers and school and working life.

1978 *Report of Committee of Enquiry into the Education of Handicapped Children and Young People* (Warnock). Recommended the integration of handicapped children into ordinary schools.

Report of Steering Committee to consider proposals for replacing GCE O level and CSE by a common system of examining (Waddell). The Committee found that a single system of examining at 16+ was feasible.

1979 *Education Act.* Conservative Government repealed 1976 Act and allowed LEAs powers to arrange for secondary school provision.

1980 *Education Act.* 'Parents Charter'. Schools to provide information about courses, LEAs to enable parents to express preference for schools with appeals procedure. Scheme of assisted places at independent schools established.

1981 *Education Act.* Dealt with children with special educational needs, following the recommendations of the Warnock Report.

Department of Employment White Paper. A New Training Initiative. A Programme for Action. Guaranteed a year's training for 16- to 17-year-old school leavers, consisting of industrial experience and off-the-job training in further education.

1982 Proposed establishment of a *School Curriculum Development Committee (SCDC)* and a *Secondary Examinations Council (SEC)* in place of the Schools Council was announced.

1983 *Secondary Examinations Council* (Chairman Sir Wilfred Cockroft) and the *School Curriculum Development Committee* (Chairman Professor R. Blin-Stoyle) were formed.

An Alphabetical Guide to Educational Terms

A

Aberdare Report
See **intermediate education.**

ability groupings
See **mixed ability grouping, setting, streaming, unstreaming.**

Abitur
The West German examination for 18- to 19-year-old school leavers. Like the **GCE A level** in England, it is a university entrance qualification as well as being recognized as a general educational qualification for entry into some kinds of employment. Unlike A level it is a broadly based examination, more like the French *Baccalauréat.*

academic
1. A teacher or researcher in **higher education**.
2. An adjective applied to scholarly activities, sometimes as a term of abuse.

academic board
A group of academic staff in a college or university normally elected in order to regulate academic affairs. Usually one of the most senior committees, possibly responsible only to the senior governing body of the institution. The **Weaver Report** recommended that academic boards should be established and properly constituted in all **colleges of education**. Academic boards rarely exist in schools, but it is sometimes suggested that such an organization would be highly desirable.

academic disciplines
See **disciplines, academic.**

academic year
Term used to indicate the annual period of attendance at institutions for study. The academic year in **higher education** institutions tends to be from October to July and in **further education** and schools from September to July, but there are variations at all levels in the starting and finishing dates. The academic year of the **Open University** is from January to December. (*See also* **half-term, semester, term, vacation.**)

accountability
A metaphor imported from business and commerce into education during the 1960s, especially in the USA. Accountability reflects an increased public concern over educational issues such as **curriculum** and not simply the large sums of money involved. (*See also* **Assessment of Performance Unit, 'Great Debate', performance contracting, William Tyndale School.**)

A. BECHER, M. ERAUT and J. KNIGHT, *Politics of Educational Accountability,* Heinemann, 1981

M. ERAUT, 'Accountability and Evaluation', in B. SIMON and W. TAYLOR (eds), *Education in the Eighties,* Batsford, 1981

action research
A study of a particular social situation (which might or might not be concerned with education) in which the intention is not simply to understand and report, but to bring about certain improvements. A well-known educational example concerned the study of **educational priority areas (EPA).** (*See also* **research and development**).

A. H. HALSEY, *Educational Priority: EPA Problems and Policies*, Vol. 1. HMSO, 1972

active learning
See **passive learning**.

active vocabulary
The words that an individual speaker not only has available in terms of recognizing their meaning and appropriateness but also is able to *use* either in speech or in writing, or in both. (*See also* **passive vocabulary**.)

administrative memorandum
A type of memorandum issued by the **DES** to **LEAs**, advising them on policy or on statutory or administrative changes. It is similar to a **Circular**.

admissions to schools
LEAs differ in their policies on admission procedures. They may either allow parents to choose schools within an area and then try to match demand with available accommodation or operate a zoning system, whereby choice is restricted to a **catchment area**. The 1980 Education Act stipulated that LEAs must publish their admittance arrangements. Under Section 5 of the Act, parents can express a preference for any school, either within the LEA or outside, though this choice is subject to a number of conditions: for example, it does not apply where schools are selective and the child does not meet the admission requirements, or if special education is needed. It applies also to special admission arrangements, as may happen in some **voluntary schools**, or if such choice would prejudice the provision of efficient education and the efficient

use of resources. Parents can use the new appeals procedure set up under the Act if they wish to do so. (*See also* **appeals against admission decisions, special educational needs**.)

adult education
Courses of an informal character provided for adults in a range of interests: these are usually held in institutions different from colleges and universities attended by school leavers. They range from leisure pursuits to higher degree qualifications. For example, there are residential colleges such as Coleg Harlech and Hillcroft College for longer term courses; the **Open University**, BBC and IBA which co-operate in providing courses involving **distance learning**; and **WEA, extra mural departments** and evening institutes, which offer short courses in many areas of knowledge. It has recently been suggested that there should be a statutory entitlement of a year's education for those over 18 years of age, to be taken as and when required. (*See also* **community college, continuing education, recurrent education, Russell Report, village college**.)

ADVISORY COUNCIL FOR ADULT AND CONTINUING EDUCATION, *Adults: their educational experience and needs, outreach*, ACACE, Leicester, 1982

C. D. LEGGE, *The Education of Adults in Britain*, Open University Press, 1982

adult literacy
The setting up of an Adult Literacy Research Agency in 1975 was the first official recognition of the large proportion of the adult population in need of literacy skills. A national campaign was mounted and local

authorities and voluntary agencies were given short-term financial assistance in starting their schemes. In 1978, an Adult Literacy Unit was established but was replaced in 1980 by an Adult Literacy and Basic Skills Unit (ALBSU), which covers other areas such as English as a second language and **numeracy**. Shortage of money and lack of physical resources has hampered the work. In 1979, it was calculated that only 8% of the adult population in need of literacy help had been receiving assistance. The Unit is also tackling the problem of numeracy. A recent survey has shown that one adult in three finds difficulty with simple subtraction, division or multiplication and one in ten cannot do simple addition. (*See also* **National Institute of Adult Education**.)

ADULT LITERACY UNIT, *Adult Literacy 1979/80: Report to the Secretary of State for Education and Science*, HMSO, 1982

advanced further education (AFE)

Term covering courses in all publicly maintained non-university higher education institutions leading to a qualification above the **Ordinary National Certificate (ONC)** or **GCE A level** standard.

advisers

Advisers, sometimes called inspectors or organizers, are employed by **LEAs** to ensure the efficient functioning of the education institutions within an authority. Whilst many aspects of advisers' work, such as inspecting and reporting on schools, advising on curriculum and other matters and improving the professional expertise of teachers, overlap with those of

HMIs, there are a number of differences. LEA advisers are responsible for supervising teachers in their first post and during the completion of their probationary period. (For untrained graduates, this task is shared with HMIs.) They assist in the appointment of staff in the authority's schools and are in a position to be knowledgeable about teachers seeking promotion. Advisers are responsible to the **Chief Education Officer (CEO)** and give advice on allocation of money in the authority's estimates and inform him of new developments, for example, in educational methods. The advisory service spans the whole range of primary and secondary schools and in some cases of further education also. Not all subject areas are covered except in the largest authorities and the size of the team varies considerably from authority to authority. A recent national survey of advisers highlighted their training needs in such areas as evaluation of teachers and institutions and in supervision skills. (*See also* **full inspection**, **probation**, **Schools Council**, **William Tyndale School**.)

R. BOLAM, G. SMITH and H. CANTER, *LEA Advisers and the Mechanics of Innovation*, NFER, 1979

Advisory Centre for Education (ACE)

A non-profit making organization stemming from the Consumers' Association, ACE disseminates information on many aspects of schooling. Its house journal *Where?* has been a sounding-board for many important issues. Since its foundation in 1960, ACE directors have included Michael Young, Brian Jackson and

Eric Midwinter. (*See also* **Home and School Council**.)

Advisory Committee on the Supply and Education of Teachers (ACSET)

ACSET is the latest in a line of such committees and councils. Between 1949 and 1965, the **National Advisory Council on the Training and Supply of Teachers (NACTST)** produced nine reports. It was revived under the title of Advisory Committee for the Supply and Training of Teachers (ACSTT) in 1973, but ceased to operate after the general election of 1979. The present Committee was set up in April 1980 and operates through sub-committees which look at, for example, **in-service education** and school staffing standards. The membership of the Committee includes a wide range of interest groups. It has not yet been resolved whether the function of the Committee is to advise the **Secretary of State** and the **DES** or to act as a sounding board for the Department's policy options.

D. SAMPLE, 'Good Advice for the DES', *Times Educational Supplement*, 18 July 1980

advisory teachers

Experienced teachers who are appointed or seconded for a short term by an **LEA** to advise school staff. They work closely with **advisers** but have the advantage of recent classroom experience.

aesthetic

A term, increasingly used in discussions of a balanced curriculum, to indicate those subjects or areas of experience by means of which a pupil is introduced to the world of 'beauty' (e.g. art, music, literature). The philosophical basis for this distinction dates back to Immanuel Kant (1724–1804), who wished to avoid the confusion of aesthetic, moral, useful and pleasurable criteria. An opposite point of view was taken in England by William Morris and John Ruskin, who did not wish to accept the separation of art and morality.

P. H. HIRST, *The Logic of the Curriculum*, Routledge and Kegan Paul, 1970

P. H. PHENIX, *The Realms of Meaning*, McGraw-Hill, 1964

affective

In Benjamin Bloom's *Taxonomy of Educational Objectives* (1956) a distinction is made between the cognitive, the psychomotor and the affective domains, the affective being concerned with emotions, feelings and attitudes rather than with cognitive processes or physical skills.

B. S. BLOOM, D. R. KRATHWOL et al., *Taxonomy of Educational Objectives*, Handbooks 1 and 2, Longman, 1956

age: chronological and mental

Chronological age is the everyday usage of an individual's age defined in terms of time since date of birth. For educational purposes, it is sometimes useful to compare chronological age with mental age or reading age. Mental age is calculated by comparing a child's score on an **intelligence test** with the average scores of children. For example, a child might have a chronological age of 8 and a mental age of 10, that is, she/he is mentally advanced for her/his years and is capable of reasoning at the same level as the average 10-year-old – she/he would thus have an above average **IQ** (*see* **intelligence**).

age of transfer
Up to 1964, the age of transfer from **primary** to **secondary schools** was between 10½ and 12 years of age. The Secretary of State in that year encouraged experiments in different sorts of schools, especially the **middle school**, which recruits pupils of between 8 and 12 or 13. The present situation is very confused. Throughout the country, transfers are made at many different ages, according to the educational planning of **LEAs**.

age participation rate (APR)
A term used in calculating demand for **higher education** (and sometimes **further education**). The age participation rate for higher education is calculated by showing the number of 18-year-olds who wish to enter higher education as a proportion of the whole group. It has often been remarked that the age participation rate for England and Wales is much lower than that of other advanced industrial societies – that is, a smaller percentage of the population attends university and other forms of higher education.

agreed syllabus
The 1944 Education Act stipulated that **LEAs** together with Church and teacher representatives, should draw up an agreed non-denominational syllabus in **religious education**, the only compulsory area of the school curriculum. Authorities were not restricted to using their own and the West Riding of Yorkshire Syllabus was widely used. More recently, the Hampshire Syllabus, which takes a broader view, drawing on different living faiths as well as Christianity, has gained popularity.

Agreement to Broaden the Curriculum (ABC)
A document drawn up in 1961 by A. D. C. Peterson, then Director, Oxford Department of Education, together with secondary school **headteachers** which aimed at allowing students to keep open their subject options as between Arts and Sciences until the end of the fifth year. This would allow **sixth form** choices to be made on the basis of previous experience. Those schools who subscribed to the document agreed to devote at least one-third of the time in sixth forms to non-specialist work.

aims
Statements of educational intentions or purposes of a more general nature than **objectives**. Although all the three terms (aims, goals and objectives) are sometimes used synonymously they are increasingly used distinctively to represent three levels of intention from the most general aims to the more specific objectives. 'Aims' became unfashionable with educational theorists in the 1960s and were explicitly avoided in the **Plowden Report**. But recently philosophers, e.g. John White and Anthony O'Hear, have returned to the concept.

A. O'HEAR, *Education, Society and Nature: an introduction to the philosophy of education*, Routledge and Kegan Paul, 1981

J. P. WHITE, *The Aims of Education Restated*, Routledge and Kegan Paul, 1982

Albemarle Report

A Departmental Committee on the Youth Service in England and Wales under the chairmanship of Lady Albemarle reported in 1960. It recommended that the Government should establish an emergency training college for youth leaders and also a Youth Service Development Council to superintend a national building programme. The report was accepted by the Government: a training college was set up at Leicester, a Council was formed and a small building programme was approved. (*See also* **McNair Report, Thompson Report, Youth Service**.)

Report of the Departmental Committee on the Youth Service in England and Wales, HMSO, 1960

A level (Advanced level examination)

The Advanced level of the **General Certificate of Education** (GCE) is an examination taken by more able pupils, usually after a two-year period of study following **O levels**. It is closely associated with the traditional sixth form of a school, replacing in 1951 the **Higher School Certificate**. A wide range of subjects is available at A level, though candidates normally choose two or three to study. This specialization and narrowness has been criticized, but attempts at its reform such as **Q and F** or **N and F** have not been successful. Passes in at least two A level subjects are normally required for admission to university or to **undergraduate** courses in polytechnics. (*See also* **General Certificate of Education, Ordinary National Certificate, Schools Council, S level**.)

all-age school

A school in which pupils would spend the whole of their school life from perhaps the age of 5 onwards. This pattern had been universal in **elementary education** in the last century, but separate **infant schools** were common by the 1920s. The **Hadow Report** (1926) recommended a break at the age of 11, though over a third of 13-year-olds were in all-age schools in 1949. All-age schools now no longer exist in the State system.

alternative education

A general term used to indicate a form of schooling which is very different from that offered by the State or other traditional agencies. Alternative education is normally, but not necessarily, associated with radical and progressive views of education such as the avoidance of a formal curriculum and formal teaching methods. (*See also* **compulsory education, deschooling, free school**.)

I. LISTER (ed.), *Deschooling: a reader*, Cambridge University Press, 1974

E. REIMER, *School Is Dead*, Penguin, 1971

ancillary staff

Non-teaching members of an institution who assist in its everyday running, for instance, **Media Resources Officers** and laboratory technicians. (*See also* **dilution**.)

AO level (Alternative O level examination)

Graded at **General Certificate of Education O level** standard, the AO level is based on a limited range of subjects and is designed for more mature candidates. The examination is usually taken by pupils of at least 17 years of age. (*See also* **General Certificate of Education**.)

appeals against admission decisions

Section 68 of the 1944 Education Act gave the individual the right to appeal to the Secretary of State if the **LEA** was acting unreasonably on admissions. Under the 1980 Education Act, a new appeals procedure (Section 7) was introduced to meet parents' wishes on choice of schooling for their children. Special local committees were set up by each LEA to hear appeals, with their decisions binding on LEAs and **governors**. The success rate for appeals is about 15 per cent. (*See also* **admissions to schools**.)

ADVISORY CENTRE FOR EDUCATION, *School Choice Appeals. An ACE Handbook*, 1982

B. PASSMORE, 'If, at first, you don't succeed', *Times Educational Supplement*, 25 June 1982

aptitude

An individual's potential ability to acquire skills or knowledge (i.e. not an existing achievement). For example, there are tests available which are designed to indicate mechanical aptitude or mathematical aptitude. One problem of such tests is, however, that although they are intended to be predictive (i.e. indicating potential rather than actual achievement), they necessarily involve performance which may be partly dependent on **skills** already learned. (*See also* **attainment test**, **performance test**.)

aptitude test
See **aptitude**.

Architects and Buildings Branch, DES

The A and B Branch, in its present form, dates from 1949, with the appointment of a professional architect, Stirrat Johnson-Marshall, as its head, jointly with a **Ministry of Education** official. A development group within the branch was established to work closely with **LEAs** on school design. The publication of its Building Bulletins made the work of A and B Branch widely known. At the end of 1981, the DES announced that A and B Branch was to disappear and become part of a new Schools Branch II. (*See also* **open plan school**.)

M. SEABORNE and R. LOWE, *The English School, its Architecture and Organization, Vol. 2, 1870–1970*, Routledge and Kegan Paul, 1977

Area Training Organization (ATO)

The **McNair Report on Teachers and Youth Leaders** recommended that Area Training Organizations (ATOs), responsible for the co-ordination and validation of teacher training, should be established in each area. From 1947, specially created **Institutes of Education**, based on existing universities, were for the most part officially recognized as the ATOs. The Institutes, which had a federal structure, also provided in-service courses for teachers and taught masters' and research degrees in all aspects of education. As a result of the restructuring of teacher training, ATOs ceased to operate from August 1975.

ascertainment
Procedures laid down by statute to

determine a child's educational needs in consequence of his or her inability to follow a normal course of education.

assembly

A meeting in school time on school premises of more than one class of pupils. The assembly may be for information or leisure activities, but the 1944 Education Act stipulated that all county and voluntary schools must begin the day with an assembly for a collective act of worship. No specific religion is mentioned in the Act and parents may have their children withdrawn from the assembly. (*See also* **Agreed Syllabus, religious education**.)

D. SULLIVAN (ed.), *Reflections on Assembly*, Christian Education Movement, 1981.

assessment

Any means based on evidence of some kind for judging how much a student has learned or benefited from some kind of learning experience. Assessment is a wide, generic term which includes some specific techniques such as examinations and continuous **monitoring**. (*See also* **attainment test, evaluation, grade, halo effect, multiple choice test, profiles, special school, special educational needs**.)

H. G. MACINTOSH (ed.), *Techniques and Problems of Assessment*, Arnold, 1974

D. SATTERLEY, *Assessment in Schools*, Blackwell, 1982

Assessment of Performance Unit (APU)

This unit was established by the **DES** in 1974 following the White Paper on Educational Disadvantage and the Educational Needs of Immigrants (Cmnd 5720). Its terms of reference were 'to promote the development of methods of assessing and monitoring the achievement of children at school and to seek to identify the incidence of under-achievement'. Much of the work of the Unit has been concerned with the first task. It set out to assess children's development in six areas (a seventh, modern languages, was added later), namely, aesthetic, mathematics, science, social and personal, physical and language. In 1978, tests were administered, covering the performance in mathematics of 11- and 15-year-old pupils in England and Wales, followed by tests in foreign languages, language and science. The work of the APU has been criticized for its emphasis on assessment of standards rather than on the needs of disadvantaged children. After much discussion, it was decided not to proceed with tests of social and personal development. (*See also* **accountability, Educational Disadvantage Unit, monitoring, performance contracting**.)

DES, Report on Education 93, *Assessing the Performance of Pupils*, HMSO, 1978

C. GIPPS and H. GOLDSTEIN, *Monitoring Children*, Heinemann Educational, 1983

assignment

A task given to a pupil or student by a teacher either as part of a learning programme or as a means of **assessment**, particularly within the **Dalton Plan**. Assignments are usually set out as individual exercises, often for homework, but co-operative assignments are sometimes set for completion by two or more students. In primary schools 'assignment' tends to be used with much the same meaning as **'project'**.

assistant(e)
A person from abroad, either a student or a **graduate**, attached to a secondary school for a period of a year in order to help in the teaching of a foreign language. There is an official system of exchange sponsored by the **DES**.

assistant master
A male member of a school teaching staff who is not a **headteacher**, **deputy head** or **senior teacher**.

Assistant Masters and Mistresses Association (AMMA)
In 1978, the AMMA was formed from an amalgamation of the Assistant Masters Association and the Association of Assistant Mistresses. Membership is open to all classroom teachers working in **primary**, **secondary** or **further education**, but **headteachers** are not recruited. The AMMA attracts mainly secondary school staff, who make up 86% of the membership. The Association has over 90,000 members and is Britain's third biggest teachers' union. It lays great stress upon professionalism and, unlike the **NUT**, it is not affiliated to the Trades Union Congress. (*See also* **teachers' associations**.)

assistant mistress
A woman member of a school teaching staff who is not a **headteacher**, **deputy head** or **senior teacher**.

Assisted Places Scheme
This scheme, which was first included in the 1974 Conservative Party manifesto, now forms part of the 1980 Education Act and is designed to assist academically able children whose families could not otherwise afford the tuition fees to attend one of the 220 independent secondary schools in the scheme. The age of entry is usually 11 to 13, though many are admitted at sixth form stage. The scheme, which came into operation in September 1981, is expected to provide for between 5,000 and 6,000 children a year. At least 60% of all assisted place pupils at a school must have entered directly from an **LEA** or **Services school**. The scheme has been criticized by advocates of comprehensive schools on the grounds that it 'creams off' some of the most able pupils from those schools. (*See also* **creaming**, **Fleming Report**, **independent school**.)

DES, *Assisted Places at Independent Schools: a Brief Guide for Parents*, HMSO, 1980

Association of County Councils (ACC)
The 47 member counties of the ACC provide the major services for nearly 31 million people living in England and Wales. The Association, founded in 1974 and formerly the County Councils Association, puts forward policies for county government after receiving approval from its Executive Committee. It discusses issues with Ministers, Civil Servants and MPs and appears before **Select Committees**. Central to the ACC's work is the problem of finance. It argues its case with the Government through the Consultative Council on local government finance and at officer level through technical working groups. It also takes part in national negotiations on pay and conditions of

service for local authority employees. (*See also* **Council of Local Education Authorities.**)

Association of Education Committees (AEC)

The leading organization for education authorities from the 1944 Education Act until its dissolution in 1977, the AEC Executive consisted of **Chief Education Officers** and chairmen of Education Committees (*see* **local education authorities**). It played a powerful part in the **Burnham Committee** proceedings and was instrumental in persuading the Ministry of Education to create the **Certificate of Secondary Education** for **modern schools**. The General Secretary, Sir William Alexander, served the Committee for more than 30 years.

Association of Headmistresses (AHM)

This Association was founded in 1874 by nine secondary school headmistresses for the advancement of girls' secondary education and for the holding of annual conferences. From the beginning, the Association welcomed a wide range of secondary schools and there never existed a division corresponding to that between the **Headmasters' Conference** and the **Headmasters' Association**. From 1976, it became absorbed into the **Secondary Heads Association**. (*See also* **teachers' associations**.)

N. GLENDAY and M. PRICE, *Reluctant Revolutionaries. A Century of Headmistresses, 1874–1974*, Pitman, 1974

Association of Metropolitan Authorities (AMA)

There are 77 metropolitan authorities in England in seven metropolitan conurbations, providing all the services of local government. The AMA, which was formed in 1974, is funded by subscription from the metropolitan authorities. Its task is to keep them informed of what is happening in Government circles and to represent the authorities at governmental and parliamentary levels. Each major area of interest has its own service committee, and specialist staff deal with education, planning, housing, social services and legal matters. (*See also* **Council of Local Education Authorities.**)

Association of Polytechnic Teachers (APT)

The Association, started in 1973, now represents a fifth of the staffs of polytechnics in England and Wales, with over 3,000 members. In June 1981, it gained its first seat on the **Burnham Committee**. (*See also* **teachers' associations.**)

Association of University Teachers (AUT)

In 1909 a meeting was called in Liverpool 'to consider a proposal to form an Association for bringing the members of the Junior Staff more in touch with one another and with the life of the University'. From this sprang the AUT, which now represents the majority of university teachers and related associated administrative grades in professional and salary matters. (*See also* **teachers' associations.**)

H. PERKIN, *Key Profession. The History of the Association of University Teachers*, Routledge and Kegan Paul, 1969

attainment test
A test which is designed to measure the degree of **learning** which has already been achieved in a particular subject area, especially English and arithmetic, rather than the potential ability of an individual which might be measured by a specific **aptitude test**. (*See also* **performance test**.)

audio-visual aids (AVA)
Equipment for using recorded sound and visual images in schools and other educational institutions. A distinction is sometimes made between AVA hardware (equipment such as film projectors, television screens and audio players) and the software (e.g. films, audio tapes, film strips, slides). Posters, wall charts and other display materials are included in AVA, but not books. (*See also* **educational technology**, **educational television**, **Media Resources Officer**, **technology**.)

L. A. GILBERT, *Educational Audio-visual Materials: Directory of National Information Agencies*, Council of Europe, Strasbourg, 1980

Auld Report
A report for the **ILEA** drawn up by Mr Robin Auld, QC, who presided over a 14-week public inquiry in 1975 into the teaching, organization and management of the **William Tyndale School.**

*The William Tyndale Junior and Infants Schools; report of the public inquiry con-*ducted by Robin Auld into the teaching, organization and management of the William Tyndale Junior and Infants Schools, Islington, London N1. ILEA, 1976

autistic
Autistic children appear to be unable or unwilling to communicate with other individuals including their own parents. Even if such children are of average or above average intelligence they are likely to be educationally retarded; in the past they would probably have been considered to be mentally subnormal or classified as feeble-minded. The causes of autism are not known, but researchers in the field of special education have established improved methods of teaching autistic children, some of whom have been enabled to make considerable progress.

F. TUSTIN, *Autistic States in Children*, Routledge and Kegan Paul, 1981

autonomy
One of the aims of education in a democratic society – according to some *the* aim – is said to be the development of a pupil's ability to make rational decisions for himself or herself ('autonomously') rather than simply carry out instructions. Moral autonomy is thus the highest level of moral development. In England, autonomy as an **aim** in education is associated with Robert Dearden (*The Philosophy of Primary Education: an introduction*, Routledge and Kegan Paul, 1968).

B

Baccalauréat

School–leaving examination in French secondary schools which is used for admission to higher education. It is more like the German *Abitur* than the English **GCE Advanced level** in that it is broadly based rather than specialized, although in recent years a greater degree of specialization has been permitted. (*See also* **essentialism**, **International Baccalaureate**.)

Bachelor of Education (B.Ed.)

The **Robbins Report** (1963) recommended that the three year courses leading to a Teacher's Certificate should be replaced by a Bachelor of Education degree. It was to be awarded by a university and include a professional teaching qualification. The first B.Ed. degrees were awarded in 1968 by five universities, but they are now also offered by other institutions of higher education. The normal pattern is for a three year course (including **teaching practice**) to result in a pass degree, with honours awarded after an optional fourth year. It can also be taken by practising teachers on an **in-service** basis. (*See also* **Postgraduate Certificate of Education**, **qualified teacher status**.)

N. EVANS, *Preliminary Evaluation of the In-Service B.Ed. degree*, NFER, 1981

D. R. MCNAMARA and A. M. ROSS, *The B.Ed. Degree and Its Future*, School of Education, Lancaster, 1982

backwardness

Educational backwardness refers to a child whose attainment in basic skills of reading and arithmetic falls below the levels of achievement of those in his or her age group irrespective of **intelligence**. Backwardness should, therefore, be distinguished from educational retardation which arises, in the main, from low intelligence. Backwardness is capable of remediation but teachers have to be alert to a wide range of causative factors which may be physical, emotional, or environmental. (*See also* **special educational needs**.)

R. GULLIFORD, *Backwardness and Educational Failure*, NFER, 1968

F. J. SCHONELL, *Backwardness in the Basic Subjects*, Oliver and Boyd, 1942

banding

The division of a school year group into two, three or four bands, mainly on the criterion of ability. Each band is subdivided into a number of classes, though not necessarily of equal ability. (*See also* **mixed ability groupings**, **setting**, **streaming**.)

Barlow Report

A Committee on Scientific Manpower was appointed by the Lord President of the Council in 1945 and chaired by Sir Alan Barlow to consider the development of scientific resources in the following decade. It recommended that the output of science graduates should be doubled, from 5,000 to 10,000 a year, and that universities should be expanded to accommodate this expansion. Priority was to be given to teaching and fundamental research, the needs of the Civil Service, both Government and industrial, and defence science. The Committee also endorsed the findings of the **Percy Report** (1945) on higher education in the public sector and requested that urgent consideration be given to the development of two or three Institutes of Technology, preferably in university cities, to provide **graduate** and **postgraduate** courses at doctoral level.

Scientific Manpower: Report of a Committee Appointed by the Lord President of the Council, 1946, HMSO, Cmd 6824

Basic English

A phrase which ought to be used as a technical term rather than as a parallel to basic maths, basic science, etc. Basic English was developed between 1926 and 1930 by C. K. Ogden as a possible international language. Its basis was the listing of 850 commonly used key words which could communicate all ideas and any kind of message. However, it was increasingly used as a means of teaching English to foreigners rather than as a complete language in its own right. It was also used in some studies of 'readability' and graded reading.

C. K. OGDEN, *Basic English*, Kegan Paul, 1930

basic skills

Usually used to refer to those skills, especially in the **three Rs**, which provide the kinds of competency, such as being able to add up and multiply, which are thought to be necessary for participation in everyday adult life. The fallacy of this approach, for example, in reading skills, is that skills are divorced from content, so that first the child is taught to read, and at a later stage is taught to read something useful. Most modern reading specialists would advocate reaching stage two very quickly. A more correct use of 'basic skills'

would be to refer to those skills in any subject which are necessary to proceed to more advanced skills in the same area.

behavioural objective

A specific statement of intent by a teacher about the changes in behaviour that a student must show as a result of a teaching programme. The emphasis is on pupil or student behaviour rather than teacher behaviour or teacher intention. An essential feature of a behavioural objective is that the behavioural change must be specified in advance, in terms of student behaviour which can be measured. Opponents of the behavioural objectives approach criticize this view of curriculum planning for a number of reasons, including the suggestion that teachers will tend to concentrate on what is easily tested, that is, the most trivial aspects of a subject. Another criticism is that human learning is a much more complex process than this simplified view would appear to suggest. (*See also* **objectives**.)

L. STENHOUSE, *An Introduction to Curriculum Research and Development*, Heinemann Educational, 1975

Beloe Report

The terms of reference of a Committee appointed by the **Secondary School Examinations Council** were 'to review current arrangements for the examination of secondary pupils other than by the **GCE** examination, to consider what developments are desirable, and to advise the Council whether, and if so, what, examinations should be encouraged or introduced, and at what age levels.' The chairman was Mr

Robert Beloe. Its report, issued in 1960, recommended that a new examination, appropriate for pupils at the end of the fifth year of a secondary school course when they would normally be aged 16, should be devised. It was to be for candidates in the next 20 per cent of the ability range below those attempting GCE O level in four or more subjects. At least four subjects were to be taken: a further 20 per cent of the age group could attempt individual subjects. Two important points were emphasized: that the examinations should not simply provide a replica of GCE examinations but should be specially designed to meet the needs and interests of the pupils, and that they should be largely in the hands of the teachers who would use them. The **Ministry of Education** accepted these recommendations and consequently the **Certificate of Secondary Education** examination was created.

MINISTRY OF EDUCATION, *Secondary School Examinations other than GCE. Report of a Committee Appointed by the Secondary School Examinations Council*, HMSO, 1960

bilateral school
A school in which any two of three main elements of secondary education, i.e. **grammar**, **technical** or **modern**, were organized in clearly defined sides. Pupils, though on the same site, remained in their allocated courses during their secondary school life. Some local authorities after the Second World War retained separate grammar schools, confining bilateral schools to the technical and secondary modern streams. (*See also* **bipartite system**, **tripartite system**.)

binary system
In a speech given at Woolwich Polytechnic in 1965, Anthony Crosland, then Secretary of State for Education, announced the Labour Government's acceptance of a plan to develop a system of **higher education** within the further education sector, separate from the university sector. Crosland's plan was based on the different traditions of the two systems, the need to raise the status of higher education and a recognition of **LEA** control, through funding of the non-university sector. In 1966, the Government's White Paper, *A Plan for Polytechnics and Other Colleges: Higher Education in the Further Education System*, Cmnd 3006, substantially added weight to the argument, leading to the establishment of 30 **polytechnics** in the next six years. A further fillip was given with the addition of former **colleges of education** and the newly formed **institutes of higher education** in the 1970s. (*See also* **polyversity**.)

bipartite system
A system consisting of selective and non-selective schools, usually of the **grammar** and **secondary modern** type respectively.

Black Papers
The title adopted for a series of occasional publications first appearing in 1969 which have attacked modern teaching methods, the **Plowden** philosophy, the alleged decline in educational standards and comprehensive schools. They advocated the retention of selection for secondary education, and the provision of super schools for the gifted. Contributors consist of academics, teachers, writers, and politicians

holding right-wing views. They include G. H. Bantock, Rhodes Boyson, C. B. Cox, A. E. Dyson, Kingsley Amis, Cyril Burt and Jacques Barzun.

C. B. COX and A. E. DYSON (eds), *The Black Papers on Education*, Davis-Poynter, 1971

black studies

Courses, either in school, FE or HE, based on a study of the history and culture of black peoples. In such studies, the stress would normally be on the positive contributions made by black nations with a view to enhancing the self-image of black pupils. Black studies are usually designed for black pupils. It is sometimes argued that white pupils also need to be made aware, for example, of the quality of the African art and culture which existed before the arrival of the Europeans. Complaints are sometimes made of courses which give the impression that African history only began when the Europeans came. (*See also* **multi-cultural or multi-ethnic education**.)

Blue Book

A term used to describe Government publications bound in blue paper. These are usually bulkier reports than **White Papers**. **Royal Commissions**, **Departmental Committees** and **Select Committees** often appear in this form. (*See also* **Parliamentary Papers**.)

boarding school

Predominantly found in the private sector of education, boarding schools normally require their pupils to be resident during term-time. Special houses belonging to the school, under the supervision of a master or mistress, accommodate the pupils. In the State sector, the majority of such provision is for children with **special needs**. (*See also* **day school**, **house system**.)

DES, *Boarding Education: Report of a DES/CLEA Working Group*, 1980

Board of Education

The need for a single coherent central authority in education was recognized by the end of the last century. Accordingly, in 1899 Parliament approved the Board of Education Act. This led in the following year to the consolidation of the former **Education Department** and the **Science and Art Department** and the appointment of a President of the new Board, charged with the superintendence of education in England and Wales. Three branches of the Board, elementary, secondary and technological, were established to carry out the work. A fourth, the university branch, was formed in 1910. One of the main functions of the Board was to put into effect the provisions of the 1902 Education Act and ensure that the new **LEAs** provided well-maintained and efficient schools. It also administered grants, withholding them from authorities failing to comply with the Board's requirements. The Board was also responsible for establishing schemes for the constitution of Education Committees and making orders for **voluntary school** managers. In 1944, the Board was superseded by a **Ministry of Education**. (*See also* **President of the Board of Education**.)

L. A. SELBY-BIGGE, *The Board of Education*, Putnam, 1927

board school
See **school board**.

borderline
1. Those points on a scale of marks near (that is, on either side of) **cut-off points.** For example, if the pass/fail cut-off point is a mark of 40, then the range of marks 36 to 44 might be regarded as borderline. Similarly, in the marking of **honours degrees** there would be a cut-off point or mark for first class/upper second but the range of marks either side of the cut-off point would be regarded as borderline and normally subject to special scrutiny.

2. Candidates who fall into the category near the cut-off point are sometimes referred to as 'borderline'.

brain drain
A tendency for highly educated professionals to leave the home country in order to work in other countries where they are likely to be paid more, or to have better working conditions. In recent years, the term has been extended to cover those highly qualified **graduates** who leave the country because they are unable to find suitable employment within the UK.

W. A. GLASER, *The Brain Drain: emigration and return*, Pergamon, 1978

brain storming
A technique, originating in the USA, designed to encourage creative solutions to a problem or series of problems. A group of colleagues would meet to discuss a problem, but agree to suspend criticism until the concluding session. The theory is that by removing the fear of criticism, ideas flow more readily and much more creative solutions are generated.

British and Foreign School Society
The first public meeting of 'The Society for Promoting the Royal British or Lancasterian System for the Education of the Poor' was held in 1808. Joseph Lancaster's system, embracing a complete scheme of primary instruction, was unsectarian though Christian, and attracted many influential supporters, including Lord Byron and James Mill. It included provision at Borough Road for training monitors. The Society was reorganized as the British and Foreign Society in 1812. Flourishing societies were established not only in Great Britain but on the Continent and throughout the Empire. (*See also* **British schools**.)

H. B. BINNS, *A Century of Education: being the centenary history of the British and Foreign School Society 1808–1908*, Dent, 1908

J. R. CARR, 'Lancasterian Schools: A Reappraisal', *Durham Research Review*, Vol. 5, No. 24, 1970

British   Association   for Commercial   and   Industrial Education (BACIE)
Founded in 1919 by representatives of 49 leading firms who realized the need for an organization that would act as a guide to employers on recruitment and training policy, the Association has expanded and now deals with all aspects of vocational education and training. BACIE has developed a range of services for its members and offers courses for the training of trainees in member companies and for others wishing to develop their interpersonal and management skills.

British Association for the Advancement of Science (BAAS)

Commonly called the British Association, it was established in 1831 by a small group of scientists who were concerned to ensure that science and technology made their maximum contribution to the life of society. Its main platform is the Annual Conference, held in different centres of Britain, which meets in 17 different sections. The Conference proceedings, which are published, are intended to inform people of recent scientific advances and to stimulate public debate.

R. MACLEOD and P. COLLINS (eds), *The Parliament of Science: the British Association for the Advancement of Science, 1831–1981*, Science Reviews, Northwood, 1981

British Council

The Council was established in 1934 to develop closer cultural relations with and promote a wider knowledge of Britain in other countries. The majority of its funding is provided by the Foreign and Commonwealth Office. A large part of its activities is devoted to education, such as the teaching of English, providing educational assistance in developing countries and maintaining and running libraries. The Council is represented in more than 80 countries.

British Education Index (BEI)

A quarterly publication listing and analysing by subject content all articles on education appearing in periodicals published in the British Isles.

British school

A shortened term for Nonconformist schools established by the **British and Foreign School Society** from 1814. The majority of them became **State schools** after the 1870 Education Act.

Brougham Reports

Henry Brougham, later Baron Brougham, successfully moved for an inquiry into the state of education among the poor in the Metropolis in the House of Commons in 1816. A **Select Committee** on the Education of the Poor was appointed the same year with Brougham as chairman. In its report, the committee demonstrated that educational endowments for the poor were being misapplied and that there was a grave shortage of **elementary schools**. A second committee in 1818 reinforced the findings of the earlier report and recommended that government schools should be established to fill the gaps. An Education Bill, introduced by Brougham in 1820, proved abortive and no action was taken on these far-sighted proposals.

Reports of the Select Committee on the Education of the Lower Orders, 1816–18, P.P. 1816, iv; 1818, iv

Bryce Report

A Royal Commission was appointed in 1894 'to consider what are the best methods of establishing a well-organized system of secondary education in England'. The Commission, chaired by James Bryce, recommended in its report the following year three major reforms: the need for a central authority for secondary education under a Minister for Education; the extension to local authorities of responsibility for secondary as well as elementary education; and the provision of scholarships to provide a ladder of opportunity for elementary pupils. It also noted the comparatively meagre supply of secondary school places for girls, though some improvements had been effected since the time of the **Taunton Report**. Although the recommendations were not adopted, they were influential in subsequent changes made at the beginning of this century. (*See also* **eleven plus examination, girls' education, ladder of ability**.)

Report of the Royal Commission on Secondary Education, P.P. 1895, xliii–xlix

bulge

A metaphor used to indicate the increase in the number of pupils reaching a stage in the educational process. The term was used in the UK to indicate the increased demand for school places resulting from the increased number of births immediately following the Second World War. There was a second but less dramatic bulge beginning in 1958. The bulge was responsible for the shortage of teachers and overcrowded classrooms in the 1940s and early 1950s; when the bulge passed out of the system, the problem of **falling rolls** produced the reverse effect, namely, too many teachers and schools having to be closed. The bulge also caused problems subsequently in the higher education sector.

Bullock Report

The Committee of Inquiry appointed in 1972 by the Secretary of State for Education and Science and chaired by Lord (then Sir Alan) Bullock was given three tasks: to consider, in relation to schools, all aspects of teaching the use of English, including reading, writing and speech, to report on how present practice might be improved and to suggest ways in which arrangements for **monitoring** the general level of attainment in these skills could be introduced. In the Committee's report, issued in 1975 under the title *A Language for Life*, more than 300 conclusions and recommendations were listed. One reiterated the earlier **Newbolt Report's** maxim that every teacher should be a teacher of English, but linked this with the need for a systematic policy in schools. Language across the curriculum was advocated, starting with pre-school children and continuing through the secondary stage. It suggested that **LEAs** should appoint specialist English **advisers**, and qualified teachers be given responsibility for supporting colleagues in language and teaching of reading. Reading clinics or remedial centres in LEAs should be provided and screening procedures for pupils instituted. Together with a recommended increase in resources for English, especially in secondary schools, greater **in-service** facilities for teachers were necessary. Attention was also drawn to the need to assist adult illiterates and co-ordinate information and support on a national scale. (*See also* **language deficit**.)

DES, HMI Discussion Paper, *Bullock Revisited*, 1982

Report of the Committee of Inquiry, A Language for Life, HMSO, 1975

Burnham Committee

Named after its first chairman, Lord Burnham, the Committee met in

1919 to draw up national pay scales for elementary school teachers. Soon after, secondary and further education teachers' pay came within the Committee's remit. In 1945, the Burnham Agreement came into force, which established a single salary scale for primary and secondary teachers. There are two committees, one for primary and secondary schools, the other for further education. Each consists of two panels, one representing management, i.e. the employing local authorities, and the other the teachers. The latter panel consists of members of the **teachers' associations**. There are two **DES** officials on each panel. In the case of a dispute, both panels must agree before the issue goes to arbitration. In the past few years, two Government committees, **Houghton** (1974) and **Clegg** (1980) have also been involved in determining the level of **teachers' salaries**.

R. SARAN, 'The Politics of Bargaining Relationships During the Burnham Negotiations', *Educational Management and Administration*, Vol. 10, No. 2, June 1982

bursar
1. Originally a treasurer of a college, the term now applies to a school or college post which involves financial responsibilities and other duties such as the maintenance of the buildings of an institution. (*See also* **registrar**.)
2. Holder of a monetary award, a **bursary**, for maintenance of an education course.

bursary
An award, granted by an educational institution or other body, which assists the student in covering expenses for a course of study. (*See also* **entrance award**.)

business education
Several official reports on business education have been published since the end of the Second World War, including Carr-Saunders (1949), McMeeking (1959), Arnold (1960), Crick (1964) and **Haslegrave** (1969). The Crick Report recommended an award in business studies similar to the Diploma in Technology. As a result, business studies degrees were established in **polytechnics** and colleges. The report also called for a less vocational and more liberal interpretation of the business studies curriculum. The Haslegrave Report suggested the setting up of a **Technician Education Council** and a **Business Education Council**. Business studies is also offered as an A level examination. It was pioneered by the Wolfson Foundation in association with Marlborough College where the A level Business Studies Project was established in 1967. At university level, there are two institutions which are concerned with this field, the London Graduate School of Business Studies and the Manchester Business School. (*See also* **National Advisory Council on Education for Industry and Commerce**.)

W. W. DANIEL and H. PUGH, *Sandwich Courses in Higher Education: CNAA Degrees in Business Studies*, P E P 1975

E. MCKENNA, *Undergraduate Business Education – A Reappraisal*, London Chamber of Commerce and Industry, 1983

Business Education Council (BEC)
Set up the year after the **Technician**

Education Council (TEC) in 1974 by the Secretary of State for Education and Science, following the Haslegrave Report, it plans and administers a national system of courses in business and public administration below degree level in England and Wales. (The corresponding body in Scotland is SCOTBEC.) There are three levels of award; general certificates and diplomas, national and higher certificates and diplomas. The Council operates through four boards – business studies, financial sector studies, distribution studies and public administration and public sector studies. Each board has developed integrated core modules and specialist option modules for its courses. The vocational aspect is strongly represented, with emphasis on numeracy, communication, problem-solving skills and work experience. Courses can be taken on a full or part-time basis. Distance learning schemes are being developed. Higher level courses are devised by colleges and validated by BEC. In 1983, BEC joined TEC to form the Business and Technician Education Council (BTEC). (See also business education, Higher National Certificate, Higher National Diploma, modular course, Ordinary National Certificate, Ordinary National Diploma.)

BUSINESS EDUCATION COUNCIL, 1974– 1976: The First Three Years, BEC, 1977

Butler Act

Name given to the 1944 Education Act, after its architect, R. A. Butler, then President of the Board of Education. It was devised during the Second World War and its main proposals were outlined in a White Paper on Educational Reconstruction in July 1943. The Act made many important changes in the system of schooling but not all parts of it have yet been put into operation. The Act stipulated that public education should be organized in three progressive stages – primary, secondary and further education – and LEAs were expected to provide for these stages. Children were to be educated according to their age, ability and aptitude. A Ministry of Education was to be formed, replacing the existing Board, with a Minister possessing much greater powers to ensure the LEAs carried out their duties. Part III Authorities, responsible for elementary education, were abolished, though Divisional Executives and Excepted Districts were allowed. The dual system continued, with voluntary schools being categorized as aided, controlled and special agreement, according to their status. Religious education was made compulsory for all schools, with an act of corporate worship beginning the school day. Fees were abolished in maintained secondary schools from April 1945 and county colleges, for continuing education, were to be set up nationally. The school leaving age was to be raised from 14 to 15 and then to 16 as soon as was expedient. The Act was silent on the organization of secondary education, though LEAs were left to provide alternatives to the tripartite system. Surprisingly, no mention of the curriculum appears in the provisions of the Act. The raising of the school leaving age was delayed for two years and the provision of county colleges has never materialized. The inclusion of religious education as a mandatory part of the curriculum was and still is a controversial issue. Nevertheless the spirit of the Act allowed for innovations and advances in education which were previously not possible.

R. A. BUTLER, *The Art of the Possible*, Hamish Hamilton, 1971

H. C. DENT, *The Education Act*, 12th edn, University of London Press, 1968

C

CAL
See **Computer Assisted Learning**.

CAMOL
See **Computer Assisted Management of Learning**.

campus
The grounds in which a school, college or university is situated, forming a self-contained entity. There are a number of school campuses which consist of buildings covering the whole age range of school life. The term originated in the USA in the late nineteenth century at Princeton University. (*See also* **split site**.)

capitation allowance
An amount given each year by the **LEA** to a school in order to buy such things as books and stationery. The amount a school receives will depend on the number of children in the school (capitation, therefore, refers to an amount 'per head'), but the amount will normally increase with the age of the children. Normally LEAs will give more for secondary school pupils than for primary school pupils, and will be more generous for **sixth formers** in secondary schools. LEAs vary considerably in the amount of freedom which they give to their headteachers in determining exactly how to spend the capitation allowance.

careers guidance
The Careers Service replaced the former Youth Employment Service (YES) under the Employment and Training Act 1973. The YES was operated by **LEAs** for those under 18 and provided careers guidance and employment and training services. This dual responsibility had disadvantages, and under the 1973 Act the latter function was transferred to the **Manpower Services Commission**. At the same time, the Careers Service was extended to include all those in further and higher education. Provision of these services is mandatory upon local authorities. One of the main aims of the Service is to help pupils and students reach informed realistic decisions about their careers. Careers officers liaise with school programmes of careers education, which often begin in the third year of secondary schooling. Both group work and individual **counselling** is carried out by officers. They also supply information about employers willing to provide work experience. The Service is very active in the **further education** sector. With the present high level of unemployment, an important aspect of the Careers Service is its involvement with un-

employed young people. Careers information is made available by the Careers and Occupational Information Centre (COIC), which forms part of the Manpower Services Commission. (*See also* **Macfarlane Report**, **vocational guidance**.)

DEPARTMENT OF EMPLOYMENT, Careers Service Branch, *The Careers Service, 1974–1979*, HMSO, 1980

J. HAYES and B. HOPSON, *Careers Guidance, the role of the school in vocational development*, Heinemann Educational, 1971

case study

1. A method of teaching in which a situation is presented to students by means of film or document as a basis for discussion.

2. A method of **evaluation** in education relying less on statistical measurement and more on other kinds of data gained by means of interview or **participant observation**.

W. A. REID and D. F. WALKER, *Case Studies in Curriculum Change: Great Britain and the United States*, Routledge and Kegan Paul, 1979

H. SIMONS, *Towards a Science of the Singular: essays about case study in educational research and evaluation,* Centre for Applied Research in Education, Norwich, 1980

catchment area

A geographical area from which a school or institution draws its pupils or students. **Primary schools** tend to recruit pupils from a compact district surrounding the school, whereas a traditional **grammar school**'s catchment area might have been very wide. One view of the comprehensive school is that it should be a **neighbourhood school** drawing pupils from the catchment areas of a small number of primary schools. The 1980 Education Act has changed the picture, for under Section 5 parents can state a preference for schools and also opt for schools in other **LEAs**.

Central Advisory Councils

These Councils, one for England and one for Wales, which replaced the **Consultative Committee** under Section 4 of the 1944 Education Act, differed from the former in that they included persons of experience from outside the education field. The Councils' functions were to advise the Secretary of State in matters of educational theory and practice referred to them and to offer advice on their own initiative. Three important reports emanating from the Councils were **Crowther** on the education of the 15- to 18-year-olds (1959), **Newsom** on the secondary modern school curriculum (1963) and **Plowden** on the state of primary education (1967). The Councils have not been reconstituted since the Plowden Report was issued. (*See also* **Gittins Report**, **Ministry of Education**.)

M. KOGAN and T. PACKWOOD, *Advisory Councils and Committees in Education*, Routledge and Kegan Paul, 1974

Central Register and Clearing House

A London-based organization which enables non-graduates to apply to institutions in the scheme offering **B.Ed.** and other courses without the necessity of approaching each one individually. The equivalent scheme for graduates wishing to pursue a course of teacher training is the **Graduate Teacher Training Registry** (GTTR).

central school

Sometimes called 'intermediate' or 'modern' schools, central schools provided an education for brighter children of the **elementary school** population who failed to secure a place at a selective secondary school or chose not to take it up. The first ones opened in London in 1911, followed by some in Manchester in 1912. The 1918 Education Act encouraged **LEAs** to make available more schools of this type. Entry was often competitive. A **general education** to the age of 15 was given. Unlike **secondary schools**, which were geared to university entrance, central schools looked to a combination of apprenticeship and technical and commercial colleges.

Centre for Educational Research and Innovation (CERI)

Created in 1968, the Centre functions within the **Organization for Economic Co-operation and Development** (OECD). It is concerned with the promotion and development of educational research, testing of innovations in education systems and promoting co-operation between member countries in the field of educational research and innovation. It has published reports such as *School and Community* (1975) and *Evaluating Educational Programmes* (1976).

Certificate of Extended Education (CEE)

This examination is aimed at students who obtained grades 2 to 4 in their **Certificate of Secondary Education** examination and who wish to continue their education. Conceived as a single subject examination taken at 17+ after a one-year course, it was criticized for its lack of core syllabus of numerical and communications skills. The **Keohane Report** (1979) recommended that these areas should be compulsorily examined, as should careers education and vocational studies. It was hoped that such an examination as CEE would be acceptable to employers and **colleges of further education**. Initially run as a **pilot scheme** by the **DES** in 1972, the CEE has failed to win the Department's approval. The DES document *Examinations 16–18* (1980) provided, in the judgement of the Department, a better relationship between employment and a course for 17+ students. The *17+, A New Qualification* (1982) discussion paper from the DES advocated the approach recommended by the **FEU**, and courses for the **Certificate of Pre-Vocational Education** began in September 1983. (*See also* **Schools Council, seventeen plus examination, vocational preparation**.)

SCHOOLS COUNCIL, *CEE: Proposals For a New Examination*, Methuen Educational, 1975

Certificate of Pre-Vocational Education (CPVE)

In May 1982, the **DES** published a statement *17+, A New Qualification* giving details of this award. It is designed as a one-year course for young people at 16+ who have few examination successes. The course, which began to operate from September 1983, is intended to prepare them immediately for a job, preferably with a training component, or to follow a particular vocational course at a later stage. 60% of the course will be common to all students, consisting of English, maths, science and technology and social studies: there will also be a choice from four broad options of a pre-vocational nature. This takes the place of the experimental **Certificate of Extended Education (CEE)**. The CPVE is administered by a joint board of **Business and Technician Education Council** and **City and Guilds**, together with representatives of the **Royal Society of Arts**, and the **GCE** and **CSE** boards. (*See also* **vocational preparation**.)

J. DEAN and A. STEEDS, *17 plus; the new sixth form in schools and FE*, NFER, 1982

Certificate of Secondary Education (CSE)

An examination introduced in 1965 for secondary school pupils of about 16 in the 40 per cent ability band below those capable of taking the **GCE examination** at **O level**. The **Beloe Report** stipulated that the examination should be specially designed to suit the needs and interests of the ability range concerned and should not attempt to replicate the GCE at a lower level. The examination is regionally operated by 12 examining boards in England, with a joint CSE/GCE Board in Wales. A grade 1 result is equivalent to a GCE grade in the range A, B and C. Candidates can be awarded one of five grades, or one ungraded, in each subject they take. In 1982, 85% of those in the last year of compulsory education obtained at least one graded result at CSE (or better). (*See also* **examination boards**, **secondary**

modern school, **sixteen plus examination**, **Waddell Report**.)

Chancellor

The nominal head of a university. The post was formerly vested with wide administrative powers, but these have diminished over time. The Chancellor is normally present on formal occasions, such as degree ceremonies and university Foundation Days. Members of the Royal Family and other eminent people are often chosen for this task. (*See also* **honorary degree**, **Vice-Chancellor**.)

charitable status

Charitable status is enjoyed by all schools and institutions which are registered as such with the Charity Commissioners or the Secretary of State for Education and Science; it is also enjoyed by (a) other colleges and institutions which are exempt from such registration under the Charities Act 1960 (e.g. Oxford, Cambridge and some other universities for which special legislation exists) and (b) voluntary schools which are exempted under the Charities (Exemption of Voluntary Schools from Registration) Regulations 1960, S. I. 1960 No. 2366. Charitable status involves certain obligations, such as the keeping of proper books of account, and also gives privileges, including 50% relief on general rates, and some exemptions from income tax. (*See also* **Charity Commission**.)

Charity Commission

The Commission, established in 1853 by the government of the day, consisted of four Charity Commissioners, at least two of whom were to be barristers, and was charged with the investigation of any charities in England and Wales. Their scope was extended in 1860 and an important aspect of their work was the making of new educational schemes and checking abuse of existing charitable funds. Following the publication of the **Taunton Report**, the Endowed Schools Act of 1869 gave powers for the formulation of schemes to a new body, the **Endowed School Commission**. Though this latter Commission effected wide reforms, its functions were transferred in 1874 to the Charity Commission, forming a department within it. Twenty years later, the **Bryce Report** recommended that the duties of the Charity Commission should be exercised by an educational authority. In 1900 a number of its powers were transferred to the new **Board of Education**. (*See also* **charity school**.)

HOUSE OF COMMONS, Expenditure Committee, *Charity Commissioners and Their Accountability*, 2 vols., HMSO, 1975

charity school
Founded by the Society for Promoting Christian Knowledge from 1699, these schools provided education and clothing for poor children. Their aim was to teach reading and writing, the Church catechism and habits of industry. Local subscriptions and endowments financed the schools, many of which originated in London. In the nineteenth century, the **Charity Commissioners** investigating these schools found that many of the endowments had been misappropriated. (*See also* **free education**.)

J. G. JONES, *The Charity School Movement: a study of eighteenth century Puritanism in action*, Cambridge

University Press, 1938 (reprinted F. Cass, 1964)

Chief Education Officer (CEO)
The principal officer of an **LEA** responsible for advising the local council on a range of educational matters, writing reports for the Education Committee and carrying out its policies. The post dates from the 1902 Education Act when LEAs replaced **school boards**. The post of CEO is enshrined in statute. Under Section 88 of the 1944 Education Act it is the duty of an LEA to appoint 'a fit person to be chief education officer . . . but shall not make such an appointment except after consultation with the Minister'. There are 104 CEOs, though not all have this nomenclature: for example, the **ILEA** post is named the Education Officer; some are called **Director of Education**.

T. BUSH and M. KOGAN, *Directors of Education*, Allen and Unwin, 1982

child-centred education
A version of **progressive education** which places the child rather than the teachers or subject matter at the centre of the educational process. In its milder versions, child-centred education may be regarded as little more than a reaction against the inhumane practices of some nineteenth-century schools: but extreme versions of the doctrine would suggest that the child's interest alone should determine what is taught in class, and therefore any kind of curriculum planning would not be appropriate. (*See also* **problem-solving**.)

H. ENTWISTLE, *Child-Centred Education*, Methuen, 1970

child guidance clinic

Child guidance clinics are multi-disciplinary centres for the diagnostic assessment and treatment of children with behavioural problems and other developmental disorders. They are usually administered by **LEAs** and staffed by psychiatrists, educational psychologists, and psychiatric social workers. Treatment may be child-centred in some cases but many clinics work on the basis of family therapy. The main referring agents are schools and family doctors but many clinics have an open-door policy so that parents and adolescents may be self-referring. A detailed history of the child guidance service is given in: O. SAMPSON, *Child Guidance, the History, Provenance and Future*, British Psychological Society, Leicester, 1980. (*See also* **school psychological service**.)

childhood, history of

Recent interest in the concept of childhood has led to the publication of a number of studies, especially in the USA. Aspects such as child rearing, socialization, the curriculum and adolescence have been explored. Writers differ in their interpretations of the history of childhood. De Mause, for instance, states that the central force for change in the status of childhood arises from psychogenic changes in personality occurring because of successive generations of parent-child interactions. Laslett notes that written evidence from the past is too slight to support such a theory and favours socio-historical influences. Neither of the authors examines the effects of the process of schooling on the family.

L. DE MAUSE, *History of Childhood*, Souvenir Press edn, 1976

P. LASLETT, *The World We Have Lost*, Methuen, 2nd edn, 1971

childminding

Childminders look after other people's children between the ages of 3 and 5 in their own homes and receive payment. If the duration is of more than two hours per day, the person is required to register with the Local Social Services Department under the provisions of the Local Authority Social Services Act 1970.

B. BRYANT, M. HARRIS and D. NEWTON, *Children and Minders*, Grant McIntyre, 1980

B. and S. JACKSON, *Childminder: a study in action research*, Routledge and Kegan Paul, 1979

chronological age
See **age: chronological and mental.**

Circular

Issued by the **DES** and signed by the **Secretary of State** or the Permanent Secretary for the guidance of **LEAs** and others on matters concerning government educational policy. A well-known example was Circular 10/65, which gave guidance to LEAs on the form **comprehensive school** reorganization might take. Circulars do not have the force of a legal requirement but represent the policy of the central authority and cannot be ignored completely by LEAs. (*See also* **administrative memorandum, Holmes Circular**.)

City and Guilds Foundation Courses

These one-year full-time courses, offered by the **City and Guilds**

Institute since 1976, are designed for fifth or sixth formers of average ability. The content of the course is similar to that of the **Certificate of Extended Education (CEE)** but includes preparation for work in a variety of fields, such as construction, distribution and agriculture. All these courses are designed in such a way that the student spends a good proportion of the time on work connected with one of the areas of employment. The Foundation Certificate consists of an externally set test in each area and the teacher's assessment of the student's performance in each area. As the title states, this is a Foundation Course and students are permitted to take examinations from other bodies. (*See also* **seventeen plus examinations**, **vocational preparation**.)

City and Guilds of London Institute (CGLI)

Founded in 1878, the Institute has from the outset been concerned with the advancement of technical and scientific education by means of **vocational preparation**. It has worked closely with the **Technician Education Council** (TEC) as well as offering its own qualifications in crafts. Recently, the Institute has developed Foundation Courses for schools. (*See also* **Royal Society of Arts.**)

J. LANG, *City and Guilds of London Institute Centenary 1878–1978*, City and Guilds of London Institute, 1978

civic universities
See **universities: history of.**

Clarendon Report
Public criticism of the **public schools** resulted in a Royal Commission being appointed in 1861, charged with the tasks of inquiring into the endowments and revenues as well as the curriculum offered, in the nine leading schools: Eton, Winchester, Westminster, Charterhouse, St Paul's, Merchant Taylors', Harrow, Rugby and Shrewsbury. Reporting in 1864, the Commission recommended that the statutes of foundations should be modified whenever they required a closer adaptation to the needs of modern society. **Governing bodies** were to be reformed and were to undertake a revision of statutes in order to remove local restrictions on masterships and **scholarships** and to reorganize the expenditure on prizes and scholarships. Of great general interest was that part of the Report which dealt with the **curriculum** of schools. The chairman of the Commission, the Earl of Clarendon, favoured a more liberal approach to the education of the élite, stating 'A young man is not well educated who cannot reason or observe or express himself correctly . . . if all his information is shut up within one narrow circle.' The Commissioners, whilst denouncing the domination of classics, agreed that it should continue to hold the principal place. The influence of the German *Gymnasien* is noticeable in their findings. Natural science was to be taught for one or two hours a week, mathematics and divinity to every boy and modern languages, drawing and music formed part of the curriculum. Ancient history and geography were to be taught in connection with classical teaching. Progress in putting some of these recommendations into practice was slow, chiefly because the old universities could not give a lead in

teaching methods in non-classical subjects. However, modern studies were encouraged by the Public Schools Act of 1868 which recast the governing bodies and the ancient statutes of these institutions. (*See also* **Taunton Report**.)

Report of the Commissioners appointed to inquire into the revenues and management of certain schools and the studies pursued and instruction given therein, P.P., 1864, xx, xxi

class
1. A group of pupils or students of varying size, but usually between 25 and 35 in number. Members of a class are normally of the same age group, except where **family grouping** is adopted, but may be of different abilities. The term is interchangeable with **form**.

2. Refers to the division of an **honours degree**, according to merit.

clearing house
An information gathering unit to enable, for example, applicants for university places to make a general application in order of choice, rather than having to apply individually to each institution. In the UK the **Universities Central Council on Admissions (UCCA)** publishes all the university courses available to students and then processes the applicants from those students in terms of their priorities and the response gained from the universities. Another example in the UK of a clearing house is the **Graduate Teacher Training Registry (GTTR)**.

Clegg Report
A Standing Commission on Pay Comparability was appointed by the Prime Minister in March 1979 at the request of the **Burnham Primary and Secondary Committees**, to establish acceptable bases of comparison with terms and conditions of work between teachers and other comparable occupations. The chairman of the Commission was Professor Hugh Clegg. In the light of the Commission's findings, new salary scales came into effect from 1 April 1979. (*See also* **Houghton Report**.)

Standing Committee on Pay Comparability, Report No. 7, *Teachers*, HMSO, 1980, Cmnd 7880

cloze
The cloze procedure is a method of testing readability of a text by requiring students to show their comprehension of a passage where a proportion of the words has been deleted. Such a process tests both the reading ability of the student and the difficulty of the passage; this is one of the limitations of the procedure.

H. GRUNDIN, 'Cloze Procedure and Comprehension', in D. FEITELSON (ed.), *Cross-Cultural Perspectives on Reading and Reading Research*, Newark, USA, 1978

coaching
Special tutorial help given to a student or students, often in preparing for an examination. (*See also* **crammer**.)

Cockcroft Report
A Committee of Inquiry into the teaching of mathematics in primary and secondary schools was established in 1978 under the chairmanship of Dr Wilfred Cockcroft. Its report was issued in January 1982 under the title *Mathematics Counts*. The Committee noted that many teachers of the subject were not adequately qualified,

a situation which should be changed by offering higher salaries to new recruits and more **in-service training** for serving teachers. On the question of **standards**, the Committee found no evidence that the 'back to basics' approach in mathematics teaching yielded better results than more enlightened methods. It did, however, advocate that more attention should be paid to mental arithmetic and to practical work. A common core of useful mathematics, covering less than is attempted in many schools, was favoured. The present examination system was heavily criticized on the ground that it destroyed pupils' confidence. The Committee suggested instead a range of examinations for different abilities ranging from a super 16+ for the most able to a system of graduated or **graded tests** for the least able. (*See also* **numeracy**.)

Mathematics Counts. Report of the Committee of Inquiry into the Teaching of Mathematics in Schools, HMSO, 1982

Cockerton Judgment
In 1900, the Local Government auditor, Cockerton, brought a law case in the High Court against the School Board for London, on the ground that it had exceeded its powers in teaching certain branches of science and art in **higher grade** and evening schools. The Court ruled that **school boards** were not empowered to teach beyond the range of elementary subjects and then only for pupils up to 16 or 17 years of age. This decision was upheld in the Court of Appeal in the following year. The judgment hastened educational reform: the 1902 Education Act abolished school boards and the new

LEAs were responsible for both elementary and secondary education.

E. J. R. EAGLESHAM, *From School Board to Local Authority*, Routledge and Kegan Paul, 1956

Codes
Until 1860, the regulations of the **Committee of the Privy Council on Education** for schools wishing to receive a parliamentary grant were in the form of Minutes. These dealt with the syllabuses of **elementary schools**, conditions of grants, instruction and advice on the training of **pupil-teachers** and students in **training colleges**. Robert Lowe, as **Vice-President**, consolidated the Minutes into a Code in 1860 which was thenceforward issued annually. From 1904, the Codes dealt only with matters of minor detail and were finally replaced in 1927 by the **Handbook of Suggestions**.

coeducation
The education of boys and girls together in a school and in 'mixed' classes within that school. In England, the term 'coeducation' tends not to be used for institutions of further or higher education. Nearly all **primary schools** are coeducational, and there has been a steady trend towards coeducation in **secondary schools**, particularly since 1944.

coeducational school
See **coeducation**.

cognitive development
The gradual growth of a child's ability to understand concepts and complex patterns of ideas. Piaget and others have theorized about stages of cognitive development, for example,

sensorimotor, preconceptual, intuitive, concrete and formal. (*See also* **cognitive map**; **enactive**, **iconic and symbolic**.)

D. P. AUSUBEL et al., *Educational Psychology: A Cognitive View*, 2nd edn, Holt, Rinehart and Winston, 1978

A. FLOYD (ed.), *Cognitive Development in the School Years: A Reader*, Croom Helm with Open University Press, 1979

cognitive map

The mental picture or diagram that an individual has of a particular environment. A cognitive map will differ from one individual to another in terms of being more or less complete; individuals will also differ from their viewpoint of the same environment. (*See also* **cognitive development**.)

College of Advanced Technology (CAT)

The White Paper *Technical Education*, 1956, called for a huge increase in advanced courses in **technical colleges**. Most of the work was to take place in Colleges of Advanced Technology (CATs) which were to be formed from technical institutions already providing substantial advanced level and postgraduate work. Eight CATs were designated by the White Paper and by 1962 they had been increased to ten. Directly funded like universities, they offered an honours award, the Diploma in Technology, validated by the National Council for Technological Awards. An important feature of the course was the **sandwich** element of a year in industry. After the **Robbins Report** the CATs became fully-fledged universities. (*See also* **Percy Report**; **universities: history of**.)

P. VENABLES, *Higher Education Developments. The Technological Universities*, 1956–1976, Faber and Faber, 1978

college of education

Following the recommendations of the **Robbins Report** the 155 teacher training colleges were renamed colleges of education. These offered three or four year courses leading to the award of the **Bachelor of Education (B.Ed.)** degree. Approximately one-third were denominational colleges, with two-thirds administered by **LEAs**. A White Paper entitled *Education: A Framework for Expansion* published in 1972 revealed that a substantial reduction in the number of teacher training places was necessary to avoid a surplus of teachers in the near future. It proposed that colleges should merge with **polytechnics** and other **FE colleges**. The present picture is a confused one. A few colleges have joined universities and the majority now form part of a polytechnic or an FE institution. There are others which have been able to diversify their courses and remain freestanding. Another pattern still has been for groups of colleges to form **colleges or institutes of higher education**. The shrinking number of students has led to the closure of many colleges, a trend which is still continuing. (*See also* **academic board**, **Area Training Organization**, **Crombie Code**, **qualified teacher status**, **Weaver Report**.)

R. ALEXANDER, M. CRAFT and J. LYNCH, *Growth and Decline: Teacher Education Since Robbins*, Holt-Saunders, 1983

H. C. DENT, *The Training of Teachers in England and Wales, 1800–1975*, Hodder and Stoughton, 1977

college of further education

A college administered by an **LEA** offering courses for those normally between 16 and 19 who wish to take **GCE** examinations or more vocational awards. (*See also* **linked course**, **sixth form**, **sixth form college**.)

college of higher education

See **institute of higher education**.

College of Preceptors

Incorporated by Royal Charter in 1849, it promotes the **in-service training** of teachers both in the UK and overseas. It is probably best known for its work as an examining body for practising teachers. During the second half of the nineteenth century, the College made a number of unsuccessful attempts to become a Registration Council for teachers. The College awards qualifications as Associate (ACP) and Licentiate (LCP), both graduate level qualifications, and Diplomas in Advanced Study in Education. Two new classes of membership are Member (MCollP), to recognize good professional practice, and Ordinary Fellow (FCollP), reserved for those who have made an outstanding contribution to education. (*See also* **General Teaching Council**.)

collegiate university

From the middle ages, the colleges of Oxford and Cambridge Universities were established by money given by pious founders. Examples are New College, Oxford, founded by William of Wykeham in 1379, and King's College, Cambridge, founded by Henry VI in 1441. Each college has much autonomy. It controls its own property, elects its own **Fellows**, chooses its own Head and, subject to university regulations, admits its own **undergraduate** students. The hallmark of such a college is its corporate identity, in contrast to that of a **federal** system. Durham University is also organized on a collegiate basis.

UNIVERSITY OF OXFORD, *Report of Commission of Inquiry I. Report, Recommendations*, Oxford, Clarendon Press, 1966.

Command Paper

A document presented 'by Her Majesty's Command' to either House, the Command Paper is in fact the responsibility of a Minister. It may be for example, a **White Paper** or a **Blue Book** and is not in pursuance of an Act of Parliament. All Command Papers bear a number, such as the White Paper, *Education: A Framework for Expansion*, 1972, Cmnd 5174.

Committee of Directors of Polytechnics (CDP)

A group formed in 1970, consisting of the heads of these 30 institutions, 'to contribute to the evolution of policy for the development of polytechnics within the total provision for higher education'. It meets from time to time to discuss matters of common interest and make representations to Government where necessary.

Committee of the Privy Council on Education

Established in 1839 to superintend grants provided by the Government for the provision of schools and **training colleges**. It consisted of four members, the **Lord President of the Council**, the Lord Privy Seal, the Chancellor of the Exchequer and the Home Secretary. Its first Secretary was Dr James Kay (later Kay-Shuttleworth). Meeting about once a month, the Council published its decisions as Minutes of the Committee of the Council on Education. It evolved a policy which ensured that grants given for specific purposes were properly used. The Council appointed the first two inspectors of schools, **HMIs**, to assist in this task. With the growth in the activities of the Committee, an **Education Department**, headed by a **Vice-President**, was established in 1856 and took over the Council's work.

P. H. J. H. GOSDEN, *The Development of Educational Administration in England and Wales*, Blackwell, 1966

D. G. PAZ, 'The Composition of the Education Committee of the Privy Council', *Journal of Educational Administration and History*, Vol. 8, No. 2, 1976

Committee of Vice-Chancellors and Principals (CVCP)

This Committee was established in 1918 and reconstituted in 1930. As the title suggests, it represents heads of university institutions. The Committee is a standing body with its own secretariat. It keeps in touch with, and expresses its views to, Government departments, research councils and other agencies concerned with **higher education**. (*See also* **Principal**, **Vice-Chancellor**.)

Common Entrance examination

An examination taken by pupils wishing to enter a **public school** or some of the **independent schools** at 13 years of age. Begun in 1904, it is set by a boys' common entrance com-

mittee and a girls' board. Some 14,000 pupils – 10,000 boys and 4,000 girls – sit the papers in a complete year. From 1981, joint papers for boys and girls were taken in English, French, mathematics and science. (*See also* **preparatory school**.)

community college/school

A concept of education which seeks to involve individuals as members of communities in educational activities, regardless of age. This notion, derived from the **village college** and recommended in the **Plowden Report**, has been translated into programmes located in community colleges or schools, with an intake of pupils usually between 14 and 18 years. Parents make use of resources during the day as well as the evening, taking part in academic and recreational activities alongside their children. As well as housing a school, the campus may include an FE college, library and sports complex. The buildings are often in use up to late at night for leisure and cultural activities and for meetings of local clubs and societies. (*See also* **adult education**, **community education**, **neighbourhood school**.)

B. JENNINGS, *Community Colleges in England and Wales*, National Institute of Adult Education, Leicester, 1980

A. YARDLEY and H. SWAIN, *Community Schools in Practice*, Home and School Council, Sheffield, 1980

community education

Educational planning which involves educational activities outside the school or beyond the **community college** or **village college**. The concept of community education is related to the ideas of **continuing**

education, namely, that education does not stop when a person finishes the period of full-time schooling but continues into adult life. Many schemes of community education would involve teaching staff venturing into the wider community as well as bringing adults into the educational institution. Another of its aims is to improve the environment and the quality of life of the community in general.

J. BOYD, *Community Education and Urban Schools*, Longman, 1977

C. POSTER, *Community Education: its Development and Management*, Heinemann Educational, 1982

Community Programme

A scheme, started in 1982, to provide temporary jobs for 18- to 24-year-olds who have been unemployed for six months or more and people over 25 who have not worked for a year or more. The **Manpower Services Commission** (MSC) provide the resources, but the work itself is found by industry, local authorities, voluntary bodies and so on. Those joining the scheme may work full or part time on the Programme, which includes such activities as working with children and maintaining equipment for **play centres**. The Community Programme replaced the Community Enterprise Programme, the main difference being that the new programme sets a limit to the average earnings of workers within any one programme, which effectively restricts them to three-quarters of a week.

Community Service Volunteers (CSV)

A national voluntary agency, founded in 1962, with the aim of supporting teachers, youth workers and others interested in developing community involvement projects with young people both inside and outside the formal education system. CSV operates through four major programmes: (1) volunteer programmes, involving young people in community service full-time for between four and twelve months; (2) an advisory service, which produces ideas and materials for schools and colleges wishing to involve their students in social action related to the curriculum; (3) a media programme, which works with television and radio companies to recruit volunteers; and (4) a youth employment programme which, with Government funding, deploys young people in full-time work. CSV receives funds from the **DES**, local authorities and private trusts.

compensatory education

The theory behind 'compensatory education' is that of 'social deficit' – that is, that some children come from homes which do not provide early learning experiences or sufficient stimulation to motivate children in the classroom. Working-class children and children from some ethnic minority groups have been singled out for 'compensatory education' programmes such as **Head Start** in the USA or **EPA** programmes in the UK following the recommendations of the **Plowden Report**. This view of compensatory education has been challenged, especially by some sociologists. For example, Basil Bernstein, 'Education cannot compensate for Society', *New Society*, 26 February, 1970, and C. Jencks, *Inequality: A Reassessment*, Basic Books, New York, 1972. (*See also* disadvantaged, enrichment programme, language deficit, positive discrimination.)

competency based teaching (CBT)

Aimed at improving teacher performance in the classroom, CBT employs many forms of teaching methods, such as **games and simulations** and **micro teaching**, which seeks to promote self-awareness and interaction skills. The essence of CBT is that 'competence' must be defined in such a way as to make it measurable.

s. v. MONJAN, *Critical Issues in Competency Based Education*, Pergamon, Oxford, 1979

comprehensive school

The 1944 Education Act, which promoted the notion of **secondary education for all**, encouraged experiments in secondary school organization. The existing **tripartite system** allocated children at the age of 11 to either a **grammar**, a **technical** or a **modern** course, each taught separately. Circular 144/1947, which set out the various forms of organization, defined a comprehensive school as 'one which is intended to cater for all the secondary education of all the children in a given area without an organization in three sides.' The first purpose-built comprehensive school was opened in 1954 at Kidbrooke in London. (*See also* **house system**, **mixed ability groups**, **upper school**.)

c. BENN and B. SIMON, *Half Way There*, Penguin, 2nd edn, 1972

P. H. JAMES, *The Reorganization of Secondary Education*, NFER, 1981

compulsory education

The 1944 Education Act stated that it was the duty of parents to ensure that children of compulsory school age should receive efficient, full-time education. This applies to all who have attained the age of 5 years and are not 16 years of age. (*See also* **alternative education**, **deschooling**, **half-time system**, **home education**, **ROSLA**, **School Attendance Committee**, **school leaving age**.)

R. SZRETER, 'The Origins of Full-Time Compulsory Education at Five', *British Journal of Educational Studies*, Vol. 13, No. 1, 1964

Computer Assisted Learning (CAL)

Sometimes also referred to as Computer Aided Instruction (CAI). The use of a computer is not only to present instructional material to students, but also to react to their responses. In the past, students tended to have to work at individual terminals linked to a central computer, but with the development of microcomputers it is now much more common for students to work with their own computer. (*See also* **CAMOL**, **computers in schools**, **educational technology**, **new information technology**, **programmed learning**.)

J. ANNETT, *Computer Assisted Learning: 1969–1975, A Report*, SSRC, 1976

Computer Assisted Management of Learning (CAMOL)

A five-year research and development project (1973–8). The project was sponsored by the **Council for Educational Technology (CET)**. (*See also* **Computer Assisted Learning**, computers in schools, educational technology, new information technology, programmed learning.)

computers in schools

In recent years, the Government has established two schemes to develop the use of microcomputers in schools. The first, the *Microelectronics Education Programme* (MEP), begun in 1980, was under the auspices of the DES. Its aim was to develop suitable programs and to familiarize teachers with the equipment. The scheme will run until 1986 at a cost of more than £20 million. A second scheme, launched in 1981, was the Department of Industry's *Micros in Schools*, which aimed at placing a micro-computer in every school. Half the cost of the computer is provided by the Department, the other half by the school. A large number of **secondary school** teachers have attended four-day training courses to learn how to use computers; **primary schools** have self-study kits and two-day training courses for teachers. There are 14 regional information centres responsible for providing courses, developing programs and demonstrating equipment. (*See also* **new information technology**.)

DES, *Microelectronics Education Programme. The Strategy*, HMSO, 1981

conditional offer

Best exemplified by the **UCCA** procedure for pupils wishing to proceed to university. Such an offer is made by the appropriate department, conditional upon the pupil obtaining stipulated grades in **GCE A level examinations** which have yet to be taken at the time of the offer. An unconditional offer means that a candidate is accepted as having fulfilled the necessary entry requirements. (*See also* **entry qualification**.)

conditioning

A form of **learning** of a very simple kind. A person would acquire the tendency to make a response to a stimulus automatically.

Confederation for the Advancement of State Education (CASE)

A **pressure group** set up in 1960 to improve the quality of local maintained schools, consisting of parents and others interested in education. Local groups operate within the framework of national CASE policy. For example, in 1966, CASE gave its support to a fully **comprehensive** system and expressed its opposition to **streaming**, **corporal punishment** and secret **school records**. (*See also* **Home and School Council**, **parents and education**.)

conscience clause

From 1833, attempts had been made to protect Nonconformist consciences from the enforced teaching of the catechism and attendance at church by those attending school. The matter was not settled until the 1870 Education Act which stated that schools receiving a parliamentary grant placed no religious conditions on the admission of children and that pupils could be withdrawn by their parents from any religious observance or instruction. The nature of that instruction was settled by Section 14 of the Act, called the Cowper-Temple clause after its promoter, that it should be one 'in which no religious catechism or religious formulary which is distinctive of any religious denomination shall be taught'.

Consultative Committee

Set up by the Board of Education Act (1899) to advise the new Board on any matters referred to it. The first Committee consisted of eighteen members, the majority of whom were from universities. After its reconstruction in 1920, and under the chairmanship of distinguished academics, influential reports, such as the **Hadow** (1926, 1931 and 1933) and **Spens** (1938), covering the whole field of elementary and secondary education, were issued. After the 1944 Education Act, the Committee was replaced by two **Central Advisory Councils** for England and for Wales.

continuing education

A term which overlaps **adult education**, **permanent education** and **recurrent education**, but is not synonymous with any of them. With continuing education, the emphasis is on the idea that education in its true form proceeds throughout an individual's life. Thus the emphasis in continuing education is to break down the barrier between formal and informal education, institutions of education and real life. (*See also* **community education**, **National Institute of Adult Education**.)

ADVISORY COUNCIL FOR ADULT AND CONTINUING EDUCATION, *Continuing Education: from policies to practice*, ACACE, Leicester, 1982

continuous assessment

See **assessment**.

convergent thinking

A way of thinking, or **problem-solving**, which concentrates on finding only one solution to a problem. This assumes that there is only one best or correct solution to any given problem. (*See also* **creativity**, **divergent thinking**.)

corporal punishment

See **punishment: corporal punishment**.

corporate management

A form of planning which affirms the unitary concept of an enterprise with a need for central allocation of the use of resources and management. The Maud Committee on Management of Local Government (1967) recommended a reduction in the number of committees in a local authority, with executive decisions being taken by a small number of councillors advised by a powerful officer. A more moderate plan was suggested by the Department of the Environment, *The New Local Authorities: Management and Structure* (1972), known as the Bains Report. Whilst most committees were to be retained, a policy and resources committee was to be set up to co-ordinate, plan and decide on priorities. A Chief Executive was to be appointed to advise the council and work with a management team consisting of the officers of the different departments. This move to PPB (Planned Programme Budgeting system) has been interpreted by local authorities in a variety of ways and the difficulties of operating such a system are recognized in the field of education. Much depends on how the chief officers' team works, the personality relationships and role clarity. There is also the problem of methods of evaluating objectives set.

J. L. DAVIES, 'Corporate Management and the Education Service in British Local Government: Analyses and Reflections', *Educational Administration*, Vol. 7, No. 2, Summer, 1979–80

correspondence course

A course of study, conducted by means of written work, between student and **tutor** through the post. (*See also* **distance learning, Open University, self-instruction**.)

R. GLATTER and E. G. WEDDELL, *Study by Correspondence*, Longman, 1971

correspondence theory

A view put forward by some sociologists of education which suggests that the major purpose of schooling, if not the only one, is to service the needs of industrial society. Thus pupils are taught in schools to be punctual, to be obedient, to work hard under supervision, so that they may become docile factory workers and clerks when they leave school.

B. DAVIES, *Social Control and Education*, Methuen, 1976

Council for Educational Technology (CET)

An organization established in 1973 for promoting the application and development of **educational technology** in all sectors of education and training in the UK. The CET is an autonomous body, though its funds come directly from Government (**DES** and, in Scotland, the **SED**.) It is essentially a development agency identifying those areas to which educational technology can make a contribution and initiating development work to help resolve the problems when they are identified. (*See also* **CAL, CAMOL**.)

Council for Education in World Citizenship (CEWC)

Founded in 1939, the Council provides information, projects and practical help on all international issues, without political bias or geographical limits. The Council holds termly national conferences for 13–15- and 16–18-year-old students on topics such as World Health and The Nuclear Dilemma; organizes teachers' seminars to discuss crucial questions relating to education for international understanding; provides speakers for schools; has a London Resources Centre of teaching material on World Studies; and disseminates information through its Information Service on topics of current or recent international concern. An earlier, and narrower, concept of citizenship was promoted by the Association for Education in Citizenship, founded in 1934, which supported the idea of 'direct training' by means of specific curriculum content rather than by indirect and more open ways.

Council for National Academic Awards (CNAA)

The **Robbins Report** recommended that opportunities for obtaining **degrees** and other academic qualifications outside the universities should be made available. The Council was established in 1964, taking over from the National Council for Technological Awards, which could award diplomas only. The majority of courses, both **first degree** and **postgraduate**, are located in **polytechnics**. Many courses include a sandwich element in them. The CNAA does not set the syllabus or examine students, but approves courses and the appointment of **external examiners**.

Colleges, after obtaining **LEA**, **RAC** and **DES** approval, submit a detailed outline of the courses, intended teaching methods and assessment procedures, the target student audience and the teaching qualifications of the staff. Usually a visitation is made by one of the 50 subject boards of the Council, each of which has a strong academic representation, to assess college resources and to discuss the submission with staff concerned. A first degree course is approved for an indefinite period, but is subject to review. A recent document from the Council, *Developments in Partnership in Validation* (1979), indicated the changing relation of the Council to the colleges, with greater sharing of responsibility between the Councils and institutions. It is now the largest degree awarding body in the country apart from London University and the **Open University**, and is responsible for degree courses for over 30 per cent of students taking such courses. (*See also* **Diploma in Higher Education**, **sandwich course**, **validation**.)

Council of Europe

An organization established in 1949 with the aim of achieving greater unity between its members, safeguarding and realizing their ideals and principles and facilitating their economic and social progress. Its headquarters are in Strasbourg and committees of ministers from the 21 member countries meet there as well as the Parliamentary Assembly. A Council for Cultural Co-operation was established in 1962 to promote cultural and educational programmes. Conferences, seminars and symposia on many issues including education are held from time to time and their proceedings are published. The Council of Europe is particularly associated with the policy of **permanent education**.

COUNCIL OF EUROPE, *A Contribution to the Development of a New Education Policy*, Strasbourg, 1982

Council of Local Education Authorities (CLEA)

In 1975, the **Association of Metropolitan Authorities** (AMA) and the **Association of County Councils** (ACC) formed this new Council so that the education authorities of England could speak with one voice. CLEA consists of nine members each from the two Associations, but has its own education officer. The Council deals with a large range of matters, from discussing teachers' conditions of service to making representations to the **Secretary of State** on issues affecting **LEAs**. (*See also* **National Advisory Board**.)

counselling

Counselling has been defined by Lovel (1976) as helping people to understand their own motives and reasons for actions so that they can come to their own conclusions about what they will do and how they can do it; it means helping them to define their needs and discover what resources are available to them to work out the best ways of making and sustaining satisfactory relationships with others. The person is central in counselling, not the problem. In a school setting, counselling is focused on personal, educational and vocational guidance. The first full-time courses for experienced teachers in Britain were established in 1965 and were much influenced by the ideas and work of Carl Rogers, the American psychotherapist. More recently, there has been a growth in part-time courses which tend to encompass pastoral care and educational welfare, reflecting the growth in pastoral care career structures. (*See also* **Education Welfare Service, pastoral system, tutor**.)

D. HAMBLIN, *The Teacher and Counselling*, Blackwell, 1974

G. LOVEL, 'The Youth Worker as first aid counsellor in impromptu situations', quoted in T. D. VAUGHAN (ed.), *Concepts of Counselling*, National Council of Social Service, 1976

county college
The 1943 White Paper on Educational Reconstruction recommended that **LEAs** should be duty bound to provide compulsory part-time education for the 15- to 18-year-olds. This revival of the **day continuation school** notion was officially accepted by the Education Act of 1944, which provided for county colleges to be opened throughout the country by 1950. However, priority was given to the **raising of the school leaving age**, and the scheme for providing these colleges was quietly dropped. The **Crowther Report** revived the notion in 1959.

county school
See **maintained school**.

course
A term which is used with a variety of meanings. Probably the most common usage refers to a 'course of study' meaning a series of **lessons**, **lectures** or **seminars**, of specified duration, often a year. Thus a **programme of studies** would consist of several courses. Ambiguity arises, however, when reference is made, for example, to a '**degree** course' when the more appropriate terminology would appear to be 'degree programme'. In recent years, some degree programmes have been organized on a **modular** or course unit basis. In this context, a course unit would normally be of a specified length (usually one year) and have a specific value within a degree programme. A student might, for example, be required to complete a minimum of three and a maximum of four units in an academic year, and be judged on his best nine units at the end of a three-year programme. (*See also* **course work**.)

course work
Work carried out by a student during a **course** of study. Its nature may range from essay writing to practical tasks. According to the course regulations, such work may be taken into account in forming a final **assessment** of the student's merit.

crammers
A name given to a private college where students of 16 years of age and over attend to prepare for school examinations and special examinations with a view to entering the professions and universities. Programmes of work in crammers are usually fairly intensive. Crammers mainly attract those who have either been badly taught at school or who need extra qualifications in a shorter space of time. (*See also* **coaching**.)

C. PALMER, *Crammers*, Duckworth, 1977

creaming

The process of selecting those pupils who are thought to be the brightest and putting them into segregated schools. It is often argued that in many **LEAs comprehensive schools** are 'creamed off' because the most academically gifted pupils are sent to surviving **grammar schools**. Another example of creaming occurs in the much criticized **Assisted Places Scheme**. (*See also* **giftedness**.)

creativity

Very largely as a reaction against the use and misuse of **intelligence tests**, which were said to measure **convergent thinking**, some psychologists developed tests which would test **divergent thinking** or **creativity**, e.g. 'write down as many uses as you can think of for a brick'. It is now generally recognized that some individuals are more creative than others, but whether Beethoven or Leonardo would be scored highly on creativity tests is a more difficult question. (*See also* **problemsolving**.)

E. PICKARD, *The Development of Creative Ability*, NFER, 1979

P. E. VERNON (ed.), *Creativity*, Penguin, 1970

credit

In USA universities a student is awarded one or more credits on successful completion of a **course**. Usually about 120 credits are needed for the award of a **degree**. In UK, most academics object to this cafeteria or fragmented system, preferring a degree programme which is more carefully planned around a central core of important knowledge. Thus the **Open University** credit system is very different from that of USA universities since credits are awarded for much longer blocks of study (only six are required for an ordinary degree and eight for an honours degree). In Open University terminology, a credit is awarded for a year's work for a part-time student who works for about ten to twelve hours a week. In 1983, the DES announced its intention to set up a study of credit transfers, that is, facilitating the acceptance of credits gained in one higher education establishment by other establishments.

credit transfers
See **credit**.

Crewe Report

The last of the **Prime Minister's Reports,** on the position of Classics in the United Kingdom, was issued in 1921. The Committee, chaired by the Marquess of Crewe, included Sir Henry Hadow, W. P. Ker, Gilbert Murray and A. N. Whitehead. Its remit 'to advise as to the means by which the proper study of these subjects may be maintained and improved', led to a wide-ranging investigation of the teaching of Classics in schools and universities. The report painted a gloomy picture. In **public schools**, Greek and Latin occupied no preponderant position, and in **secondary schools**, whilst the position of Latin was not discouraging, Greek was threatened with extinction. It recommended that while French would normally be the first foreign modern language, liberty of experiment should be encouraged and Latin should be taught first. Some teaching of formal grammar was desirable in elementary schools, whilst in secondary schools greater stress was to be laid on the historical and archaeological backgrounds to the texts.

Report of the Committee appointed by the Prime Minister to inquire into the position of Classics in the educational system of the United Kingdom, HMSO, 1921

criterion-referenced test

A test designed to establish a candidate's performance in terms of a given level or **standard** rather than being better (or worse) than of other candidates. In England, the driving test is often quoted as the most familiar example of a test which demands performance at a certain level on a number of known criteria. A criterion-referenced test may express the notion of 'pass' either in terms of a 'cut-off point' or test score, or in terms of reaching a standard of competence on a number of related criteria (such as the use of mirror and braking in the driving test). (*See also* **norm-referenced test**.)

R. SUMNER and T. S. ROBERTSON, *Criterion-Referenced Measurement and Criterion-Referenced Tests: some published work reviewed*, NFER, 1977

critical learning period

One theory in **child development** suggests that there are limited times in childhood when individuals may acquire particular skills. If that opportunity is missed during the 'critical period' it is then thought to be difficult or perhaps impossible to acquire the skill at a later stage. Critical learning periods are likely to exist in other animals, but some pyschologists doubt their existence in human beings. Language acquisition is sometimes suggested as the most important example of a critical learning period, but this is by no means established.

Crombie Code

The Colleges of Education (Compensation) Regulations 1975, which came into operation on 1 August of that year, set out the terms of redundancy compensation for college lecturers arising out of the reorganization of higher education.

Cross Report

In 1886, Sir Richard Cross, then Conservative Home Secretary, was appointed chairman of a Royal Commission 'to inquire into the working of the Elementary Acts, England and Wales'. Both the Catholic and Church of England authorities were concerned at the position of **voluntary schools** under the 1870 Education Act; as a result, religious interests were well represented on the Commission. Because of divisions of opinion within the Commission, two reports were issued in 1888. The majority report supported voluntary schools and a minority report voiced Nonconformist objections to allowing Church schools to have a share of the rates. However, there was agreement on a number of issues. Whilst recommending the eventual abolition of '**payment by results**', it favoured the retention of standards, and a core curriculum, consisting of the **three Rs**, needlework for girls, history, geography and elementary science. The teaching of Welsh was officially sanctioned. The Commission also called for a definition of the term 'elementary' by Parliament. (*See* **university day training college**.)

Reports of the Royal Commission on the Elementary Education Acts, 1886–8, P.P. 1886, xxv; P.P. 1887, xxix, xxx; P.P. 1888, xxxv–xxxvii

Crowther Report

Sir Geoffrey Crowther was chairman of the **Central Advisory Council** (England) which issued a Report in 1959 on the education of boys and girls between the ages of 15 and 18. One of its chief recommendations was that the **school leaving age** should be raised to 16 between 1966 and 1968 to encourage pupils to continue at school until 18, with compulsory part-time day education to this age to be provided in **county colleges** for those who had left school. The second volume of the report provided valuable statistical and sociological evidence of the importance of home background on educational achievement. (*See also* **numeracy**.)

Report of the Central Advisory Council for England (England): 15 to 18, HMSO, 1959

culture

By definition any society possesses a culture or way of life which members of that society share (to some extent). Culture refers to **knowledge**, beliefs and attitudes, passed on from one generation to the next. In a complex industrial society this transmission process is much more complex than in a technologically and economically simple society. In a complex society not all values and beliefs are held in common – there are **sub-cultures** within the major society. But there are always some cultural features held in common, that is, a common culture as well as sub-cultures. (*See also*

curriculum, multi-cultural or multi-ethnic education.)

D. LAWTON, *Class, Culture and the Curriculum*, Routledge and Kegan Paul, 1975

R. WILLIAMS, *Culture and Society 1780–1950*, Penguin, 1961

curriculum

A narrow definition would limit curriculum to a 'programme for instruction'; wider definitions would include all the learning that takes place in a school or other institution, planned and unplanned. In recent years curriculum has increasingly been defined as a selection from the **culture** of a society; and the curriculum is planned by a process of cultural analysis. (*See also* **syllabus**.)

D. LAWTON, *Curriculum Studies and Educational Planning*, Hodder and Stoughton, 1983

curriculum: common curriculum

A **curriculum** planned to cater for all pupils in a school. It is 'common' in the sense that all pupils study certain subjects or have certain educational experiences 'in common' by the end of the period of compulsory schooling. 'Common curriculum' can also be used nationally to indicate the desirability of all children in the country having certain planned experiences 'in common'. Both uses depend to some extent on the idea of a common **culture**. Common curriculum should not be confused with 'uniform curriculum', **compulsory curriculum** or **core curriculum**.

M. HOLT, *The Common Curriculum*, Routledge and Kegan Paul, 1978

curriculum: compulsory curriculum

The idea that a properly planned **curriculum** would either be wholly compulsory, or, more probably, that there would be compulsory elements distinguished from the optional or fringe subjects or topics. The term is sometimes used without making clear whether the curriculum would be compulsory for schools (that is, a nationally prescribed curriculum) or compulsory for pupils within a particular school.

J. P. WHITE, *Towards a Compulsory Curriculum*, Routledge and Kegan Paul, 1974

curriculum control

Part of the study of the **politics of the curriculum**. In any society there are decision-makers who control or influence the content of what is taught in schools. In the UK, teachers are said to control the curriculum, but they have always been constrained by examinations, governors and others. Recently it has been suggested, especially by **DES**, that there should be more central control or influence over the curricula of primary and secondary schools.

D. LAWTON, *The Politics of the School Curriculum*, Routledge and Kegan Paul, 1980

B. SALTER and T. TAPPER, *Education, Politics and the State*, Grant McIntyre, 1981

curriculum: core curriculum

Often confused with **common curriculum**, but is usually used as a weaker term to indicate that there are some subjects which are more important that others, and therefore

should be compulsory. Hence the familiar secondary school curriculum pattern for fourth and fifth year pupils of 'core plus options'. This approach to curriculum has been much criticized by **HMI**, particularly in documents published by **DES**, such as *Curriculum 11–16*, 1977, and *Aspects of Secondary Education*, 1979. (*See also* **Munn Report**, **options**.)

curriculum development project

A study of a particular subject or area of the **curriculum** often with a view to improving that part of the curriculum by supplying teachers with attractive teaching materials sometimes in the form of 'packages'. In the UK, many curriculum development projects have been financed by the **Nuffield Foundation** or the **Schools Council**. In recent years there has been less emphasis on 'materials' but greater efforts to encourage teachers to rethink aims and methods for themselves. (*See also* **dissemination**, **Man – A Course of Study project**.)

curriculum: hidden curriculum

An ambiguous and confusing term. One meaning implies that there are certain kinds of learning (often regarded as important) which are not included in the timetable, but will be transmitted by such institutional arrangements as **prefect** systems or by so-called extra-curricular activities such as the Combined Cadet Force (CCF). A related meaning refers to the possibility of pupils acquiring attitudes and behaviour patterns not intended by school authorities. (*See* *also* **curriculum: paracurriculum**, **timetabling**.)

curriculum: paracurriculum

A term invented by David Hargreaves because he was dissatisfied with the term '**hidden curriculum**'. The term 'paracurriculum' is gaining acceptance as a more general term, that is, 'hidden' as well as more subtle socialization effects. (*See also* **curriculum**.)

D. HARGREAVES, 'Power and the Paracurriculum' in C. RICHARDS (ed.), *Power and the Curriculum*, Nafferton, 1978

curriculum planning

The process of designing and organizing the whole curriculum either at national level or within a single school. School-based curriculum planning would involve in descending order of generality the whole curriculum, **syllabuses** year by year for different areas or subjects within the whole curriculum, schemes of work and individual **lessons** prepared by each teacher.

D. LAWTON, *Curriculum Studies and Educational Planning*, Hodder and Stoughton, 1983

curriculum: spiral curriculum

Learning planned in such a way that a pupil would encounter important concepts at a number of stages – concrete before abstract, simple before complex, easy before difficult. Bruner's intention was to indicate that important concepts should not be regarded as something to be learned on a single occasion and then taken for granted; concepts need to be encountered in a variety of contexts, over a period of time, and gradually assimilated rather than suddenly learned.

J. BRUNER, *The Process of Education*, Harvard University Press, 1961

cut–off point

A point on a mark list or rank order which is used to separate 'passes' from 'failures' or first class from second class, etc. For example, a group of examiners, after looking at a number of examination papers, might decide that a mark of 40% would be the lowest level of pass and all candidates with 39% would fail. 40% would thus be the cut-off point, but probably all candidates with marks of, say, 37 to 43% would be regarded as borderline, and submitted to special scrutiny. In such a case, the examiners would have certain criteria or standards in mind which would justify passing some and failing others: the mark of 40% would be arbitrary, but the standard it represented would not.

D

Dainton Report

A Committee chaired by Sir (then Dr) Frederick Dainton, set up in 1965 to inquire into the flow of candidates in science and technology into higher education. Its report issued three years later warned of the harm both to individuals and society of the relative decline in the study of science and technology, especially in the **sixth forms**. This 'swing from science', it suggested, could be dealt with by introducing a broad span of studies in sixth forms and delaying premature specialization. Schools and **LEAs** should also ensure that the majority of secondary school pupils should come into early contact with good science teaching and should study mathematics until they leave school. (*See also* **Swann Report.**)

COUNCIL FOR SCIENTIFIC POLICY, *Enquiry into the Flow of Candidates in Science and Technology into Higher Education*, HMSO, 1968, Cmnd 3541

Dalton Plan

A system of teaching and learning devised by Helen Parkhurst and first introduced at Dalton High School, Massachusetts, in 1920. It was based on two major principles: first, that the pupil must be free to continue without interruption upon any subject that may arise in the course of her/his study and second, that the Plan would transform the learning process into a co-operative adventure. The basis of the Plan was that the curriculum was divided up into jobs and the pupil accepted the task appointed for his class as a contract. The contract job comprised a whole month's work,

designed to accord with the pupil's ability. The Plan postulated the establishment of laboratories, one for each subject in the curriculum, with a specialist in that subject attached to each laboratory. Helen Parkhurst's scheme was rapidly taken up in England, notably by Rosa Bassett at Streatham School for Girls, London. (*See also* **individualized learning**, **problem-solving**.)

H. PARKHURST, *Education on the Dalton Plan*, Bell, 1922

dame schools

Traceable as far back as the seventeenth century, these schools were for young children, usually in rural areas, and staffed by unqualified women. The standard of instruction given was normally very low.

J. H. HIGGINSON, 'Dame Schools', *British Journal of Educational Studies*, Vol. 22, No. 2, 1974

day continuation school

A Consultative Committee on Attendance at Continuation Schools, reporting in 1909, favoured the 'systematic encouragement of suitable and practical kinds of continued education beyond the now too early close of the elementary school day course.' It was, however, less decisive on the question of compulsory or optional courses. The **Lewis Report** in 1917, examining post-war educational needs, suggested compulsory attendance for youths between 14 and 18. Opposition from industrialists limited the proposed scheme contained in the 1918 Education Act; the upper age limit was reduced to 16 years and annual hours of attendance were reduced from 320 to 280. **LEAs** were given up to seven years to implement these provisions. A few authorities, notably Stratford, Rugby, London, Kent, Birmingham, Swindon and West Ham, set up day continuation schools. However, by 1921 the need for economic cutbacks, the practical difficulties in operating the scheme and the fading enthusiasm of its supporters led to the end of this educational innovation. (*See also* **county college**.)

B. DOHERTY, 'Compulsory Day Continuation Education: An Examination of the 1918 Experiment', *The Vocational Aspect of Secondary and Further Education*, Vol. 18, Spring 1966

E. A. WATERFALL, *The Day Continuation School in England. Its Functions and Future*, Allen and Unwin, 1923

day nursery

Unlike other types of nursery education, day nurseries are normally organized by local authority Social Services Departments. They are for children under 5 in special need, and have qualified staff. They are open often throughout the year from 8 a.m. to 6 p.m. Another type of day nursery is that provided by either private enterprise or employers' organizations for children of parents going to work. They are usually heavily subsidized and are registered with a local authority. (*See also* **child-minders**, **National Nursery Examination Board**, **nursery class**, **nursery school**, **playgroups**.)

C. GARLAND and S. WHITE, *Children and Day Nurseries*, Grant McIntyre, 1980

day release

A method of organizing courses in **further** or **higher education** whereby students on courses are in employment and are released for perhaps one or two days a week during the term for training or general education or to pursue a formal qualification. (*See also* **sandwich course**.)

K. EVANS, *Day Release – A Desk Study*, FEU, 1980

day school

Term generally applied to most **maintained schools**. Their main characteristic is that pupils attend during school hours and do not normally board at the school. (*See also* **boarding school**.)

Dean

1. Person responsible for a **faculty** or department in a university or higher education institution.

2. A **Fellow** or senior member of a university who supervises the conduct and discipline of students.

deficit model

A theory put forward to account for the 'under-achievement' of certain minority groups and working-class children. The theory suggests that failure is connected with certain cultural 'deficits' which handicap them in the learning process at school. The theory was implicit or explicit in many of the well-known reports on education such as **Crowther**, **Newsom** and **Plowden**. Some sociologists have reacted to this model by suggesting that schools often fail to provide adequate teaching for certain groups of children, or that society itself is at fault in various other ways. Whereas the deficit model 'blames' the family of an under-achieving child, later theories tend to blame teachers or society in general. (*See also* **compensatory education**, disadvantage, **enrichment programme**.)

degrees

Awarded by universities and other institutions of higher education as the result of successful completion of a course of study: the candidate may be tested by examination, **continuous assessment**, a **viva**, a **thesis**, or a combination of any of these. There are three levels of degrees:

1. *Bachelor*, usually a **first degree**, except for degrees such as B.Phil. and B.Litt. and for some Scottish universities. The course is normally of three years' duration. Examples are the Bachelor of Arts (B.A.) and Bachelor of Science (B.Sc.) degrees.

2. *Master,* usually a **higher degree** obtained after one or two years of study and may include an element of research. In Scotland, the M.A. (Master of Arts) is mainly a first degree. At Oxford and Cambridge, it is awarded seven years from the time of **matriculation** upon payment of a fee.

3. *Doctor*, usually awarded on the basis of a thesis, the result of research. The initials Ph.D. or D.Phil. (Doctor of Philosophy) indicate such an award. There are also *higher doctorates*, such as Doctor of Laws (LL.D.) and Doctor of Literature (D.Litt.), which are awarded on the basis of the submission of publications.

Medical practitioners are as a matter of convention entitled to be called doctors on becoming qualified, even without obtaining a doctorate qualification in Medicine (M.D.). Degrees are normally awarded in a **faculty** and may be indicated by abbreviations following the title. For in-

stance, the Bachelor degree in the Faculty of Economics at London University is written as B.Sc.(Econ.). The majority of degree courses are for internal students, but some universities, notably London, offer **external degrees** for both home and overseas candidates. (*See also* **diploma, external degree, graduate, honorary degree, honours degree, postgraduate, undergraduate, university department of education, validation**.)

delegacy

A group of individuals in a university who are given responsibility for a particular task or organization. For example, in some universities extramural studies are organized by a delegacy; in others, school examinations are the responsibility of a delegacy; although these responsibilities are delegated. A report back is normally made to another university committee, perhaps the Senate.

Departmental Committees

Similar to **Royal Commissions**, except that they deal with subjects of lesser importance and do not enjoy the same prestige. A Departmental Committee is appointed by a Minister to investigate a topic, drawing on a range of specialist advice. Its report may be either a **Command Paper** or a non-parliamentary publication and is usually referred to by the name of its chairman. (*See also* **Parliamentary Papers**.)

Department of Education and Science (DES)

In 1964, the **Ministry of Education** became the Department of Education and Science. In addition to absorbing the Ministry for Science, the DES took over from the Treasury responsibilities relating to the **UGC**. There is a **Secretary of State**, a Minister of State (Arts) and three Parliamentary Under Secretaries. The DES works in partnership with **LEAs**, but has powers under the 1944 Education Act to intervene where authorities or schools have failed to discharge their duties. The 1979, 1980 and 1981 Education Acts have further strengthened the powers of the DES. Its main tasks are to formulate policies for non-university education in England and for universities in England, Wales and Scotland and to determine priorities in the allocation of resources to the education service. It is responsible for approving building projects in England, the supply and training of teachers and the qualifications of teachers in England and Wales. The DES commissions research relating to policy matters and monitors **standards** in educational establishments through **Her Majesty's Inspectorate** (HMI), a body independent of the DES. There is a separate Secretary of State for Wales. (*See also* **Department of Education Northern Ireland, Scottish Education Department, Welsh Office**.)

DES, *The Educational Systems of England and Wales*, HMSO, 1982

W. PILE, *The Department of Education and Science*, George Allen and Unwin, 1979

Department of Education Northern Ireland

The Department of Education administers public education in Northern Ireland, apart from that given in the universities. The education system is governed by the Education and Libraries (Northern Ireland) Order, 1972, which came into effect from 1973. The Order created five education and library boards, which are responsible locally for ensuring that there are sufficient schools and other facilities in their respective areas. They also manage controlled schools and are responsible for the maintenance of most **voluntary schools** and ensure that an efficient library service is available. The boards consist of representatives of district councils, teachers, libraries, transferors of school and maintained school authorities. The Department oversees the boards and is responsible for all aspects of schooling, teacher training, teachers' salaries, youth services and so on. The Inspectorate is based at the Department and, unlike **HMI**, is not an independent body. (*See* **Department of Education and Science, Scottish Education Department, Welsh Office**.)

deputy head
A post in the hierarchy of a secondary school between the **head** and **second master/mistress**. There is no one standard job definition, but the holder of the post often acts as liaison between the head and the rest of the staff and frequently exercises powers delegated by the head. In large schools nowadays there are often two or more deputy heads. Primary schools normally have one deputy head. (*See also* **induction schemes**.)

R. MATTHEW and S. TONG, *The Role of the Deputy Head in the Comprehensive School*, Ward Lock Educational, 1982

deschooling
A term invented by Ivan Illich (1971)

in *Deschooling Society* to encourage the idea of developing true education without schools. Schools, according to Illich, are too bureaucratic and expensive as well as being very inefficient means of educating the young. Developing countries in particular, in his view, would be better off without schools. Some of his followers have concentrated instead on changing schools by weakening the links between schools and the job-market. (*See also* **alternative education, compulsory education, free schools**.)

I. D. ILLICH, *Deschooling Society*, Calder, 1971

developmental testing

A kind of **formative evaluation** particularly used by the **Open University**. Teaching materials are tried out on students on a trial basis before the final version is put into production. The trial group of students is asked to comment on particular difficulties or confusing passages which are then analysed by educational psychologists and others skilled in textual presentation.

Devonshire Report

The Devonshire Commission took its name from its chairman, the seventh Duke of Devonshire, who was interested in the application of science to industry. The Royal Commission on Scientific Instruction and the Advancement of Science issued a series of reports between 1872 and 1875 on many aspects of scientific education, including the universities. Many of its recommendations were forward-looking. The **Revised Code** had prevented the development of science in **elementary schools**. Advances

were to be made by the recruiting of scientifically qualified men for the Inspectorate and professorships were to be established in order to produce a supply of well-qualified science masters. It also deplored the lack of science teaching in endowed schools and recommended that laboratories should be built for practical instruction in physics and chemistry. (*See also* **Samuelson Report**.)

Reports of the Royal Commission on Science Instruction and the Advancement of Science 1872–5, P.P. 1872, xxv; P.P. 1875, xxviii

diagnosis

The analysis of pupils' abilities in school attainment. This may be done by using specially designed **attainment tests**, and **diagnostic tests** in the basic subjects. Pupils can be referred to **child guidance clinics**, staffed by educational psychologists, for an investigation of physical, psychological or emotional dispositions which may affect school performance. Schools are also being urged to establish programmes to meet the individual needs of these children. (*See also* **school psychological service**.)

diagnostic test

A test designed to discover an individual pupil's strengths and weaknesses in a particular subject area, often arithmetic or reading. Such a test is not designed to find out a pupil's competence or where he stands in relation to the rest of an age group. It is designed as a teaching aid. (*See also* **attainment, diagnosis, child guidance clinic**.)

difficulty index

Measure of the difficulty of an item in a test. It might be measured by the percentage of candidates answering correctly according to some models of test construction. An item with either a very low or a very high difficulty index would be omitted from the final version of the test. (*See also* **facility index**.)

dilution

A fear that if unskilled or untrained helpers are employed in schools to do some of the less professional work previously done by teachers, then the whole of the profession will become 'diluted'. For this reason many professional teachers' organizations are officially opposed to the employment of teachers' aides or classroom helpers of any kind. The opposing argument is that if more non-professionals were employed in schools this would release teachers for their more skilled professional duties. (*See also* **ancillary staff**.)

diploma

1. A qualification granted by an institution at the end of a course of study. Diplomas may be of sub-degree standard or may be confined to graduates, e.g. **PGCE**. Many professional associations grant their own diplomas.

2. A document describing a candidate's performance following a course of study.

(*See also* **degree**.)

Diploma of Higher Education (Dip HE)

Introduced in 1974, the Diploma is a two-year course of study at **degree** standard offered by 62 institutions, either universities, polytechnics or institutes of higher education. There is a wide range of subjects to choose from in the social and physical sciences, the arts, humanities and technology. Most of the courses are **CNAA** validated. The majority of students go on to study for a degree and some institutions have specially designed degree courses to which successful Diploma students can transfer. The Diploma is especially useful for school-leavers who wish to continue with their studies but wish to delay making a definite choice in the first instance. Entry qualification is two **GCE A levels**, though this is not always enforced.

direct grant college

The **DES** provides direct finance to the voluntary colleges, formerly teacher-training institutions but now offering diversified courses, in England and Wales. In addition, there are ten non-denominational further education institutions in this category, which includes the Royal Academy of Music and the Royal College of Music.

direct grant school

A type of secondary school, usually a selective **grammar school**, first established in 1926, which received a grant direct from the **DES**. The arrangement included a guarantee that a proportion of places was reserved for children from **primary schools** to be paid by **LEAs** or the schools' governors in accordance with the Direct Grant Regulations 1959. From September 1976 this arrangement ceased to operate: direct grant schools either joined the maintained system or became private schools. (*See also* **independent school**.)

E. ALLSOPP, *Direct Grant Grammar Schools*, Fabian Society, 1966

direct method

This method of teaching modern languages stemmed from work done in Germany towards the end of the last century. It avoids the analysis of grammar, but stresses the employment by the teacher of oral techniques, especially conversation and question and answering: in this way the pupil becomes immersed in the language itself. The direct method was very popular in English schools between 1900 and 1914: by the 1920s it was under attack, to be finally laid low by a staff inspector at the Board of Education, HMI Mr F. H. Collins, between the years 1929 and 1932. (*See also* **language laboratory**.)

director

1. Director of Education, an alternative title to **Chief Education Officer**, the leading officer of an **LEA** Education Department.

2. Director of Studies, a person in a school or college responsible for a course or advising a group of students in academic matters.

3. A title for the head of an educational establishment, particularly in universities and polytechnics.

disadvantaged

Those whose life chances are diminished by various social, physical, economic or family handicaps, or a combination of them, from birth. The 'cycle of deprivation' hypothesis is often linked to the 'culture of poverty' argument, both laying stress on family process. Another view is that society and its structure are most to blame. The chances of avoiding disadvantage depend much on the individual's external avenues of escape. (*See also* **compensatory education, deficit model, enrichment programme, EPA, language deficit, positive discrimination**.)

J. ESSEN and P. WEDGE, *Continuities in Childhood Disadvantage*, Heinemann Educational, 1982

M. RUTTER and N. MADGE, *Cycles of Disadvantage; a Review of Research*, Heinemann Educational, 1982

discipline

In schools, usually a term used to indicate 'classroom control' or 'keeping order'.

J. W. DOCKING, *Control and Discipline in Schools*, Harper and Row, 1980

disciplines, academic

Areas of human knowledge, for example, history, geography, physics or geology, which have been developed, often in universities, as separate subject areas for purposes of teaching and research. A discipline would be associated with **learned journals**, professional associations and perhaps written or unwritten codes of practice. Some philosophers, for example, Paul Hirst, have tried to avoid the ambiguity of 'disciplines', preferring to subdivide knowledge into forms and fields. (*See also* **disciplines of education, interdisciplinary studies**).

B. SIMON, 'The Study of Education as a University Subject in Britain', *Studies in Higher Education*, Vol.8, No.1, 1983

R. WHITFIELD (ed.), *Disciplines of the Curriculum*, McGraw-Hill, 1971

disciplines of education

The subject areas that, according to one view of professional training, all teachers should be introduced to as part of their initial training. The disciplines were traditionally considered to be philosophy, psychology and history of education; but since the late 1950s and early 1960s, sociology has tended to be included, sometimes at the expense of history. (*See also* **academic disciplines**.)

J. W. TIBBLE (ed.), *The Study of Education*, Routledge and Kegan Paul, 1966

discretionary award

In contrast to a **mandatory award**, **LEAs** give discretionary awards according to their own determined policies and cases are considered individually. These are for a variety of courses, usually below first degree level. For example, an award might be given to enable 16 to 18-year-old students from low income families to attend an **A level** course at a local college. (*See also* **entrance award**, **maintenance grant**.)

discrimination index

A measure of the success with which an item in a test can discriminate between 'good' and 'poor' candidates on the test as a whole. The easiest way of measuring the discrimination is to see to what extent success on a particular item correlates with success on the test as a whole. In some test models, items that do not discriminate are omitted from final versions of the test.

disruptive unit

Children who cause undue disruption in ordinary schools may be placed in a disruptive unit, either on a part- or full-time basis. Units may be part of the **campus** of an ordinary school or in segregated provision. There are more than 1,000 of these units throughout the country. There is a high staff-pupil ratio and the educational treatment provided combines a therapy and management approach coupled with an appropriate curriculum. They are, in the main, regarded as temporary measures: some units aim to rehabilitate children to main schooling, others towards employment.

DES, *Behavioural Units: A Survey of Special Units for Pupils with Behavioural Problems*, HMSO, 1978

R. GUNSELL, 'Suspensions and the Sin Bin Boom: soft option for schools', *Where?*, No. 153, 1979

dissemination

Part of the process of curriculum development. A well-planned scheme of curriculum development would consist not only of planning the desired change and preparing materials and methods to implement change, but also of planning the means of getting these new ideas across to a large number of teachers. In the early days of curriculum development, it was thought that this process of spreading ideas would occur naturally by a process of diffusion, but this proved to be an unwarranted assumption and plans for dissemination in an active way were built into later **curriculum development projects**. (*See also* **research and development**.)

B. MACDONALD and R. WALKER, *Changing the Curriculum*, Open Books, 1976

J. RUDDOCK, *Dissemination of Innovation: the Humanities Curriculum Project*, Methuen Educational, 1976

dissenting academy
The passing of the 1662 Act of Uniformity deprived some **Oxbridge** tutors of their fellowships and clergymen of their livings. A number therefore set up their own academies and brought with them a liberal and broadly based curriculum, which often included both history and science. The academies became very popular throughout England, offering up to five years' study. One of the most famous was Warrington Academy, which included on its staff Joseph Priestley, the discoverer of oxygen. By the beginning of the nineteenth century the movement was in decline, partly through lack of endowments and partly through sectarian differences.

J. W. A. SMITH, *The Birth of Modern Education: the contribution of the Dissenting Academies 1600–1800*, Independent Press, 1954

dissertation
A treatise based on research submitted in connection with an award or qualification. Although the terms dissertation and **thesis** are often interchangeable, the latter is often more demanding. In some universities, a dissertation is shorter than a thesis. (*See also* **degrees**, **viva**.)

distance learning
The most obvious kind of distance learning is the **correspondence course**, but the term now includes other media besides the written and the printed word, such as television, video tapes and radio programmes. Distance learning normally is based on a pre-produced course which is self-instructional, but where organized two-way communication takes place between the student and a supporting institution. The **Open University** is a good example of this form of learning. Cable and/or satellite television may prove to be very important in distance learning in the future. (*See also* **PICKUP**, **study skills**.)

B. HOLMBERG, *Status and Trends of Distance Learning*, Kogan Page, 1981

A. KAYE and G. RUMBLE, *Distance Teaching for Higher and Adult Education*, Croom Helm in association with the Open University Press, 1981

distractor
In a **multiple choice test** each question will be followed by one correct answer but several incorrect answers or distractors. The candidate has to choose the correct answer from the incorrect, and at least some of the incorrect answers should be sufficiently plausible to distract a candidate. If all the incorrect answers were too obviously wrong, then the candidate would be able to 'guess' at the correct answer without really knowing the right answer.

divergent thinking
A thinking process which tends to look for a variety of solutions rather than a single correct answer. Liam Hudson in his book *Contrary Imaginations*, Penguin, 1972, contrasted the **convergent thinking** of boys who tended to become scientists and those who as a result of his tests were

classified as divergers. These tended to be better at art subjects. (*See also* **creativity**.)

don

Originating from the Spanish word 'don', to denote a nobleman, it was later applied to **Oxbridge Fellows**, but has now been extended to include university teachers in general.

Donnison Report

Whilst the **Public Schools Commission** under the chairmanship of Sir John Newsom was deliberating, its terms of reference were extended to include **direct grant** and **independent day schools**. Members of the Commission, in their second report published in 1970, were divided in their opinions on the funding and status of direct grant schools. The return to office of a Conservative Government shortly after this report was published ended further consideration of the proposals, though after the Labour victory in 1974 the direct grant arrangements were terminated. (*See* **Assisted Places Scheme**, **Fleming Report**.)

PUBLIC SCHOOLS COMMISSION, *2nd Report, Vol. 1, Report on Independent Day Schools and Direct Grant Grammar Schools*, HMSO, 1970

Down's Syndrome

A condition, known also as mongolism, named after the nineteenth-century physician who wrote up case studies of the condition. The condition is now believed to be caused by chromosomal abnormalities resulting in flattened facial features, stubby fingers and mental retardation. Children of this kind used to be taught in **special schools**, but recently attempts have been made to integrate especially those with the milder forms of Down's Syndrome in normal classes.

C. CUNNINGHAM, *Down's Syndrome: an introduction for parents*, Souvenir Press, 1982

drill

Drill flourished in elementary schools, particularly during the nineteenth century. It was encouraged on the grounds of promoting good health as well as discipline. The 1871 Education Code allowed forty hours of drill a year, the title being changed four years later to 'military drill'. Instruction was often given by drill sergeants, hired by the **Education Department** from the War Office. Drill was confined to boys only, girls having physical exercises. By the end of the century, military drill had been generally supplemented by more imaginative physical training. (*See also* **truant school**.)

J. S. HURT, 'Drill, discipline and the elementary school ethos', in P. MCCANN (ed.), *Popular education and socialization in the nineteenth century*, Methuen, 1977

dual system

The existence of Church and State schools alongside each other dates from the time of the 1870 Education Act. Under this Act, Church schools were given building grants for new buildings. By the 1902 Act, rate-aid was extended to Church schools, in return for concessions such as the nomination of school **managers** by the **LEAs** and their supervision of non-religious aspects of the curriculum. The 1944 Act modified the system by dividing **voluntary** schools into three categories – **aided**, **controlled** and **special agreement** – according to the type of financial arrangement desired in return for concessions made with the LEA. It should be noted that the Act introduced compulsory religious worship and instruction in all **county** and voluntary schools. Legislation in 1959 and 1967 allowed for building grants to Church schools for the first time in a century. (*See also* **religious education**.)

M. CRUICKSHANK, *Church and State in English Education: 1870 to the Present day*, Macmillan, 1963

Duke of Edinburgh's Award

A scheme begun in 1956 'to help the young generation, first to discover their talents and then how to use them, particularly in the service of others'. The scheme is available to organizations and individuals between the ages of 14 and 20. Awards – bronze, silver and gold – are given in a range of interests which includes, for instance, life-saving, youth leadership, drama, sailing and expeditions on land or sea.

Dunning Report

Published in 1977, this report complemented the work of the **Munn Committee**. The remit of the Committee, under its chairman Mr J. Dunning, was to identify the aims and purposes of assessment and certification in the fourth year of Scottish secondary education, the higher grade Scottish Certificate of Education and the Certificate of Sixth Year Studies. The Committee's recommendations were quite radical. The O grade examination should be replaced by a three-level Certificate, foundation, general and credit, according to ability. Assessment of the examination would be based on a combination of internal and external marks. Teachers would be assisted in ensuring standards by the recommendation that national guides in each subject were to be prepared. (*See* **Munn Report, Scottish Education Department**.)

SCOTTISH EDUCATION DEPARTMENT, *Report of the Committee to Review Assessment in the Third and Fourth Years of Secondary Education in Scotland. Assessment for All*, HMSO, 1977

dyslexia

Defined by the World Federation of Neurology in 1968 as 'a disorder in children who, despite conventional classroom experience, fail to attain the language skills in reading, writing and spelling commensurate with their intellectual abilities.' In the UK, some doubt has been expressed on whether a clearly defined syndrome exists. The **Bullock Report** rejected the term and the **Warnock Report** preferred the use of a more general term, 'children with special learning difficulties'. 'Dyscalculia' is the term applied to those children who have similar difficulties with mathematics.

L. KOSE, 'Developmental Dyscalculia', *Journal of Learning Difficulties*, Vol. 7, No. 3, 1974

P. TANSLEY and J. PANCKHURST, *Children with Special Learning Difficulties. A Critical Review of Research*, NFER, 1981

E

educability

A measure or crude estimate of the extent to which an individual pupil or a group might be capable of responding to or benefiting from a given educational programme.

Education Act, 1944

See **Butler Act**.

Education Acts

Since the last century, a series of Education Acts, passed by Parliament, have signalled reform and re-organization of all aspects of education. The earliest ones, 1870, 1876 and 1880, were mainly attempts to establish adequate school accommodation and to enforce attendance. The 1902 Act laid the foundations for a coherent education system, bringing hitherto disparate elements under a central body, the **Board of Education**, as well as creating **LEAs**. Welfare aspects were dealt with by the 1906 Act (school meals) and 1907 (medical treatment), whilst the school leaving age was raised by those of 1918, 1936 and 1944. This last Act will be dealt with separately (*see* **Butler Act**) but it is important to note that it organized education in three stages – **primary**, **secondary** and **further**. The Education Act, 1980, has a number of significant features. It compels LEAs to provide information about admissions to their schools. Parents and teachers must be included in all school governing bodies; parents are given the opportunity to send their children to schools outside their **catchment area**; and the Secretary of State is empowered to assist bright pupils to attend certain **independent schools**. The 1981 Education Act set out to make a legal framework for the aims stated in the **Warnock Report** concerning the **special educational needs** of children and young people. (*See also* **legal aspects of education**.)

G. TAYLOR and J. B. SAUNDERS, *The Law of Education*, Butterworths, 8th edn, 1976, supplement 1980

educational administration, as a study

The study of educational administration, according to Baron (1979), deals with the range of education from nursery to university, and is marked off from other forms of administration, such as public administration or social administration, by the unique relationship which exists between teacher and taught. It draws on a number of other disciplines, especially in the field of social sciences, as the study of educational administration emphasizes the behavioural, economic, managerial and political. Examples of research areas include the government of education institutions, the major interest groups involved in the decision-making process at local and national levels and staff development.

G. BARON, 'Research in Educational Administration in Britain', *Educational Administration*, Vol. 8, No. 1, Autumn 1979

D. A. HOWELL, *A Bibliography of Educational Administration in the United Kingdom*, NFER, 1978

Educational Disadvantage Unit (EDU)

A unit set up in 1971 by the **DES** to investigate the needs of children considered to be 'educationally disad-vantaged'. The early work of the **APU** was associated with EDU but it gradually distanced itself from the question of the **disadvantaged**.

Educational Institute of Scotland (EIS)

Represents about 80 per cent of all Scottish teachers in primary, secondary and further education, totalling over 40,000 members. The committees dealing with teachers' salaries and conditions of service have a majority of EIS members and the committee for college lecturers has 8 of the 19 places filled by EIS representatives.

educationally subnormal (ESN)

Children described as educationally subnormal will be intellectually impaired in either a moderate (M) or severe (S) form. The majority of such children will have associated disorders in areas of physical and emotional development. Approximately one-third of mildly mentally retarded children have significant problems in the area of behavioural disorders and may have problems of physical co-ordination. The severely mentally retarded are usually multiply-handicapped and some need nursing and social care rather than educational management. Children in both categories are usually taught together in special classes, which may be in **special schools**, but more are now being integrated into ordinary schools. (*See also* **special educational needs, Warnock Report**.)

educational priority areas (EPA)

In 1967, the **Plowden Report on** **Primary Education** had drawn attention to the schools in run-down areas with poor buildings, high staff turnover and children with multiple handicaps. The report advocated **positive discrimination** in order to 'make schools in the most deprived areas as good as the best in the country'. In 1968 an **action research** programme was approved by the Government in London, Birmingham, Liverpool, the West Riding and Dundee. **LEAs** have different sets of criteria for defining an educational priority area, that of the **Inner London Education Authority** being the most sophisticated. Schools in areas designated receive extra financial and social support. (*See also* **compensatory education, disadvantage, enrichment programme**.)

A. H. HALSEY, *Educational Priority: EPA Problems and Policies*, Vol. 1, HMSO, 1972

E. MIDWINTER, *Projections: an Educational Priority Area at Work*, Ward Lock, 1972

Educational Publishers Council

Established in 1969 and forming part of the Publishers Association, the Council is concerned with assessing and putting forward the co-ordinated views of educational publishers and making known generally the nature and importance of publishers' work in this field. In recent years, the Council has issued a series of publications analysing schoolbook spending by **LEAs** in different areas in England.

educational technology

Rowntree (1982) states that educational technology 'is a rational problem-solving approach to education, a way of *thinking* sceptically and systematically about learning and teaching'. It is not concerned solely with hardware, such as **audio-visual aids,** and software, such as tapes, but also with helping pupils to achieve educational **objectives** through appropriate learning strategies, such as problem-solving. (*See also* **CAL**, **CAMOL**, **computers in schools**, **new information technology**.)

D. ROWNTREE, *Educational Technology in Curriculum Development*, Harper and Row, 2nd edn, 1982

D. UNWIN, 'The future direction of educational technology', *Programmed Learning and Educational Technology*, Vol. 18, No. 4, 1981

educational television (etv)
A term used in two very different ways. The first refers to any television programme that is intended to be educational, for example, documentary films or discussions about politics. The second meaning is the group of television films which are made specifically for educational purposes in schools and other educational institutions. The latter may often be referred to as 'school television'. (*See also* **audio-visual aids**.)

Education Committee
See **local education authority**.

Education Department
The **Committee of the Privy Council on Education** was set up in 1839 to administer grants to **voluntary schools**. With the growth of its responsibilities, particularly the amount of money to be allocated, the Council was replaced by an Education Department in 1856. It was represented in the Commons by a **Vice-President of the Council**, who was virtually the **Minister of Education**, and a **Lord President** in the Lords. The Department continued to flourish until the Board of Education Act (1899) established a Board, headed by a President, responsible for elementary, secondary and technological education. (*See also* **Office of Special Inquiries and Reports**.)

A. S. BISHOP, *The Rise of a Central Authority for English Education*, Cambridge University Press, 1971

G. W. KEKEWICH, *The Education Department and After*, Constable, 1920

education vouchers
A scheme whereby vouchers are given to parents to enable them to purchase education at schools of their choice. A two-year study of vouchers carried out in the Ashford area of Kent in 1977 showed that apart from the expensiveness of the scheme, it would be difficult to administer. Teacher opposition to the plan in the area was high. For those parents wishing to send their children to **independent schools**, the extra cost was to be borne by them, not the **LEA**. The voucher plan was operated in the Alum Rock school district of San José, California, from 1972 to 1976. One interesting feature was the development of 'mini-schools' within larger schools, offering alternative programmes. Two of the main difficulties encountered were the shortage of buildings, and meeting the demands for the multitude of courses.

B. ATKINSON, 'Vouchsafing School Choice', *Times Educational Supplement*, 18 Feb. 1983

KENT COUNTY COUNCIL, *Education Vouchers in Kent: a feasibility study*, Maidstone, Kent County Council, 1978

Education Welfare Service

At its extremes, the Service is required, on the one hand, to exercise enforcement powers of school attendance through court proceedings, and on the other hand to provide material benefits, such as necessitous clothing allowances and **maintenance grants**. Other duties include child employment certification, transport of children and assessment for free meals. More recently, the Service has been perceived as having an important function in developing home-school liaison, rather than being regarded by parents as an instrument of the school. The Service is staffed by Education Welfare Officers (EWO), of which there are now over 3000 in England and Wales. Their job description includes **counselling** and guidance with pregnant school girls, monitoring child employment, group work with persistent non-attenders or disruptive pupils and liaising with social service agencies.

K. FITZHERBERT, *Child Care Services and the Teacher*, Temple Smith, 1977

K. MACMILLAN, *Education, Welfare Strategy and Structure*, Longman, 1977

EFL
See **English as a Foreign Language**.

Eldon Judgment
In an attempt to widen the school's curriculum, the governors of Leeds Grammar School put forward a scheme to Chancery in 1797 which would have allowed mathematics and modern languages to be taught. Eight years later Lord Eldon, the Lord Chancellor, ruled that Greek and Latin only could be taught. In 1840, a Grammar School Act allowed for the introduction of a broader curriculum.

R. S. TOMPSON, 'The Leeds Grammar School Case of 1805', *Journal of Educational Administration and History*, Vol. 3, No. 1, 1970

elementary school
A type of school which existed until 1944 offering an education for children from 5 to 14 years of age. Neither the 1870 nor the 1902 Education Acts defined 'elementary education', but the curriculum normally consisted of the **three Rs**, history, geography, physical education, elementary science and manual instruction for boys with home economics for girls. Foreign languages and the different sciences were not included. The 1944 Education Act made provision for **primary education** for all up to the age of 11 and **secondary education** thereafter. (*See also* **overpressure in education**, **'payment by results'**.)

F. SMITH, *A History of English Elementary Education, 1760–1902*, University of London Press, 1931

'eleven plus' examination
Term commonly used for tests administered by **LEAs** for entrance into selective secondary schools. From the time of the **Technical Instruction Acts**, committees were set up locally to select promising pupils, partly based on their performance in examinations. Sidney Webb, chairman of the London Technical Education Board, favoured an 'educational ladder' which aspiring working-class children could climb.

During the years 1895 to 1906, the number of such scholarships provided by LEAs increased from 2,500 to 23,500. In 1907, the Liberal Government introduced the Free Place Regulations, which required secondary schools in future to offer up to 25 per cent of their places free to pupils from public elementary schools. Although it was necessary for pupils to pass an attainment test, it was envisaged by the President of the Board of Education, Reginald McKenna, as a qualifying rather than a competitive examination; local authorities were free to interpret entrance tests in their own ways. By 1920 there was widespread demand for secondary school places and methods of selection were stiffened. The use of the new psychological tests became part of the procedure, besides written papers, through the work of P. B. Ballard, Cyril Burt and Godfrey Thomson. In 1932, the regulations were changed: candidates no longer needed to have attended public elementary schools and parents were means tested. Competition now became more fierce. The name of the award 'Free Place' became 'Special Place' from this time. Widespread dissatisfaction with the eleven plus examination was further fuelled by the 1944 Education Act, which offered **secondary education for all**. The introduction of **comprehensive schooling** has meant the ending of selection procedures by the majority of LEAs. However, they still exist in areas where secondary schools have not yet been reorganized. (*See also* **Bryce Report**, **ladder of ability**, **verbal reasoning**.)

P. GORDON, *Selection for Secondary Education*, The Woburn Press, 1980

K. LINDSAY, *Social Progress and Educational Waste*, Routledge and Kegan Paul, 1926.

Emergency Training Scheme
Anticipating the shortage of teachers at the end of the Second World War, the Government launched this scheme in 1943 to recruit teachers from the Forces and other forms of national service. Special Emergency Training Colleges were set up, giving a one-year course of training. By the time the scheme ended in 1951, some 54,000 students had attended these colleges.

emeritus
A title conferred on a **professor** on his or her retirement. In some universities it is also conferred on **readers**.

enactive, iconic and symbolic
The American psychologist, Jerome Bruner, put forward a theory of children's intellectual development in which he distinguished three modes of representing experience which were sequential: first, the enactive mode, during which a child experienced the world by means of purely motor responses; the iconic (which involved pictorial images or models); and, finally, the symbolic, which involved language or abstract formulae. An example which is often given to illustrate these three modes is that of 'balance'. At a very early stage of intellectual development, a child might experience balance in terms of a see-saw, the enactive mode. Later he could understand some of the principles of balance by looking at various pictures and diagrams, the iconic mode. Finally, he might be able to make calculations about various kinds of balance by purely math-

ematical formulae; he will have reached the symbolic mode. Bruner's modes clearly have much in common with Piaget's stages of development, but some teachers have found them to be more useful in classroom planning. (*See also* **Piagetian**.)

J. BRUNER, *The Process of Education*, Harvard University Press, 1960

encyclopaedism

A view of schooling which suggests that up to the compulsory school leaving age all education should be general and should be planned to cover the major kinds of **knowledge** and experiences. Thus a good education would be a balanced selection from all known forms of human knowledge and experience. (*See also* **essentialism**.)

Endowed Schools Commission

The **Taunton Commission** reported in 1868 on the need to reform the endowed schools. Following the passing of the Endowed Schools Act in 1869 a Commission, consisting of three full-time members, was set up to frame a number of model schemes as a basis for making sweeping reforms in matters of charitable endowments. There was much opposition from the larger foundations and the work of the Commission soon became a political issue. With the return of a Conservative government in 1874, the Commission was dismantled and its duties were transferred to **Charity Commission**.

P. GORDON, 'Some Sources for the History of the Endowed Schools Commission', *British Journal of Educational Studies*. Vol. 14, No. 3, 1966

English as a Foreign Language (EFL)

EFL is a commonly used abbreviation describing the teaching of English either to foreign students in the UK or in overseas countries. In the USA, ESL (English as a Second Language) is often preferred but the two are by no means identical. In recent years an attempt has been made to cover both fields by the term ESOL (English to Speakers of Other Languages), since it is not always possible to make sensible distinctions between those for whom English is a foreign language and those for whom English is a second language, but not a foreign language. The problem is particularly acute in countries such as the UK and USA where large immigrant communities exist using their first, native language but for whom English is not a 'foreign' language.

S. G. DARLAN, *English as a Foreign Language: history, development and methods of teaching*, University of Oklahoma Press, 1972.

enrichment programme

A programme of school activities designed either to compensate children from a deprived background, e.g. the American **Head Start** programme, or, in Britain, the Schools Council Research and Development Project in Compensatory Education. The most important example of an enrichment programme in this country was probably that associated with the **Plowden Report's educational priority areas**. Gifted children also need extra stimulus and this is catered for in programmes such as the Schools Council Curriculum Enrichment Programme for Gifted Children. (*See also* **compensatory** education, disadvantage, positive discrimination.)

M. CHAZAN (ed.), *Compensatory Education*, Butterworths, 1973

entrance award

At Oxford and Cambridge, financial awards may be made to certain applicants who are successful at the colleges' entrance examinations. These awards are either Scholarships or Exhibitions, the former being of greater value. There are both open and closed awards. Open awards are given solely on the basis of merit whilst closed awards are restricted to certain categories, either of subject or of students from a particular school. Entrance awards are given normally for one or two years; they are also renewable yearly or can be awarded retrospectively depending on performance in later examinations. (*See also* **bursary**, **discretionary award**, **entry qualification**, **mandatory award**.)

entry qualification

Most courses in **higher education** have prerequisites of some kind in the form of entry qualifications or entry requirements. For example, most Masters' **degrees** would require a second class honours degree at Bachelor's level; most first degrees would require students to have passed at least two **A levels.** Some courses would require other kinds of qualifications and/or experience, for example, some courses in teacher education would require that the student be a '**qualified teacher**'. The theory behind such a process is that higher level courses are 'incremental'; in other words, do not start from scratch, but build upon previously

acquired knowledge and/or experience. (*See also* **entrance award**, **graduate**, **mature student**, **open admission**, **Open Tech**, **Open University**, **undergraduate**.)

ERIC

Acronym for Educational Resources Information Centre, an American-based system which issues a monthly abstracting journal *Resources in Education* on various aspects of educational research. Many libraries are also linked into the system. (*See also* **information retrieval**, **resource centre**.)

M. R. LAUBACHER, *A Glossary of ERIC Terminology*, ERIC Clearinghouse of Information Sources, Syracuse University, 1978.

Equal Opportunities Commission (EOC)

The Sex Discrimination Act 1975 (Sections 53–61 and Schedule 3) provided that a Commission, consisting of not less than eight or more than 15 members, should be appointed by the Home Secretary to work towards the elimination of discrimination on the grounds of sex or marital status, to promote equality of opportunity between men and women and to keep under review the working of the Sex Discrimination Act and the Equal Pay Act 1970. The EOC helps and advises **LEA**s and schools who plan courses or conferences on ways of promoting equal opportunities in education. The Commission submits proposals to the Secretary of State to amend these Acts where necessary. It also produces research bulletins, e.g. *Gender and the Secondary School Curriculum*, Spring 1982. There is a separate Commission for Northern Ireland. (*See also* **girls' education**.)

essentialism

1. The belief that there is an 'essential' body of knowledge that all pupils (or possibly students in higher education) should acquire. It is sometimes not clear whether it is the knowledge which is important or the hard work necessary to attain the knowledge. The term is sometimes employed in comparative education to refer to continental school systems such as the Soviet or the French. The view is sometimes also referred to as **encyclopaedism**, which suggests that where there is a compulsory system of education, then this should be general education up to the compulsory leaving age. Schemes of specialization and 'options' common in English comprehensive schools will be condemned in terms of their narrowness or lack of breadth. (*See also* **culture**.)

2. In philosophy of education, the term used to describe Plato's theory that words have meaning only by reference to the resemblance of a particular object or quality to an ideal Form. This kind of essentialism rests on the assumption that ideal Forms exist in some meaningful sense. The curricular implications of this theory are that art and poetry are inferior to mathematics: whereas mathematics focuses upon the abstract form, art and poetry are concerned with imitation and therefore stray further and further away from ideal Forms or 'the truth'.

A. BRENT, *Philosophical Foundations for the Curriculum*, Unwin Educational, 1978

ethnography, ethnology, ethnomethodology

Ethnology may be described as the comparative study of human cultures. In modern sociology, ethnographic studies refer to small-scale microstudies of the school or classroom. Ethnomethodology is a branch of sociology, invented by Garfinkel, which concentrates on the sociology of everyday social life. The stress in these studies would be in the way that participants interpret the situation. There is therefore sometimes a link between ethnomethodology and **phenomenology**.

H. GARFINKEL, *Studies in Ethnomethodology*, Prentice-Hall, 1967

R. TURNER (ed.), *Ethnomethodology*, Penguin, 1974

European Economic Community (EEC)

The EEC was established in 1957 with the aim of promoting the development of economic activities, enhancing the standard of living and encouraging closer relations between the ten Member States by creating a Common Market. There is a permanent Commission at Brussels. Member States are represented by a Council of Ministers as well as a European Parliament, which is composed of 434 members. The EEC publishes studies and pamphlets on a range of social and economic issues of conern to Member States.

evaluation

An ambiguous term which may either refer to the whole process of judging the worth of an educational programme, including judgements about the quality of its content, or more specifically to measurements of the effectiveness of learning experiences – what is often described in the UK as **assessment** of student **attainment**. In recent years, evaluation has been divided into two kinds – the more quantitative approach (sometimes referred to as the agricultural or botanical model); and the approach which insists that the measurement of educational experiences is much more complex and demands interviews and whole studies of the context of the experience (illuminative evaluation). Another distinction is made between formative and summative evaluation. **Formative evaluation** takes place during the course of the development of an educational project or the production of materials (at a time when changes can still be made); **summative evaluation** occurs at the end of the learning experience or the completion of the project, by which time, clearly, it is too late to make any adjustments to that particular project, although lessons may be learned for the future.

B. S. BLOOM et al., *Handbook on Formative and Summative Evaluation of Student Learning*, McGraw-Hill, 1971

P. BROADFOOT, *Assessment, Schools and Society*, Methuen, 1979

evening class

A class for those of post-school age which provides further education, cultural or leisure facilities, usually on a non-examination basis. Such classes may be held in **LEA** evening institutes, further education colleges or community colleges.
(*See also* **continuing education**, **recurrent education**.)

H. J. EDWARDS, *The Evening Institute, its place in the educational system of England and Wales*, National Institute of Adult Education, 1961

examination boards

Bodies responsible for the conduct of examinations. The best-known are the **General Certificate of Education** (GCE) and **Certificate of Secondary Education** (CSE) boards. There are 7 GCE boards and 12 CSE boards for England whilst in Wales the GCE and CSE examinations are conducted by a single board. For purposes of the new **16+** **examination**, the system is to be administered by four groups of examination boards in England and one in Wales. Each of the examining groups will be associated with the territory covered by the CSE boards in the group, but will be required to accept entries from institutions anywhere in England and Wales. (*See also* **examinations: history of, examinations: modes of, General Certificate of Education, national criteria**.)

examinations: history of

Examinations in schools and universities first became popular in the nineteenth century. The degree reforms at Oxford and Cambridge were followed by the introduction of examinations into schools. At the elementary level, the system of **'payment by results'** began in 1862 and lasted until the end of the century. In secondary schools, 'Local Examinations' were introduced by Oxford and Cambridge and Durham in 1858 and London established the **matriculation** examination in the same year. The present century has witnessed the growth of public examinations at secondary school level. From 1917 to 1951, the **Secondary School Examinations Council** supervised the **School Certificate examination** for 16-year-olds and the **Higher School Certificate** for 18-year-olds. These were replaced in 1951 by the **General Certificate of Education (GCE) O level** and **A level** examinations, which are the responsibility of seven examining boards. For pupils not capable of taking these examinations, a **Certificate of Secondary Education (CSE)** was introduced in 1965 for 16-year-olds. In 1980, the Secretary of State accepted that a single **16+ examination** was desirable in the near future. Other bodies concerned with more vocationally oriented courses for the 16–19 age groups, such as the **City and Guilds Institute**, the **Royal Society of Arts**, the **Technician Education Council (TEC)** and the **Business Education Council (BEC)**, (now BTEC), also offer examinations.

In 1972, a pilot one-year course for 16-year-olds, the **Certificate of Extended Education (CEE)**, started, but never received official blessing. The **DES** announced in May 1982 a new 17+ examination, the **Certificate of Pre-Vocational Education (CPVE)**. Since the advent of the Certificate of Secondary Education, the forms of assessment used in examinations have become more varied; the traditional written answers are now supplemented by, for instance, **multiple choice** questions, **oral examinations**, **project work** and **continuous assessment**. (*See also* **national criteria**, **Norwood Report**.)

R. MONTGOMERY, *Examinations: an account of their evolution as an administrative device*, Longman, 1965

J. ROACH, *Public Examinations in England 1850–1900*, Cambridge University Press, 1971

examinations: modes of

The traditional form of public examination in England and Wales is that a **syllabus** is agreed and examination papers set and marked by **examination boards** rather than by teachers themselves in their own schools. With the development of the **Certificate of Secondary Education (CSE)** teachers were encouraged to be more involved at all levels of the examination process. In particular, teachers were allowed to propose their own syllabuses, to set papers for their own pupils and to mark them. This became known as Mode III examining (in contrast to the traditional Mode I). Mode II was a compromise whereby teachers worked out their own syllabus, but papers were set and marked by the board. (*See also* **examinations: history of**, **graded test**.)

H. G. MACINTOSH (ed.), *Techniques and Problems of Assessment*, Arnold, 1974

C. H. SMITH, *Mode Three Examinations in the GCE and CSE: A Survey of Current Practice*, Schools Council Bulletin 34, Evans/Methuen Educational, 1976

examiner, external

1. At school level, a person responsible for marking the examination scripts or other forms of presentation of candidates where the examination has been externally set. For example, **GCE** and **CSE** boards recruit experienced teachers for this work.

2. At post-school level, particularly in higher education, examiners appointed from other similar institutions to ensure that the **standards** of

examiner, internal
(*See also* **examinations: mode of, examiner, internal**.)

examiner, internal
1. A member of a school or college staff responsible for marking candidates' scripts or other forms of presentation of an internally set examination.

2. At post-school level, particularly in higher education, a member of staff who undertakes the marking of her/his students' examinations. They are then moderated by an **external examiner**. (*See also* **examinations: mode of.**)

exceptional children
These can be regarded in one of two ways. The first (Hallahan and Kauffman, 1978) is that they are markedly different from other children, in that they are, for example, mentally retarded, gifted or physically handicapped. The second (Wall, 1980) regards most children as differing in degree rather than in kind from each other, with the differences traceable to the result of the normal process of learning which are made different in their effects by physical, genetic or environmental factors. (*See also* **enrichment programme, giftedness, high flier, special needs education**.)

D. P. HALLAHAN and J. M. KAUFFMAN *Exceptional Children, Introduction to Special Education,* 1978

W. D. WALL, *Constructive Education for Special Groups,* Harrap/UNESCO, 1980

Exhibition
See **entrance award**.

expressive
Expressive attitudes are contrasted with instrumental attitudes; expressive attitudes satisfying emotional needs rather than gaining some extrinsic or instrumental rewards. Elliott Eisner made a similar distinction between expressive **objectives** and instructional objectives. With expressive objectives, there is no measurable outcome but there may be a change in pupil attitude which is very important but not measurable.

E. EISNER, 'Instructional and expressive educational objectives', in W. J. POPHAM et al. (eds), *Instructional Objectives,* Chicago, Illinois, Rand McNally, 1969

extended day
A scheme introduced by some **LEAs** following the recommendation of the **Newsom Report** whereby some secondary schools remain open after normal school hours to enable pupils to study or take part in leisure activities. Supervision is undertaken by school staff. (*See also* **school day**.)

external degree
A **degree** for which the candidate does not follow a formal course of study within an institution, but sits the requisite examinations to gain a qualification. One of the most popular methods of study for external degree is the **correspondence course**. The University of London external degree system has been widely used throughout the world since the last century. (*See also* **degree**.)

C. DUKE, *The London External Degree and the English Part-Time Degree Students,* Leeds University Press, 1967

external examiner
See **examiner, external.**

extra-mural department
A department of a university which provides courses for the general public, mostly in the field of liberal **adult education**. Most of the departments were established between the two World Wars and employ both full- and part-time tutors and cater for a geographical region. The names of the departments vary, e.g. Continuing Education, Adult Education. The 'new' universities have not developed separate departments, but some work through existing departmental structures. There is an increasing interest within universities in the study of adult education as an academic discipline. (*See also* **universities: history of, university extension.**)

D. LEGGE, *The Education of Adults in Britain*, The Open University Press, Milton Keynes, 1982

A. H. THORNTON and M. D. STEPHENS (eds), *The University in its Region. The Extra-Mural Contribution*, Department of Adult Education, Nottingham, 1977

extrinsic
See **intrinsic/extrinsic.**

F

facility index
A calculation of the ease with which any particular item in a test can be answered. It might be expressed in terms of the percentage of candidates (in a **pilot scheme**) answering that item correctly. (*See also* **difficulty index.**)

factory school
The 1802 Factory Act, the first of its kind, required compulsory instruction of apprentices in cotton and woollen mills in the **three Rs**. Many factory owners ignored this requirement, though Robert Owen opened a school at New Lanark in 1816 which was divided into infant, junior and upper departments. The Factory Act of 1833 made school attendance a condition of employment. (*See also* **half-time system, industrial school, school of industry.**)

faculty
1. A large division in a higher education institution which includes all the teaching staff, e.g. Faculty of Medicine. Colleges themselves are sometimes organized into faculties which may cover a range of allied subjects, e.g. Faculty of Humanities; many secondary schools organize their work on a faculty basis.

2. Term once used in psychology to describe mental attributes.

falling rolls
The decline in the annual number of births in England and Wales since 1964 has had its impact on schools. It has been estimated that the school population will fall to 7½ million by the end of the 1980s, compared with 9 million in 1977. This has already resulted in lower intakes in all types of schools, a drop in demand for teacher recruitment and the closure or amalgamation of a number of smaller schools. In 1981, the **DES** issued Circular 2/81 urgently re-

questing **LEAs** to undertake a review of overprovision. The Public Expenditure White Paper (March 1982) set the Government's target of removing almost half a million school places by March 1983. To avoid falling rolls resulting in a deterioration in the quality of secondary education, some LEAs have adopted the policy of 'staffing the curriculum'. (*See also* **bulge**, **middle school**, **natural wastage**, **redeployment**, **pupil:teacher ratio**.)

E. BRIAULT and F. SMITH, *Falling Rolls in Secondary Schools*, Parts 1 and 2, NFER, 1980

NATIONAL UNION OF TEACHERS, *Falling Rolls*, London, 1980

family grouping

An alternative, found especially in lower **primary schools**, to grouping by age in different classes. Where family grouping operates, a child remains in the same class, with the same teacher, for the whole of his or her time in that part of the school or for a period of several years. An alternative name for this system of organization is vertical age grouping.

L. RIDGWAY and I. LAWTON, *Family Grouping in the Primary School*, Ward Lock Educational, 1968

feasibility study

A preliminary study which is often undertaken before launching a major research project. Such a study provides the team with preliminary data, and may suggest alternative strategies which can be adopted. It will also test the viability of the larger project before financial resources are committed. (*See* **pilot study**.)

federal university

As distinguished from a **collegiate university** such as Oxford or Cambridge. In a federal organization, there is central control over the whole university whilst constituent colleges look after their internal affairs. London University is a good example. The University Court is the body which decides on the distribution of monies to the colleges. There is a Senate consisting largely of teachers of the university which gives approval to boards of faculties' recommendations and sanctions the appointment of **professors** and **readers** to the university. There is also a network of other committees which ensures that matters affecting the colleges can be discussed. (*See also* **universities: history of**.)

Fellow

1. A senior member of an Oxford or Cambridge college who has a voice in the running of the college. Fellows teach and give **tutorials** to **undergraduates**. Before the University Test Act of 1871, Fellows had to be unmarried.

2. A member of a learned or professional society, such as Fellow of the Royal College of Physicians and Fellow of the Royal Historical Society.

3. A member of a college or university engaged in funded research with the title of **Research Fellow**.

field study

A form of work undertaken in an environment outside school or college. For example, geographical and biological studies may involve students in carrying out practical activities in either a rural or an urban setting. (*See also* **field trip**.)

field trip

A journey or excursion to a particular place by students as part of a **field study**.

Finniston Report

A Committee of Inquiry, chaired by Sir Monty Finniston, was asked by the Government in July 1977 to investigate the requirements of British industry for professional and technical engineers, how far they were being met, and the role of engineering institutions in the education and qualification of engineers. Arrangements in other industrial countries, particularly in the **EEC**, were to be examined. The Committee's report, issued in 1980, stated that training schemes provided by industry were inadequate and that the talents of graduates were often wasted. It recommended closer links between industry and higher education institutions. New degrees, the B.Eng. and M.Eng., with a substantial practical and training element, should replace the present B.A., B.Sc. and M.Sc. in engineering. Below degree level, the organization of engineering education was to be carried on by the **Technician Education Council**, offering higher certificate and higher diplomas. In secondary schools, too, the curriculum should reflect the industrial and economic aspects of the economy. A statutory Engineering Authority was to be set up to advance the case of engineering nationally. Academic and postgraduate courses would be inspected by the Authority. Subsequently, an Engineering Council, though not a statutory body, was established. (*See also* **industry: links with schools**, **Swann Report**.)

Engineering Our Future. The Report of the Committee of Inquiry into the Engineering Profession, HMSO, 1980, Cmnd 7794.

first degree

An initial **degree**, usually a Bachelor's, obtained by following a course of study at a higher education institution or by private study. (*See also* **external degree**, **higher degree**, **undergraduate**.)

first school

The **Plowden Report** (1967) recommended that primary education should be restructured in the light of the then existing unsatisfactory age of transfer to secondary education. **Nursery** education should be available for children between 3 and 5 years to be followed by attendance at a first school from 5 to 8 years. From there the pupils would attend a **middle school** from 8 to 12 years. Children should enter the first school in the September following their fifth birthday. Where middle school reorganization has not occurred, the traditional **infant school** still exists, spanning the age group of 5 to 7. An HMI Survey, published in 1982, concluded that whilst first schools should not revert to infant or **junior** with infant schools, their number should not be increased.

T. BLACKSTONE, *First Schools of the Future*, Fabian Society, 1972

DES, *Education Five to Nine: an illustrative survey of 80 first schools in England*, HMSO, 1982

flashcard

Cards bearing words or letters used in schools in connection with the teaching of reading, especially word recognition. (*See also* **Gestalt**.)

Fleming Report

A Committee appointed by Lord (then Mr) R. A. Butler, President of the Board of Education, in July 1942 to consider ways in which the association between **public schools** and the general educational system of the country could be developed. It was also asked to include within its brief girls', as well as boys', public schools. The Committee was chaired by Lord Fleming and reported in 1944. Two schemes were put forward for achieving closer links between the systems. Under Scheme A, **LEAs** would have had the right to reserve a number of places, day or boarding, at schools accepted by the Board. Schools participating in this scheme would be required either to abolish tuition fees or grade them according to parents' income. LEAs would make payments direct to the schools concerned. Scheme B applied to acceptable boarding schools, which qualified pupils, previously educated for two years at grant-aided primary schools, could attend. **Bursaries** would be granted by the Board of Education to cover fees and boarding costs. Another condition was that schools accepted for this scheme were to offer a minimum of 25 per cent of their annual admissions to primary school pupils. These recommendations were not generally welcomed by the schools and by parents and the links between the two sectors were never forged. (*See also* **Assisted Places Scheme, Donnison Report, Newsom Report on Public Schools**.)

Report of the Committee on Public Schools appointed by the President of the Board of Education, HMSO, 1944

flexible grouping

Organizing the teaching of a large number of pupils (for example, a whole year group) in such a way that they could sometimes be taught in very large numbers, sometimes broken down into conventional classes of 25 or 30, sometimes working in much smaller groups, and sometimes as individuals. (*See also* **timetabling**.)

form

An alternative word for a **class** of pupils in a school. The term is invariably used for the highest class, the **sixth form**, which caters for those of 16 and over. (*See* **Remove**.)

formative evaluation/summative evaluation

The process of making judgements about the value of a new curriculum project or new teaching materials with the intention of improving the project or the materials for the future. In formative evaluation the intention is not to make a judgement about the final value of a project; it is intended to provide useful feedback to those preparing materials or working on the project so that improvement can be made before a summative evaluation takes place. (*See also* **developmental testing, evaluation**.)

T. BATES and M. GALLAGHER (eds), *Formative Evaluation of Educational Television Programmes*, Council for Educational Technology, 1978

B. S. BLOOM, J. T. HASTINGS and G. F. MADAUS, *Handbook on Formative and Summative Evaluation of Student Learning*, McGraw-Hill, 1971

foundation course

A basic, introductory, course usually

designed to prepare students for more advanced courses. The foundation course may be a prerequisite for more advanced courses in the same area. An **Open University** foundation course is required, for example, in arts/humanities before students may proceed to more advanced work in English literature. (*See also* **general education**.)

free education

Moves to provide national **elementary education** which would be both secular and free began with the foundation of the Lancashire Public Schools Association in 1846. With the return of a Liberal Government in 1868, a National Education League, based on Birmingham, added its voice to the debate. The 1870 Education Act did not grant free education, but remitted fees to necessitous children attending **school board** and denominational schools. Although the 1876 Education Act withdrew this concession from the latter type of school, it encouraged regular attendance and a longer period of schooling by offering free education for three years to children of 11, subject to passing the **three Rs** in the fourth or the fifth Standards, and fulfilling certain attendance requirements. From 1885 free education became a political issue in election campaigns, and in 1891 the Education Act gave parents the right to demand free education for their children. (*See also* **charity school**, **Welsh circulating school**.)

J. LEWIS, 'Parents, children, school fees and the London School Board', *History of Education*, Vol. 11, No. 4, 1982

free period

Can refer to the time allocated either to teaching staff for preparation or marking of **lessons** or to pupils for undertaking private unsupervised study.

Free Place system

The Regulations for Secondary Schools introduced by a Liberal Government in May 1907 stated that **grammar schools** receiving State grants should offer 25 per cent of their places free to pupils from public **elementary schools**. No definite age of entry was laid down, but applicants were required to pass an entrance test of **attainment** and proficiency, and **intelligence tests** were later used in many **LEAs**. These tests became popularly known as the **'eleven plus' examination**. The system was replaced by the **Special Place** examination in 1932.

P. GORDON, *Selection for Secondary Education*, Woburn Press, 1980

free school

A type of school which emerged in the early 1970s for parents interested in **alternative education**. It also caters for some children who had made little progress in State schools, having a freer curriculum. A number exist in London, such as White Lion Street Free School, Islington, opened in 1972, and in other large cities; they are mainly financed by local enterprise, though the White Lion Street School is now wholly funded by the **ILEA**. (*See also* **deschooling**.)

R. BARROW, *Radical Education. A Critique of Free Schooling and Deschooling*, Martin Robertson, Oxford, 1978

P. NEWELL, 'A free school now', *New Society*, 15 May 1975

full inspection

Term used to describe the visit of a team of inspectors, either central or local, representing a range of subject or phase interests, to an educational institution. The findings of the team are normally enshrined in a report. From January 1983, reports of HMI became publicly available. (*See also* **advisers, Her Majesty's Inspectors**.)

DES, *HMI Inspectors today: Standards in Education*, HMSO, 1983

full-time equivalent (FTE)

In those institutions of **higher education** or **further education** where full-time and part-time students are recruited, it is important from the point of view of staffing requirements and other resources to calculate the whole student body in terms of full-time equivalents. Frequently part-time students would count for half a full-time student. In further education it is frequently possible to convert part-time students into FTE in terms of 'contact hours'. In universities this is rarely calculated since most part-time students can be converted into fte in terms of the length of the course rather than the amount of instruction which they receive.

functional literacy

The level of skill in reading and writing that any individual needs in order to cope with adult life. It is clearly very difficult to arrive at a satisfactory definition of functional literacy, but in the USA there have been prosecutions brought by parents against a school or school system for failing to equip a child at school leaving age with functional literacy. The idea behind that view of schooling is that functional literacy would be a right of all normal pupils and that it would be the duty of the school to provide it. (*See also* **literacy**.)

further education (FE)

A term covering all types of post-school education apart from that given in universities. Much of it is vocationally orientated though not exclusively so. During the last two decades, the growth of **higher education** in this sector, especially the expansion of **polytechnics**, has been a notable feature.

L. M. CANTOR and I. F. ROBERTS, *Further Education Today: A Critical Review*, Routledge and Kegan Paul, 1979

Further Education Curriculum Review and Development Unit (FEU)

The Unit was established in 1977 to serve as a focal point for **further education** curricular matters. It determines priorities for action to improve the total provision, reviews curricula in this sector and identifies duplication and deficiencies, assists in curricular experiments, contributes to the evaluation of the attainment of objectives and disseminates information on curriculum development. Although the Unit was financed by and housed in the **DES**, it was free to operate independently from the Department's policies. From January 1983 the Unit became an agency independent of the DES. It is now a limited company and has the title of Further Education Unit. (*See also* **PICKUP, profiles**.)

G

games and simulations

A technique used in teaching for presenting occurrences in a given order so that pupils can gain insights into human interaction. Games are usually highly structured with set-out rules, for example *Monopoly*, which is concerned with property development and financial decisions. Simulations involve participants taking on roles and are more open-ended than games. A group may wish to examine the benefits or disadvantages of siting an airport, an old people's home or an asbestos factory and allocate appropriate roles to individuals. In practice, games and simulations are often indistinguishable or a session may make use of a mixture of both approaches. They cover most areas of the curriculum and are commercially available, though many teachers prefer to devise their own. (*See also* **competency based teaching**.)

A. DAVISON and P. GORDON, *Games and Simulations in Action*, Woburn Press, 1978

R. WALFORD and J. L. TAYLOR, *Learning and the Simulation Game*, Open University Press, 2nd edn, 1978

Gaussian curve

The shape of a graph showing a normal distribution. Sometimes also referred to as **normal curve**. It is a bell-shaped curve which is typical of a graph showing how many people obtain each possible score on a measured variable such as height. Psychologists also assume that **intelligence** falls into a normal distribution and therefore express **IQ** scores in terms of the Gaussian curve so that very few people are shown as extremely intelligent and very few as extremely dull, but the curve rises to a hump around the average score (in terms of IQ the score of 100). Opponents of IQ testing frequently complain that it is simply an assumption, not an established fact, to suppose that intelligence falls into the same kind of curve as height. (*See also* **intelligence test**, **parametric statistics**.)

'Geddes Axe'

A Committee on National Expenditure was appointed by the Prime Minister, Lloyd George, in August 1921 to advise on Government economies in the coming year. By the end of the year, the Committee, chaired by Sir Eric Geddes, a former Minister of Transport, had drawn up a report. The most controversial proposals, for education savings, the lowering of teachers' salaries and the exclusion of children under 6 from elementary schools, were rejected by the Cabinet. Part of the £6½ million reduction in education estimates was achieved by teachers contributing 5 per cent of their salary towards superannuation and by increasing the size of elementary school classes to 50.

B. SIMON, *The Politics of Educational Reform 1920–40*, Lawrence and Wishart, 1974

General Certificate of Education (GCE)

The GCE was introduced in 1951, replacing the **School Certificate**. Unlike the School Certificate, GCE is a single-subject not a group-subject examination. Of the eight GCE **examining boards** six are associated with universities. Both schools and colleges may enter candidates for any of the examinations. The **O (Ordinary) level** is designed for the most able 20 per cent of 16-year-olds. The **AO level** is graded at O level standard, usually for 17- and 18-year-olds. **A (Advanced) level** is normally a two-year course after O levels; it is a normal requirement for those wishing to go on to higher education. **S (Special) level** can be taken in conjunction with A level subjects and is intended to help universities select potential honours students.

general education

Perhaps best described as the opposite of 'specialized or specialist education'. Many educationalists believe that before embarking upon a specialist course of study it is important to have covered a wide range of subject matter. This would apply particularly for the first three or four years in **secondary schools** in the UK. In some universities a **foundation course** would be provided in the first year to provide general rather than specialist courses. (*See also* **liberal education**.)

General Teaching Council

From 1860, attempts have been made to found a General Teaching Council for England and Wales, analogous to the General Medical Council, to govern the profession. The Council was to deal with matters such as the training, supply and qualifications of teachers, the establishment of a code of conduct and the raising of professional standards. A disciplinary committee was to be given powers to strike teachers off the register. The Council would have dealt with all types of schools, from public to elementary. It was suggested that the **College of Preceptors** should take the initiative in obtaining a Scholastic Registration Act, but it failed to do so. Three further attempts by the College – in 1879, 1881 and 1890 – were similarly unsuccessful. In recent years, teacher union opposition has been expressed to the proposed composition of the membership of such a Council, and attempts to overcome this difficulty have not been successful. A Scottish General Teaching Council has existed since 1965, though its achievements have been limited. (*See also* **qualified teacher status**, **teachers' associations**.)

G. BARON, 'Teachers' Registration Movement', *British Journal of Educational Studies*, Vol. 2, No. 2, May 1954

Gestalt

Gestalt is the German word for 'configuration'. At the beginning of the twentieth century a school of psychology developed in Germany, its main assumption being that the human brain has a tendency to organize experience into patterned configurations or wholes. The word 'Gestalt' is often used to refer to the whole of a perception or thought process rather than the individual items within it. In education, Gestalt psychologists have been influential in their campaign against concentrating pupils' attention on the parts rather than the whole (the Gestalt). In reading, this tended to concentrate teachers' attention on 'look and say' or looking at the whole sentence rather than **phonic methods** of reading. (*See also* **flashcard, learning theory, reading age, reductionism**.)

giftedness

An ambiguous term, sometimes referring to children of high **IQ** for whom schools should make special provision; sometimes used to identify children with specific talents in fields such as music or dancing. The 'gifted' are also sometimes included in the generic terms '**exceptional children**', or 'children with **special educational needs**'. (*See also* **creaming, high flier, National Association for Gifted Children**.)

DES, Matters for Discussion 4, *Gifted Children in Middle and Comprehensive Secondary Schools*, HMSO, 1977

D. H. GRUBB (ed.), *The Gifted Child at School*, Oxford Society for Advanced Studies in Education, Oxford, 1982

girls' education

It is generally acknowledged that there is evidence of differences in school experience between the sexes, often to the disadvantage of girls. Two official surveys in 1975, by the **DES** in England and in Scotland by the **SED**, showed that, particularly in the secondary school, boys' subjects are mathematics, science and technical subjects and girls' subjects literature, language and domestic subjects. The DES survey concluded that pupils' choice should be based, as nearly as is practicable, on a real equality of access to experience, information and guidance. The Sex Discrimination Act of 1975, which set up the **Equal Opportunities Commission**, has helped to draw attention to these anomalies. (*See also* **Bryce Report, Girls' Public Day School Trust, Girls' School Association, Taunton Report, Thomson Report, women's studies**.)

DES, Education Survey 21, *Curriculum Differences for Boys and Girls*, HMSO, 1975

M. B. SUTHERLAND, *Sex Bias in Education*, Blackwell, Oxford, 1981

Girls' Public Day School Trust (GPDST)

This Trust was established in 1872 to promote a scheme for a public day school for girls at Chelsea. The **Taunton Report** had disclosed the grave shortage of suitable educational institutions for girls of middle-class families and the Trust had developed from the National Union for the Education of Girls of all Classes above Elementary, founded in 1871. By the beginning of the present century, there were 38 such schools. (*See also* **Bryce Report, girls' education, Girls' School Association**.)

L. MAGNUS, *The Jubilee Book of the Girls' Public Day School Trust 1873–1923*, Cambridge University Press, 1923

Girls' School Association (GSA)

An association concerned with the policy and administration of independent girls' schools. Membership is open to heads who are members of the **Secondary Heads Association** (SHA) and whose schools are represented in the Association of Governing Bodies of Girls' Public Schools (GBGSA). (*See also* **Bryce Report, girls' education, Girls' Public Day School Trust**.)

Gittins Report

In August 1963 the **Central Advisory Council for Education (Wales)** was asked by Sir Edward Boyle, then Minister of Education, to examine the state of **primary education** and the transition to **secondary education** in Wales. Its terms of reference were identical with those of the **Plowden** Committee. In its report, *Primary Education in Wales* (1967), the Committee agreed with its English counterpart and commended the notion of **first** and **middle schools**. It also endorsed the principle of a fully bilingual education. The teaching of Welsh, as a first or second language, was to be encouraged as well as its gradual introduction into all schools.

Report of the Central Advisory Council for Education (Wales), Primary Education in Wales, HMSO, 1967

governors

All schools have by law a board of governors. The 1944 Education Act provided for the constitution of governors to be prescribed in an **instrument of government** and the function of governors in relation to **LEAs** and headteachers was set out in articles of government. The term 'governor' was reserved for secondary schools (primary schools had **managers**). The 1980 Education Act stated that the term 'governor' applied henceforth to both secondary and primary school bodies. Their functions vary from place to place, but much depends on the attitude of the LEA concerned. Three major areas of involvement are the appointment of staff, the curriculum and finance. A study by Baron and Howell (1974) showed that there were wide variations in the degree of involvement in selecting staff; that heads maintained that they were responsible for what was taught; and that governing bodies had little real power in financial matters. Some LEAs group two or more schools under one governing body; some have separate bodies for each school. In 1977, the **Taylor Report** indicated that the composition of governing bodies needed revising. Section 2 of the 1980 Education Act stipulated that elected parents and teachers should be governors. The position of public servants as governors was left unclear by the related DES Circular 4/81 and LEAs have interpreted the Circular in different ways. One frequent criticism of the present system is that there is an undue proportion of political appointees as compared with the general lay element on these bodies. (*See also* **Manager, National Association of Governors and Managers**)

G. BARON and D. A. HOWELL, *The Government and Management of Schools*, Athlone Press, 1974

K. BROOKSBANK and J. REVELL, *School Governors*, Councils and Education Press, Harlow, 1981

grade

1. A mark given to students to denote their level of achievement. A grade may be in alphabetical or numerical form. (*See also* **assessment.**)

2. The name of year groups in USA schools. These range from Grade 1 for the first year of schooling (6 years) to Grade 12 of high school (18 years).

3. Classification of secondary schools recommended by the **Taunton Re-**

port corresponding to the three grades of society, i.e. first grade, second grade and third grade.

graded post
An appointment · formerly awarded to assistant teachers for taking on extra responsibilities. It carried an extra salary. The number of appointments was governed by the size of the school. These have now been replaced by **scale posts**.

graded reader
Reader in this context is a book rather than a person. A graded reader is a book which is graded in terms of difficulty. Such books are usually produced as a series so that a pupil progresses from one level of difficulty to the next. The pupil is gradually stretched, but does not encounter too many difficulties in the same page or chapter of the book.

graded test
An alternative to the five-year course of secondary school study leading to either **CSE** or **GCE** examinations, graded tests allow pupils to progress at their own pace. They can be taken at any time; if successful, the pupil can move on to the next area of study. The main users of such tests are the bottom 40 per cent of the ability range; **LEAs** and **examining boards** are collaborating in promoting tests in English and mathematics. A widely known type of graded test of a different kind is that for music, set by the Associated Board of the Royal Schools of Music. The **Cockcroft Report** favoured the use of such tests. (*See also* **examinations: modes of.**)
SCHOOLS COUNCIL, *Review of Graded Tests. Graded Objectives in Modern*

Language, Methuen Educational, 1983

graduate
In Great Britain, a person who has undertaken a period of study under the auspices of a higher education institution and has been awarded a **degree**. (*See also* **dissertation**, **postgraduate**, **thesis**, **undergraduate**, **viva**.)

Graduate Teacher Training Registry (GTTR)
The GTTR, based in London, helps **graduates** and **undergraduates** in the final year of their degree course to obtain admission to an initial course of teacher education at institutions offering a **Postgraduate Certificate in Education (PGCE)** course in England and Wales. The scheme is designed to ensure that candidates' applications are dealt with as quickly as possible: candidates submit one application for consideration by the institutions of her/his choice. (*See also* **Central Register and Clearing House**, **clearing house**.)

grammar school
The term was first used in England in the fourteenth century for a type of school, endowed by pious founders to provide free education to children of a locality, which developed in connection with and was largely dependent on the Church. Latin was the universal language and as this subject loomed large in the curriculum, they became known as grammar schools. Endowments were made by other institutions, such as the gilds or chantries. By the nineteenth century, many grammar schools were in a parlous condition: the value of endowments had de-

clined, the founders' wishes were often flouted, and because of the **Eldon Judgment** the curriculum was restricted. The Grammar School Act of 1840 was a step forward; henceforth, **governing bodies** were allowed to introduce a wider range of subjects into schools. Both **boarding** and **day schools** had developed and from the former emerged the **public schools**. The nine large ones were identified by the **Clarendon Commission**, 1864; the public and grammar schools after the **Taunton Commission** of 1868 developed in different ways. The 1902 Education Act gave the new **LEAs** power to provide secondary schools, on grammar school lines, emphasizing the humanities. Later, the development of the **tripartite** system of secondary education, stemming from the **Spens** and **Norwood** philosophies, supported the academic curriculum in grammar schools. The spread of **comprehensive education** has led to the disappearance of the grammar type in many areas, though its demise has not been welcomed universally. (*See also* **creaming**, **upper school**.)

N. CARLISLE, *A Concise Description of the Endowed Grammar Schools in England and Wales*, 2 Vols., London, 1818, reprinted Richmond Publishing, Richmond, 1972

R. DAVIS, *The Grammar School*, Penguin, 1967

grants

From 1833, parliamentary grants were awarded to voluntary bodies for the purpose of erecting school buildings. These increased from £30,000 a year in 1839 to more than £800,000 by 1861. From the latter date, the **Code** stated that grants would be related to attendance and attainment of pupils with proven efficiency in stipulated areas of the curriculum. There were eventually three types of grants:

1. *General* From 1862, two-thirds of grants paid to schools were based on examinations in the **three Rs**. The money was paid to the managers and not, as formerly, to teachers, thus affecting the latter's status.

2. *Specific* Introduced in 1867 to relieve the narrowness of the curriculum caused by '**payment by results**'. They were defined as 'sufficiently distinct from the ordinary Reading Book lessons to justify the description as a "Specific Subject of Instruction"'. Extra payments were made if such work was undertaken. At first, only upper forms were allowed to take these subjects and were limited to two in number.

3. *Class* Dating from 1875, a grant was given for certain subjects which were examined on a class, as distinct from individual, basis. Grammar and history were two examples.

graphicacy

A term invented as a parallel to **literacy**, **numeracy** and **oracy**. Graphicacy covers the ability to think visually and spatially as well as the mastery of certain basic skills.

D. BOARDMAN, *Graphicacy and Geography Teaching*, Croom Helm, 1983

'Great Debate'

At a speech given at **Ruskin College**, Oxford, on 18 October 1976, James Callaghan, then Prime Minister, called for a public debate on education. Criticism had been voiced by a number of groups, including employers, trades unions and parents, on educational **standards** and the relevance of the school **curriculum** to modern society. The Ruskin speech was followed by eight one-day regional conferences in February and March 1977, attended by a wide section of interests. Four subjects chosen for debate were: the school curriculum 5–16, the assessment of standards, the education and training of teachers and school and working life. Subsequently, in July the same year, a Green Paper, *Education in Schools. A Consultative Document*, Cmnd 6869, was presented to Parliament. It contained a number of proposals and recommendations arising out of the conferences. The variations in the design and management of the school curriculum were noted and the **Secretaries of State** proposed a review of curricular arrangements by **LEAs**. It recommended a more coherent and soundly based means of assessment for individual pupils, and drew the attention of LEAs to the need to examine the problems that occur at the point of **transition between primary and secondary schools**. On the education and supply of teachers, the **Green Paper** envisaged an all-graduate profession with preference being given to applicants with ex-

perience of the world outside education. LEAs were encouraged to develop **in-service training**. It also emphasized the need for schools to become more open to the community. One immediate outcome was the issue of Circular 14/77 by the **DES** and the **Welsh Office**, which required LEAs to collect and submit to the Department information about their policies and practices in curricular matters. The results were published in 1979 under the title *Local Authority Arrangements for the School Curriculum* (HMSO). (*See also* **accountability**, **industry: links with schools**, **parents**, **politics of education**, **school records**, **Yellow Book**.)

'Greats'
The name given to the final honours degree examination in Classics and classical philosophy at Oxford University. The official title of this degree course is *literae humaniores*.

Green Paper
Sets out Government proposals for future policy in the form of a discussion document, without commitment to action. The more important are **Command Papers**, and may be presented to both Houses of Parliament. (*See also* **Parliamentary Papers**.)

H

Hadow Reports
During the inter-war period, when Sir William Hadow, Vice-Chancellor of Sheffield University, was chairman of the Consultative Committee

of the Board of Education, three important reports were issued. The first, *The Education of the Adolescent*, was published in 1926, the second, *Primary Education*, in 1931 and the third, *Infant and Nursery Schools*, in 1933. The return of the first Labour Government in 1924, committed to a policy of **secondary education for**

all, led to a study of the organization, objectives and curriculum of children up to the age of 15. (The leaving age at this time was 14.) As secondary schools were outside the Committee's remit, the study was only a partial one. Psychological evidence was prominent in the Report. Its introduction includes the statement, 'There is a tide which begins to rise in the veins of youth at the age of eleven or twelve. It is called by the name of adolescence'. The Committee recommended a separation of **primary** and **secondary** education at the age of eleven. Some type of secondary education should be available to all, either **grammar** or **modern**: pupils would be allocated as the result of an examination. The **curriculum** would differ between the schools, the modern being more 'realistic'. A leaving age of 15 was recommended by the Report, but this was postponed and did not come into force until 1947. The findings were accepted by the Board, and from the 1930s schools were reorganized on Hadow lines. With the break in school life at 11 now official policy, the Consultative Committee's 1931 report on the primary school turned its attention to the consequences flowing from this move. It advocated close co-operation between the primary and secondary stages and the transfer of children at 7 from the **infant** department. The curriculum was to be thought of 'in terms of activity and experience rather than of knowledge to be acquired and facts to be stored'. Differences in intellectual capacity between pupils, it believed, should be dealt with by dividing an age group into streams by the age of 10. The third Hadow Report examined infant and **nursery**

schools. It encouraged enlightened approaches, giving approval to Froebelian and Montessorian methods, and stressed the need for separate infant schools. Perhaps the most far-sighted recommendation was that a national system of nursery schools should be provided, a recommendation which still awaits implementation. (*See also* **all-age school**.)

half-term
A short holiday given by schools in the middle of each **term**. (*See also* **academic year**, **semester**, **vacation**.)

half-time system
An attempt in the nineteenth century to limit the amount of time spent by children in employment. The 1833 Factory Act stated that two hours schooling on six days a week should be given for those between 9 and 11; eleven years later, another Factory Act extended the time to three hours' education on five days a week. This was the real beginning of the half-time system. From the time of the 1870 Education Act, public demand for more compulsory attendance and raising of the minimum age of employment resulted in legislation in the following ten years which went far to meet these wishes. However, the half-time system for older pupils continued in some areas until its abolition by the Fisher Education Act of 1918. (*See also* **factory school**.)

E. and R. FROW, *A Survey of the Half-Time System in Education*, E. J. Morten, 1970

H. SILVER, 'Ideology and the factory child: attitudes to half-time education', in P. MCCANN (ed.), *Popular*

Education and Socialization in the Nineteenth Century, Methuen, 1977

hall, university

1. A building, either on or away from the **campus**, for students' residence.

2. At Oxford and Cambridge, formerly a place, not a college, where students lived under the supervision of a Master of Arts. The title still exists in the names of some of the present colleges, such as Trinity Hall and St Edmund Hall.

halo effect

The psychologist, R. L. Thorndike, observed that in the process of various kinds of **assessment** the judgements of an assessor tend to be biased by a previous assessment (even if the assessment was of a totally unconnected ability). The halo effect can thus be either negative or positive.

Handbook of Suggestions

The ending of '**payment by results**' left the elementary school teacher free to pursue her/his work without central regulation. The first *Handbook of Suggestions for Teachers* was issued by the **Board of Education** in 1905 to inform teachers of good practice. All aspects of the elementary curriculum were dealt with, whole chapters being devoted to individual subjects. The *Handbook* was frequently revised, the last one appearing in 1937.

Hansard

Verbatim reports on the debates in both Houses of Parliament which are published daily by Her Majesty's Stationery Office. Since 1943, the Parliamentary Debates, Official Reports, have had the name *Hansard* on their covers. This is a reference to the printer, Luke Hansard, who printed the journals of the House of Commons from 1774. *Hansard* is a very useful reference source for researchers on many aspects of education. (*See also* **Hansard Society**.)

Hansard Society

The Hansard Society for Parliamentary Government is a non-party organization, founded by an Independent MP, Commander (later Lord) King-Hall in 1944. Set up at a time when Britain was at war, the Society's original aim was to encourage people to read the daily *Hansard* reports of parliamentary debates. It now has wider aims, providing information on the workings of British democracy and assessing how well the system continues to serve today's needs. The Society played a leading part in promoting political education in schools, and has a Curriculum Review Unit to monitor trends in teaching politics. (*See also* **Hansard**.)

Haslegrave Report

In 1967, the **National Advisory Council on Education for Industry and Commerce** appointed a Committee on Technician Courses and Examinations 'to review the provision for courses suitable for technicians at all levels . . . and to consider what changes are desirable in the present structure of courses and examinations'. Its report, issued in 1969, stated that the existing pattern of technician courses and examinations was unsuitable for meeting not only existing needs, but also changing needs and new needs which were likely to arise in the future. The main recommendation was that there should be a unified body for each of the main two sectors, technical and business, responsible for planning and co-ordinating courses. The Secretary of State for Education and Science was advised to set up as soon as possible a **Technician Education Council** (TEC) and a **Business Education Council** (BEC). (*See also* **business education**.)

Report of the Committee on Technician Courses and Examinations, HMSO, 1969

Hawthorne effect

In the early days of industrial psychology it was observed in one study of the Hawthorne works in the USA that when individuals are being observed they tend to perform better. This is important in educational studies because if a new teacher method or a new curriculum project is introduced into a classroom and the pupils improve their performance, this may not be caused by the value of the new approach but simply because the pupils are receiving extra attention. Hawthorne effect is sometimes extended to mean simply the effect of the novelty of a new set of materials which eventually wears off.

head boy/girl

A pupil, elected or appointed as leader of **prefects** in a school. His or her duties are often concerned with maintaining **discipline** and the orderly running of the school.

Headmasters' Association (HMA)

Established in 1890, the Association had close links with the **Headmasters' Conference**; all members of the Conference were members of the HMA, but the reverse did not hold true. The HMA drew its membership from secondary schools, and from 1976 became part of the **Secondary Heads Association** (SHA). (*See also* **headteacher**.)

Headmasters' Conference (HMC)

Originally set up in 1869 to oppose the investigations of the **Endowed Schools Commission** into **grammar** and endowed schools, the Conference consists of headmasters of leading **public** and grammar schools. The main mover of the Conference was Edward Thring of Uppingham and the first gathering took place in his school. Annual meetings are still held. (*See also* **Headmasters' Association**, **headteacher**.)

A. C. PERCIVAL, *The Origins of the Headmasters' Conference*, Murray, 1969

head of department

Heads of department in schools and colleges are persons who are in charge of their subject at all levels and co-ordinate the work of the department's staff. They are responsible for helping to formulate academic policy in relation to the overall school policy, encouraging **curriculum development** and often assisting the head or principal in deciding on matters affecting the whole institution. A head of department normally holds departmental **staff meetings** to discuss matters of common concern to teachers working in the department. As with all teaching posts, there is no precise role-definition available at the national level. (*See also* **post of responsibility**.)

K. LAMBERT, 'The Role of Head of Department in Schools', *Educational Administration Bulletin*, Vol. 3, Summer, 1975

M. MARLAND, *Head of Department*, Heinemann Educational Books, 1971

head of house, head of year
See **pastoral system**.

Head Start
A nationally funded programme started in the USA in 1964 which provided **disadvantaged** pre-school children with educational and social services. In its early years, notably through a study undertaken by Ohio University and the Westinghouse Learning Corporation, it was believed that **compensatory education** programmes had little effect. However, follow-up studies since 1975 have revealed the long-term benefits of Head Start in achievement in primary and secondary schools as well as in out-of-school behaviour. In 1980 there were 400,000 children within the 1,200 Head Start programmes across the country. (*See also* **educational priority area, enrichment programme**.)

J. S. PAYNE, *Head Start: a Tragicomedy with Epilogue*, Behavioural Publications, N.Y. 1973

E. ZIGLER and J. VALENTINE (eds.), *Project Head Start: a Legacy of the War on Poverty*, Collier–Macmillan, 1979

headteacher
The official appointed leader of teachers in a school. Most schools, until the beginning of the nineteenth century, consisted of a master and his pupils: it was only when schools became bigger and **assistant teachers** were recruited, at his own expense, that the role expanded. Dr Thomas Arnold at Rugby became the model for other headmasters in **public schools**; although later heads had not necessarily to be in Holy Orders, traces of that tradition still remain, with, for example, the head conducting the daily act of worship. The responsibilities of a headteacher were made clear by the setting up of the **Headmasters' Conference** in 1869, which consisted of the leading members of the prominent schools of the time. The term 'headteacher' today covers both headmaster and headmistress and applies to those in **primary** as well as in **secondary schools**. The head is expected to provide effective leadership, though systematic training for this role is by no means universal. Research also shows that heads differ widely in their conception of the relative importance of the different aspects of their work. It is now generally agreed that training in the skills of headship is needed in such areas as interpersonal and management skills and knowledge of how to evaluate a school's performance. In March 1983, the **Secretary of State** announced that a national centre for training heads and senior staff was to be established at Bristol. Materials produced at Bristol will be disseminated to 19 local centres in England and Wales. (*See also* **Headmasters' Association, National Association of Head Teachers, Secondary Heads Association**.)

R. S. PETERS (ed.), *The Role of the Head*, Routledge and Kegan Paul, 1976

P. WHITAKER, *The Primary Head*, Heinemann Educational, 1983

Health Education Council

The Council was set up in 1968 by the then Secretary of State for Health and Social Services to advise on priorities for health education, to advise and carry out regional and local campaigns with the appropriate authorities, to promote health education in schools, colleges and polytechnics and to act as the national centre of expertise and knowledge in all aspects of health education. The Council consists of a chairman and 25 members, appointed by the Secretary of State for Social Services from the fields of health, education, local government, the media and business. The Council operates in England, Wales and Northern Ireland.

Her Majesty's Inspectorate (HMI)

HM Inspectorate dates back to 1839, when inspectors were appointed to supervise the proper spending of public money for the education of the poor. Since the passing of the 1944 Education Act, the Inspectorate's responsibilities have been widened: all schools and colleges maintained from public funds are open to inspection. From the beginning HMIs have been called 'the eyes and ears of the Department', and an important function is to give advice to the **Secretary of State** and officials of the **DES**. As HMIs are appointed by Order in Council, they are not Civil Servants and are thus able to form independent judgements on educational issues. Although the Inspectorate has only about 400 members, their work includes providing **in-service training** courses for

teachers, carrying out inspections of institutions, preparing reports and discussion documents for publication, liaising with **LEA**s, servicing the **Assessment of Performance Unit** and serving as observers on many bodies. As HMIs are concerned with national developments, their work differs in many respects from that of local **advisers**. Examples of this are the two recent national surveys undertaken by HMI of primary and secondary schools, where 10 per cent of each type of school were inspected (see DES: *Primary Education in England* (1979), HMSO, and DES: *Aspects of Secondary Education in England* (1979)). In this way, it is possible to form opinions on national **standards**. Inspectors are appointed to one of the seven divisions into which England is divided, and will have general, specialist and liaison tasks. There is a Senior Chief Inspector, six Chief Inspectors with overall responsibility for the Inspectorate's work in the different fields and some 60 Staff Inspectors who have national responsibility for a particular phase or subject. There is a separate Welsh Inspectorate on loan to the **Welsh Office** by the DES; it consists of about 60 men and women headed by a Chief Inspector. A scrutiny of the work of the Inspectorate by Lord Rayner recently led to the recommendation that the number of inspectors should be brought up to its full strength of 430. The report agreed with the Inspectorate's policy of carrying out general surveys in order to render advice to Ministers rather than conducting inspections of individual institutions. Rayner also suggested that HMI reports on schools and colleges should be published, though in fact this had already been done since January 1983. One interesting recommendation is that HMI should make more surveys of whole LEAs. (*See also* **full inspection, 'payment by results'**.)

DES, *Study of HM Inspectorate in England and Wales* (Rayner Study), HMSO, 1983

DES, *The work of HM Inspectorate in England and Wales. A Policy Statement by the Secretary of State for Education and Science*, HMSO, 1983

heurism/heuristic method

A method of teaching science advocated by H. E. Armstrong, a teacher at Finsbury Polytechnic, from the 1880s, in which pupils are, as far as possible, placed in the attitude of a discoverer instead of merely being told about things. Although this method was treated with some scepticism by his contemporaries much of Armstrong's philosophy is to be found in the **Nuffield Science** projects.

W. H. BROCK (ed.), *H. E. Armstrong and the Teaching of Science 1880–1930*, Cambridge University Press, 1973

higher degree

A **postgraduate degree** obtained, either by research or following a taught course, at the masters' or doctoral levels. (*See also* **dissertation, graduate, university department of education, viva**.)

higher education (HE)

This term is usually used to distinguish the work in universities and **polytechnics** which results in the award of a **degree, diploma** or similar advanced qualification, from various kinds of **further education (FE)**.

higher elementary school

A type of school bridging the elementary-secondary sectors in its curriculum, legalized in 1900. The Code of 1905 suggested the development of higher elementary schools which would provide education between the ages of 12 and 15 for brighter children who had previously attended an ordinary public elementary school. The Consultative Committee's Report on Higher Elementary Schools (1906) suggested that the course should consist of three strands, humanistic, scientific and manual, and in the case of girls, domestic. Previously, these schools were required to offer predominantly scientific instruction.

Report of the Board of Education Consultative Committee upon Questions Affecting Higher Elementary Schools, HMSO, 1906

higher grade school

In 1882, a seventh Standard was added to the **Code** to enable older pupils to extend their stay at elementary schools. As an increasing number continued after passing the seventh Standard, ex-Standard classes were formed. In many cases, **school boards** gathered such pupils into one school called 'higher grade' and offering an education until at least 15. In 1894, there were 60 of these schools in England. (*See also* **standards**.)

F. G. LANDON, 'Higher Grade Schools', in T. A. SPALDING, *The Work of the London School Board*, P. S. King, 1900

Higher National Certificate (HNC)

A post-school vocational award, in

science, technology or business studies, requiring at least two years' part-time study beyond **Ordinary National Certificate (ONC)**; it is roughly of degree standard. It is sponsored by the **DES** and the professional institution concerned (in Scotland, most courses are administered by the Scottish Technical Education Council). The award is being replaced by **BEC** and **TEC** qualifications. (*See also* **Business Education Council, Higher National Diploma**.)

Higher National Diploma (HND)

A higher level qualification than the **HNC**. It was usually regarded as roughly equal to the standard of a university pass degree and requires the equivalent of two years' full-time study. This award is being replaced by **BEC** and **TEC** qualifications.

Higher School Certificate

Introduced by the **Secondary School Examinations Council** in 1919, the Higher School Certificate was awarded to pupils who had previously taken the **School Certificate** examination and had subsequently successfully completed a two-year course of study, usually to 18 years of age. The course was of a more specialized nature than that of the School Certificate and candidates sat examinations in 2, 3 or 4 subjects at main or subsidiary levels. It was replaced by the **GCE A level** examination in 1951.

high flier

Term used for a very able pupil with high attainments. (*See also* **giftedness, exceptional children**.)

high school

A term formerly widely used by grammar and independent schools. It now more commonly describes junior secondary schools, catering for the 11- to 14-year-olds. In Leicestershire, the high schools span the 10–14 age range. (*See also* **Leicestershire Plan**.)

history of education

When the history of education became a subject of university study in the early decades of the present century, much attention was given to developments in schooling in earlier times, particularly to the origins of the English **grammar school** and **public school**. There were also studies of the consequences of the provision of universal **elementary education** after 1870 and of the later Education Acts. Much of the work was descriptive, concentrating on administrative and structural aspects of education. One result of this approach was that in the 1960s the study of the history of education lost ground in **university departments of education** and in **colleges of education** to the newer disciplines of philosophy and sociology of education. There has however been a revived interest in this field during the last decade. This may be attributed to two factors: first, historians of education now regard education as a process requiring a study of practices at different levels of the system which includes informal agencies of education, and second, research in other academic disciplines has suggested fruitful approaches to historical studies. For example, the notion of 'social control' has led to studies in the socialization provided 'from above' of working-class children in schools. The relationship between the economy and education and the provision of appropriate forms of schooling have been examined. Recently attention has been drawn to the comparatively unexplored topic of the school **curriculum**, its content and its pedagogy. Studies in literacy levels at different periods have also proved to be valuable. Other work has included analyses of the effects of policy changes at central government level, the impact of psychometrics on schooling, the **politics of education**, **pressure groups** and the relationship between the development of educational thought and practice.

B. SIMON, 'The History of Education in the 1980s', *British Journal of Educational Studies*, Vol. 30, No 1, 1982

HMI
See **Her Majesty's Inspectorate**.

Holmes Circular
In May 1910, Edmund Holmes, the Chief Inspector of Elementary Schools of the Board of Education, wrote a confidential memorandum for all the Board's Inspectors on the status and duties of **LEA** inspectors. Holmes claimed that this body was on the whole inefficient and lacked the type of school and university education which characterized **Her Majesty's Inspectors**. Extracts from the Circular appeared in the Press shortly afterwards and the matter was taken up in the Commons. Holmes had by this time retired but Robert Morant, the Permanent Secretary to the Board who had signed the Circular and who had made enemies of elementary school teachers, was transferred to the new-

ly formed National Insurance Commission. Walter Runciman, the Liberal President of the Board, who handled the affair badly, was removed to the Board of Agriculture. The contents of the Circular were not fully revealed until nearly 70 years later.

P. GORDON, 'The Holmes-Morant Circular of 1911', *Journal of Educational Administration and History*, No. 1, 1978

Home and Colonial Infant School Society
Established by Dr Charles Mayo and his sister in 1836, the Society opened schools working on Pestalozzian principles and a **training college** in connection with the Church of England. However, the latter admitted men and women of different religious denominations.

Home and School Council
A partnership of three **pressure groups**, the **Advisory Centre for Education** (ACE), the **National Confederation of Parent-Teacher Associations** (NCPTA) and the **Confederation for the Advancement of State Education** (CASE). The Council, formed in 1967, produces a number of practical guides for those interested or involved in home-school matters.

home education
The 1944 Education Act (Section 36) stated that 'it shall be the duty of the parent of every child of compulsory school age to cause him to receive efficient, full-time education suitable to his age, ability and aptitude, either by regular attendance at school or otherwise'. The final two words give

parents the opportunity to educate their children at home in accordance with their own principles. **LEAs** differ in their attitude towards home education; some request detailed curriculum, others are content with a statement of broad **aims**, and some take parents to court. An organization for like-minded parents on this issue was formed in 1977 with the title of 'Education Otherwise' and has a thriving membership. (*See also* **compulsory education**.)

homework

Originally called 'home lessons', the practice of setting extra work out of school began in the early nineteenth century. After the system of **'payment by results'** had been instituted in 1862, the volume of homework increased in **elementary schools**: the establishment of the Oxford and Cambridge 'Local' examinations from 1857 had a similar effect on **secondary schools**. By the 1880s, medical reasons were being advanced against the imposition of homework but with little effect. A law case, *Hunter v. Johnson* 1884, decided that it was illegal for a pupil to be kept in after school for failing to hand in homework. In the present century, several government reports dealing with aspects of education have commented on the effects of homework on children's out-of-school life, but no action has followed. A recent survey by HMI in Wales (May 1982) found that few schools had a clearly formulated homework policy. The issue is still very much a live one. (*See also* **examinations: history of**, **overpressure in education**.)

F. COULTER, 'Homework: a neglected research area', *British Educational Research Journal*, Vol. 5, No. 1, 1979

P. GORDON, 'Homework: Origins and Justification', *Westminster Studies in Education*, Vol. 4, 1981

honorary degree

A **degree** awarded by a higher education institution to persons distinguished in their own field. The degree is conferred at a public ceremony, usually by the **Chancellor** or head of the institution.

honours degree

An examination of a higher standard than a pass **degree** which may have a different syllabus. Honours degrees are usually divided into different classes, the first being the highest, followed by second (often subdivided into upper and lower) and third. (*See also* **class**.)

Houghton Report

A Committee of Inquiry, appointed in June 1974, chaired by Lord Houghton of Sowerby, to examine the pay of non-university teachers in Great Britain. The report was completed within six months and its findings were swiftly implemented. It was the first independent committee on teachers' salaries for 30 years. At a time when counter-inflation legislation was in force, the committee regarded teachers as a 'special case' after comparing their salary with rewards in similar fields of employment. It recommended periodic reviews on teachers' pay to be made independently of the established negotiating bodies and a common grading structure for **further education** establishments and **colleges of education**. (*See also* **Burnham Report**, **Clegg Report**, **Pelham Report**.)

Committee of Inquiry into the Pay of Non-University Teachers, HMSO, 1974, Cmnd 5848

house system
Originally an essentially **public school** phenomenon, where pupils are allocated to boarding houses under the supervision of a housemaster, the house system is found in the great majority of **comprehensive schools**. These schools may be divided into a number of houses, either located in individual buildings or not, for social and academic activities. All members of staff are attached to houses and most of them look after a **tutor** group of up to thirty children for the rest of their school lives. Tutor groups may consist of pupils of the same age group or of a large age range. (*See also* **boarding school**.)

humanities
A term usually employed to group together a number of **disciplines** or subjects, all of which are concerned with some aspect of human life. History, human geography, literature and philosophy, and sometimes the social sciences are included in the term humanities. One influential curriculum development project in this field was the Humanities Curriculum Project (HCP) directed by Laurence Stenhouse.

I

iconic
See **enactive, iconic and symbolic**.

impression marking
In the marking of essays there are broadly two approaches. The first is to mark the essay as a whole and give an overall mark or grade for style, content and presentation. The alternative is a more analytic approach which sets down beforehand what kind of points a candidate should make and then marks are awarded for each of those points made, possibly with marks being added or deducted for style, spelling and other 'automatic errors'. The fairest or most accurate method is said to be a combination of both ways of marking, namely, a group of examiners some of whom use the analytic style and some the impressionistic marking, and then averaging the marks for each candidate. This is, however, a very expensive way of treating scripts and is only rarely used.

J. BRITTON et al., *Multiple Marking of English Compositions*, Schools Council Examination Bulletin No. 12, HMSO, 1966

inaugural lecture
A lecture given by the new holder of a chair on some aspect of her/his discipline. Although inaugural lectures were delivered as early as the eighteenth century, the first chairs in education, those of S. S. Laurie at Edinburgh and J. M. D. Meiklejohn at St Andrews, date only from 1876. Theirs are the earliest surviving inaugural lectures in education. None can be traced in full for the period 1914 to 1945, but a number of universities, for example, Birmingham, Bristol, London and Sheffield, have since made the lectures available

in pamphlet form. (*See also* **professor**.)

P. GORDON, *The Study of Education. A Collection of Inaugural Lectures*, 2 vols, Woburn Press, 1980

Incorporated Association of Preparatory Schools (IAPS)

The Association consists of over 500 **headteachers** of **preparatory schools** and since January 1981 represents girls' as well as boys' schools. It keeps heads informed of developments in education. Till April 1978, IAPS insisted, as a condition of membership, that schools were not only 'registered' but were also 'recognized as efficient'. Such recognition has ceased to exist, but an Independent Schools Joint Council, representing all the associations of **independent schools**, now conducts it own accreditation system. (*See also* **preparatory school**, **registration of independent schools**.)

independent learning

See **individual learning**.

independent school

Strictly defined, schools not in receipt of grants from Government or **LEAs**. These include **public schools** and some former **direct grant schools**. However, a number of **preparatory schools** opted to join the **Assisted Places Scheme** and therefore receive funds from the Government. (*See also* **education vouchers**, **maintained school**, **registration of independent schools**.)

individualized learning

There are at least two somewhat different meanings to this term. The first focuses on the pupil working on his own, perhaps by means of work sheets, perhaps by programmed materials of some kind. The second meaning refers to the need to allow children to learn not only at an individual pace, but also to make use of different approaches, styles of learning and personality differences. The latter is much less common than the former. The first of the two meanings is sometimes also referred to as independent learning. (*See also* **Dalton Plan**, **mastery learning**, **programmed learning**.)

induction scheme

Some **LEAs** have in the past held short courses for newly qualified teachers and newly appointed **headteachers** or **deputy heads**. The **James Report** of 1972 recommended that all newly qualified teachers should, in the first year at school, be given a light timetable and be enabled to spend one-fifth of the teaching week in some kind of further training. The James Report also recommended that teachers undergoing this induction year should be supported by specially appointed 'professional tutors' in the school, possibly one of the deputy headteachers. This aspect of the James Report has never been completely implemented, but a few **pilot schemes** of induction have been tried out with varying degrees of success. Schemes even more modest than the James proposals are, however, quite expensive and many schemes suffered from the financial problems faced by LEAs in the late 1970s and early 1980s. (*See also* **probation**, **teacher tutor**.)

R. BOLAM and J. K. TAYLOR, *The*

Induction and Guidance of Beginning Teachers, University of Bristol School of Education Research Unit, 1972

industrial school

Successors to **schools of industry**, they were often established by philanthropic individuals and were residential in character. The Industrial Schools Act (1857) empowered magistrates to send to these schools children who were truants, beggars or who had committed a misdemeanour. The 1876 Education Act introduced day schools for boys and girls which had a largely vocationally based curriculum.

Industrial Training Board (ITB)

The training of employees in industry either at their place of work or in vocationally orientated courses in **further education**. The Industrial Training Act (1964) was intended to increase the amount of industrial training as well as its quality. Industrial Training Boards were set up to organize training and to share the cost of training more fairly. Over 13 million workers were covered by the scheme. The Act was regarded as only partially successful and was modified by the Employment and Training Act (1973). ITBs were threatened by the general attack on **quangos** in 1980 to 1981 and in 1982 the Government decided to wind up the majority of the Boards, replacing them with 'voluntary arrangements'. (*See also* **Finniston Report, industry, links with schools**.)

industry, links with schools

Throughout the twentieth century and particularly since the 1944 Education Act, schools frequently made a distinction between education, which was the concern of schools, and training, which was the concern of industry itself. Any kind of vocational training within schools was particularly offensive to many teachers and their professional organizations. The Industrial Training Act of 1964, whilst increasing the quantity and quality of industrial training, kept industry and its training separate from the work of schools. **Industrial Training Boards** were established, but schools and **LEAs** were not involved. In the later 1960s and throughout the 1970s, however, a number of attempts were made to establish links between schools and the world of industry. Various schemes of work experience were tried out, some more successfully than others. One of the points raised in the **Ruskin College** speech of 1976 by the Prime Minister (James Callaghan) was the insufficient regard by schools for the adult world, particularly the world of work. From this time onwards, **DES** official documents emphasized the need for schools to be concerned with the world of work. At the same time, the **Manpower Services Commission** (MSC) and its various training programmes seemed to be preserving the barrier between school and training for work. This continued until in 1982 a proposal was made to introduce technical education, financed by MSC, into schools as well as **colleges of further education**, starting with the 14–year-old pupils in some selected schools. The DES and LEAs were not directly involved in the planning of these new curricula. (*See also* **Finniston Report, 'Great Debate', industrial training, SATROs**.)

I. JAMIESON and M. LIGHTFOOT, *Schools and Industry*, Methuen Educational for Schools Council, 1982

A. G. WATTS (ed.), *Work Experience and Schools*, Heinemann Educational, 1983

infant school

From the early nineteenth century it was recognized that young children needed to be educated apart from older ones, a view endorsed by the **Hadow Reports** of 1926, 1931 and 1933. The infant school caters for children, both boys and girls, between the ages of 5 and 7. The number of separate infant schools has steadily diminished since the 1920s; the majority now form part of a **primary school**, with a **junior** department and perhaps a **nursery**. (*See also* **kindergarten**, **reception class**, **'rising fives'**.)

D. and E. GRUGEON, *An Infant School*, Macmillan Education, 1971

N. WHITBREAD, *The Evolution of the Nursery-Infant School*, Routledge and Kegan Paul, 1972

information retrieval

Devices which facilitate the location of multi-media materials and information and their retrieval. These are commonly needed in, for example, libraries and **resource centres**. Information retrieval involves classifying, indexing and cataloguing. The devices range from the simple card index to elaborate systems made possible by computing. (*See also* **ERIC**.)

F. W. LANCASTER, *Information Retrieval Systems: characteristics, testing and evaluation*, Wiley, 1979

M. MARLAND (ed.), *Informational Skills in the Secondary Curriculum*, Methuen, 1981

Initial Teaching Alphabet (i.t.a.)

An alphabet of 44 characters, each representing a sound in the English language, devised by Sir James Pitman. It claims to bypass some of the difficulties encountered by young children learning to read using the ordinary alphabet. Since the early 1960s, the system has been operated in a minority of schools.

J. DOWNING, *The Initial Teaching Alphabet Explained and Illustrated*, Cassell, 5th. edn, 1965

F. W. WARBURTON and V. SOUTHGATE, *i.t.a.: An Independent Evaluation*, John Murray, 1969

Inner London Education Authority (ILEA)

The largest education authority in England, the ILEA was established when the **London County Council** was merged into the Greater London Council. It covers 13 London boroughs. The Authority consists of 48 GLC councillors, representatives of Inner London councils and co-opted members. It has been Labour-controlled for most of its existence. In 1980, the Conservative Secretary of State, Mark Carlisle, set up an interdepartmental committee to consider the future of the ILEA. The Committee, chaired by Baroness Young, then Minister of State at the **DES**, later recommended that the Authority should continue, whilst noting the weakness in accountability of the present arrangements. (*See also* **local education authority, Local Government Acts**.)

In-service Education of Teachers (INSET)

For many years one of the constant complaints about the teaching service was the lack of provision of **continuing education** and training for teachers. It was alleged that many teachers took no courses after their initial qualification to update their professional skills or to broaden their educational horizons. The **James Report** of 1972 was particularly concerned with the provision of professional courses for teachers throughout their careers. INSET is generally taken to include short courses run by the **DES** or the local authority; short courses or day conferences at **teachers' centres**; and secondment to study for **diploma** and **higher degrees** in education either on a full-time or a part-time basis. (*See also* **INSTEP**.)

R. BOLAM (ed.), *School-focused In-Service Training*, Heinemann, 1982

C. DONOUGHUE (ed.) et al., *In-Service: the Teacher and the School*, Kogan Page, 1982

INSTEP

Acronym of In-Service and Training Educational Panel, established in 1976 by the **DES** at Leicester for co-ordinating and validating **in-service training** for full-time youth and community service personnel. (*See also* **INSET**.)

institute

1. An institution, frequently though not exclusively, of university status, which specializes in a particular field of study, e.g. Institute of Archaeology.

2. A professional association for qualified practitioners, e.g. Royal Institute of British Architects.

Institutes of Education

Set up following the recommendations of the **McNair Report** in 1944, Institutes of Education consisted of a federation of teachers, colleges or institutions in a particular region, with the university playing a major part. The Institutes, many of which appointed new staff, were recognized **Area Training Organizations** (ATOs). Amongst their tasks were the validation and award of education qualifications, such as **B.Ed.** degrees and diplomas; recommending to the **DES** the granting of **qualified teacher status**; providing research facilities for higher degree students and the mounting of in-service courses. With the dismantling of ATOs in the mid 1970s, the Institutes ceased to exist. The Cambridge Institute of Education, which was always different from other institutes in not being attached to a university, receives a direct grant from the DES. The London University Institute of Education is different from the Institutes described above and might more properly be called a **School of Education**. It has a long history, dating back to 1902, when it was opened as a **day training college**, and is now the largest postgraduate educational establishment in the UK.

Institutes of Higher Education

Colleges and Institutes of Higher Education (the nomenclature varies) arose from the recommendations of the **James Report** which, amongst other objectives, called for a more flexible and open-ended pattern of courses, not confined to the education of teachers, than was offered by the **colleges of education**. In London, for example, two Institutes, West London and Roehampton, have been established, based on an amalgamation of former colleges. **Degree** courses are offered in teacher education, the humanities and sciences as well as the **Diploma in Higher Education**. Courses are validated either by a university or the **Council for National Academic Awards**. (*See also* **validation**.)

The Colleges and Institutes and Higher Education 1980 Guide, Eyre and Spottiswoode

instruction

An ambiguous term, sometimes used to indicate the same kind of process as 'teaching', but generally in a more limited and less ambitious sense. Thus in English educational terminology instruction is to training as teaching is to education.

instructor

Term for those not holding recognized teacher qualifications. The majority of these are women, particularly those teaching commercial studies, though there are instructors in the fields of craft design and technology (CDT).

instrumental learning

Instrumental in this sense implies not for its own sake but to achieve some other goal. An example of instrumental learning might therefore be for an individual to learn a foreign language not because he or she found any pleasure in that learning, but because it might be useful for travelling abroad. Most educationists would prefer expressive learning, that is, the kind of learning where no external reward or motivation is needed, but the learning process is valuable and satisfying in its own

right. There would be a connection, therefore, between instrumental learning and extrinsic motivation; expressive learning and intrinsic motivation. (*See also* **intrinsic/extrinsic**.)

instrument of government

The Education Act of 1944 (Section 17) laid down that every **primary school** should have an instrument of management and every **secondary school** an instrument of government, which set out the constitution for bodies of **managers** and **governors**. Primary schools were to have rules of management and secondary schools articles of government dealing with the powers and size of the bodies and how membership should be determined. The 1980 Education Act made a number of changes in nomenclature. The term 'managers' was abolished and now both primary and secondary schools have governors. Similarly, the governors of both types of schools operate under instruments and articles of government.

integrated day

The conventional school **timetable** is replaced, under an integrated day system, by a more flexible approach which enables pupils to integrate their knowledge, explore resources and work at their own pace. This approach is found mainly in **primary schools**. (*See also* **integrated studies**.)

I. ALLEN et al., *Working an Integrated Day*, Ward Lock Educational, 1975

integrated studies

During the 1950s and 1960s various attempts were made, especially in secondary modern schools and comprehensive schools, to break down the existing subject barriers by planning courses across a wider range. Some of these were based on the humanities, such as the University of Keele Integrated Studies Project; others focused on science (The Schools Council Integrated Science Project); many were much less organized and simply organized secondary school teaching by way of projects. These tended to be much less successful. In the primary school there had been a longer tradition of approaching teaching by way of projects rather than through subjects. One such approach was described as the integrated day which virtually abolished the formal timetable and emphasized topics, projects and interest based learning. (See also interdisciplinary studies.)

D. N. HUBBARD and J. SALT (eds), *Integrated Studies in the Primary Schools*, Sheffield University Institute of Education, 1970

D. WARWICK (ed.), *Integrated Studies in the Secondary School*, University of London Press, 1973

integration

Integration can be perceived in a number of ways: as a slogan or battle cry; an educational goal; a social movement; and a summary description of various educational procedures, ranging from social functions where handicapped and non-disabled children are brought together from time to time, to the intended complete assimilation of disabled pupils into an ordinary school. Integration is seen as one aspect of the moves to 'deinstitutionalize' handicapped persons; it has an even closer affinity with the North American concept of 'mainstreaming' children with special educational needs into ordinary classes and schools. Integration thus attempts to shift the emphasis of special services from handicapping conditions and problems to children's learning needs. (See also Warnock Report.)

L. BARTON and S. TOMLINSON (eds), *Special Education: Policy, Practices and Social Issues*, Harper and Row, 1981

S. HEAGARTY, K. POCKLINGTON and D. LUCAS, *Integration in Action*, Nelson-NFER, 1982

intelligence

A term which is widely used but often with insufficient clarity. It has been defined as 'general mental ability' or 'the ability to see relationships' or even 'what intelligence tests measure'. It may be useful to use the distinction between intelligence A, B and C. Intelligence A is an individual's innate, genetic potentiality (which must exist but can never be measured). Intelligence B is the result of the interaction of an individual's intelligence A and his environmental experiences; it is what is often described in common sense terms as intelligent behaviour. Finally, Intelligence C is what intelligence tests measure. If it is a good test then C will be close to B, but it may be a long way from A. (See also age: chronological and mental, Gaussian curve, IQ, memory, normal curve, regression to the mean, spatial ability, underachiever, verbal reasoning.)

D. W. PYLE, *Intelligence: an Introduction*, Routledge and Kegan Paul, 1979

P. E. VERNON, *Intelligence and Cultural Environment*, Methuen, 1969

intelligence test

Intelligence tests were first constructed in France by Alfred Binet (1857–1911) to assess children's educability in schools. Binet's intention was more specific than that of many later psychologists; he was also much more optimistic about the chances of 'teaching **intelligence**'. An intelligence test is **standardized** and a score given as an **IQ** or intelligence quotient. Tests and testing have been increasingly criticized since they appear to favour certain social groups such as whites in USA and middle-class children in UK. (*See also* **free place system**, **Gaussian curve**, **Koh's blocks**, **memory**, **meritocratic education**, **nature-nurture controversy**, **psychology of education**, **reliability**, **spatial ability**, **underachiever**, **validity**, **verbal reasoning**.)

L. KAMIN, *The Science and Politics of IQ*, Penguin, 1977

P. E. VERNON, *Intelligence Testing 1928–1978: What Next?*, Scottish Council for Research in Education, Edinburgh, 1979

interdisciplinary studies

Studies in which two or more disciplines are studied together focusing upon certain common **projects** or topics: for example, philosophy and psychology; or politics and science (perhaps looking at problems of conservation or pollution of the environment). The essential aspect of an interdisciplinary study is that the disciplines are studied in such a way as to produce planned interaction. It is quite different from a multidisciplinary approach in which several disciplines are employed to examine the same topic from their own separate perspectives. (*See also* **integrated studies**.)

intermediate education

A **Departmental Committee** chaired by Lord Aberdare was appointed in 1881 to enquire into the provision in Wales of education intermediate between elementary and university education, that is, secondary education. The Committee also investigated higher education provision and as a result two university colleges were opened, at Cardiff in 1883 and Bangor in 1884. Recommendations concerning intermediate education were slower to be implemented but many were incorporated in the Welsh Intermediate Act, 1889. To encourage the number of school places, the Act created joint education committees to act as local authorities for county and county boroughs in Wales. The committees were to submit schemes for secondary and technical education and were given powers to levy a rate of up to ½d. in the £, subject to county council approval, for this purpose. The sum of money raised was matched by the Treasury on condition that annual inspections took place. In 1896, a Central Welsh Board for intermediate education was formed. This pattern of local control in secondary education was adopted in England some 14 years later, in 1903.

L. W. EVANS, *Studies in Welsh Education: Welsh Educational Structure and Administration*, University of Wales Press, Cardiff, 1974

Intermediate (I) level examination

A scheme introduced by the **Schools Council** in 1980 which would broaden the studies of those taking the **A level** examaination and also provide an examination for those for whom a full A level course is too difficult. It was envisaged that it would also cater for **late developers** and could be combined with some **O level** examination work. The Government has not yet (1983) announced when this examination will be established.

internal degree
A **degree** for which the student follows the formal course of **instruction** at an institution of higher education and takes the prescribed examinations.

internal examiner
See **examiner, internal**.

International Baccalaureate (IB)
An examination designed for students in their last two or three years at secondary school in the UK and in International Schools abroad, and intended to qualify them for entry to **undergraduate** courses not confined to British universities. Six academic subjects are covered in the course: two languages, mathematics, an exact or experimental science, a human science and a subject of the student's choice. Three of these are examined at a higher level and three at subsidiary level. More than 30 institutions now offer this diploma. (*See also Baccalauréat*.)

A. D. C. PETERSON, *The International Baccalaureate: an experiment in international education*, Harrap, 1972

International Institute for Educational Planning (IIEP)

Established by **UNESCO** in 1963 in Paris to act as an international centre for advanced training and research in the field of educational planning. It co-operates with training and research organizations all over the world and publishes reports, such as *Population growth and cost of education in developing countries* (1972).

intrinsic/extrinsic
Some theories of human motivation make a distinction between intrinsic motivation to perform well or to engage in an activity for its own sake, and the kind of motivation which operates for the sake of some external reward (extrinsic motivation). Ultimately most educators will want pupils to be stimulated by intrinsic motivation, but on the way to that goal various kinds of extrinsic motivation (for example, a desire to please the teacher or to get good marks) may legitimately be employed provided they do not become ends in themselves. (*See also* **instrumental learning**.)

invigilator
An official who supervises pupils or students whilst they are answering examination papers.

IQ (intelligence quotient)
A measure of an individual's performance on a **standardized intelligence test**. Since tests were originally developed mainly for children it was convenient to express a child's score in terms of mental age (MA) rather than chronological age (CA); the score can be converted into a percentage using the following formula:

$$IQ = \frac{MA}{CA} \times 100$$

Thus a child with an average score will have an IQ of 100; a child above average will score more than 100. Tests are usually **standardized** so that two-thirds of the normal population will score between 85 and 115. (*See also* **age: chronological and mental**, **Gaussian curve**, **meritocratic education**, **normal curve**, **underachiever**.)

G. SUTHERLAND, 'The Magic of Measurement, Mental Testing and English Education, 1900–40', *Transactions of the Royal Historical Society*, 5th Series, Vol. 27, 1977

item

A question or problem in a test. Item analysis is the process of studying students' responses to each item in order to improve the test, and then removing items that are seen as too difficult or too easy. An item bank is a collection of test questions. New tests can be composed not by creating new items but by making a selection from the item bank.

C. LACEY and D. LAWTON (eds), *Issues in Evaluation and Accountability*, Methuen Education, 1981

item bank
See **item**.

J

James Report

The Committee of Enquiry into Teacher Education and Training under the chairmanship of Lord James of Rusholme reported in 1972. Its terms of reference included a consideration of the content and organization of college courses, whether intending teachers should be educated alongside students following other careers and the extent to which institutions other than **colleges of education** should be concerned with teacher education. The report outlined a completely new system of teacher education. It envisaged three cycles:

1st Cycle. Students were given the choice of taking a degree at a college or university or a **Diploma in Higher Education**, the latter course lasting two years and being located within the further education system.

Entry to both courses required a two **GCE A level** minimum qualification.

2nd Cycle. A one-year course of professional studies and training. Successful candidates would become for the second year licensed teachers with restricted timetables, and be monitored by a professional tutor. After the second year of this cycle, teachers would be awarded a B.A. (Education) degree.

3rd Cycle. Paid in-service training, consisting of one term every seven years, was an essential aspect of the scheme.

There was opposition to the concept of consecutive rather than concurrent training which was clearly spelt out in the scheme. Teachers questioned the status of the proposed new degree and the Diploma in Higher Education. The suggested administrative structure of teacher education, a National Council with Regional Councils to replace existing **Area**

Training Organizations (ATOs), was also criticized. (*See also* **induction schemes, McNair Report**.)

J. P. PARRY. *The Lord James Tricycle: some notes on teacher education and training*, Allen and Unwin, 1972

Report of a Committee of Enquiry into Teacher Education and Training, HMSO, 1972

Joint Four Secondary Association

The name given to the body which negotiated salaries and spoke on a range of matters for four associations representing secondary school staff interests, the Assistant Masters' Association (AMA), the Association of Assistant Mistresses (AAM), the **Association of Headmistresses** (AHM) and the **Headmasters' Association** (HMA). There are now only two such associations because of amalgamations: the **AMMA**, representing the assistant masters and mistresses, and **SHA**, representing secondary heads.

junior school

A school catering for children between the ages of 7 and 11. After the 1918 Education Act, when the **school leaving age** was raised to 14, LEAs began to create junior departments of **elementary schools**, and this movement received a great impetus after the Hadow Report of 1926. The **Hadow Report on the Primary School** five years later adumbrated an educational philoso-

phy for this age range based on enlightened approaches. In 1945, half the junior schools in England were separate from **infant schools**, but the majority are now under one headship.

H. PROBERT and C. JARMAN, *A Junior School*, Macmillan Educational, 1971

junior technical school

From 1913, the Regulations of the Board of Education recognized a new type of day technical school, the junior technical. These schools prepared boys for trades within industry, such as engineering and building. A much smaller sub-category was the *junior technical (trade) school*, for boys and girls entering occupations such as printing and tailoring. Unlike the pure junior technical schools, approximately 50 per cent of the curriculum was devoted to craft work. Another category was the *junior housewifery school* which prepared girls for home management. Lastly, the flourishing *junior commercial schools* offered entry to commercial life for potential shorthand typists and clerks. Some junior technical schools had four-year courses leading to the **School Certificate** examination. They were much praised by the **Spens Report** and formed the basis later of the **technical high school**.

BOARD OF EDUCATION, Educational Pamphlet 111, *A Review of Junior Technical Schools in England*, HMSO, 1937

K

Keohane Report

A study group, under Professor K. W. Keohane, was set up by the Secretary of State for Education in April 1978 to consider the **School Council**'s proposals for a **Certificate of Extended Education** and to consider possible developments in the provision of relevant courses and examinations in schools and further education. In its report *Proposals for a Certificate of Extended Education* published in December 1979, it recommended the development of non-compulsory vocationally-oriented syllabuses and compulsory tests of efficiency in English and mathematics, with pupils able to select other aspects of their studies as appropriate. The proposal was rejected by the **DES**. In a consultative paper *Examinations 16–18* issued October 1980, the **Secretary of State** preferred the emphasis placed on vocational education by a study group of the **Further Education Curriculum Review and Development Unit** (FEU) in its document *A Basis for Choice* (1979): this was clearly shown in the DES discussion paper *17+ A New Qualification*, issued in 1982. (*See also* **seventeen plus examinations, vocational preparation**.)

Study Group on the Certificate of Extended Education, *Proposals for a Certificate of Extended Education*, HMSO, 1979, Cmnd 7755

kindergarten

A system of education for infants resulting from the work of Froebel. It is based on the child's inclination to play with others, so games are used to develop the body, mind and spirit. It was introduced into England in 1854, two years after Froebel's death. Twenty years later, the School Board for London appointed an instructor for teachers in their **infant schools**.

E. MICHAELIS and M. KEATLEY MOORE, *Froebel's Letters on the Kindergarten*, Swann, Sonnenschein, 1904

knowledge

Knowledge is often contrasted with **skills** and with attitudes and values, but this is an artificial and sometimes unhelpful distinction since knowledge overlaps both those categories. A somewhat more helpful distinction is between 'knowing how' and 'knowing that', the former being more closely connected with skills. It is impossible to discuss the nature of knowledge without making some reference to the human being's means of acquiring knowledge. This was Piaget's major interest and formed the basis of his work on stages of development. The conventional pre-Enlightenment view of knowledge was that it was created by God and only discovered by man through the use of his reason. Traces of that view survive in some popular attitudes to education which tend to see knowledge as a commodity to be collected by a pupil. Post-Reformation science encouraged a move away from a unified view of knowledge to a subdivision of knowledge into science, theology, law and so on. In the twentieth century the educational argument about knowledge has frequently centred on the relation between the structure of knowledge and the content of the curriculum, particularly subjects. In the USA, Phenix's work on 'realms of meaning' has been influential; in the UK, Hirst's seven forms of knowledge approach has been much discussed. The sociology of knowledge is concerned with the two ideas that the perception of reality is filtered through cultural constraints which differ from one society to another; and secondly, that within any society an individual's view of knowledge and reality is related to his own social position. The danger of these views is an extreme form of relativism – that one view of reality is as good as any other. In education, particularly in studies of the **curriculum**, the danger exists of moving from the recognition of class-based tastes and prejudices to statements that the whole of school knowledge is merely 'bourgeois'. Some Marxist writers such as Gramsci, however, saw that the future of education had to be concerned with making available to everyone those kinds of essential knowledge which had been part of élite education in the past. (*See also* **academic**, **culture**, **disciplines**, **encyclopaedism**, **essentialism**, **phenomenology**, **praxis**.)

H. ENTWISTLE, *Class, Culture and Education*, Routledge and Kegan Paul, 1977

R. PRING, *Knowledge and Schooling*, Open Books, 1976

Koh's blocks
A non-verbal **intelligence test** in which an individual has to construct from a number of coloured blocks certain patterns presented to him from a booklet.

L

labelling
A term much used in the **sociology of education** to indicate the tendency to classify an individual as a member of a category, and then treat him as a type rather than a person. The stereotypes which are particularly mentioned in this respect are 'slow learning child', 'culturally deprived child' 'linguistically deprived child', or 'delinquent'. The obvious danger of a teacher treating children in this way is that of **self-fulfilling prophecy**. (*See also* **mixed ability grouping**, **setting**, **streaming**, **unstreaming**.)

ladder of ability
A term associated with the meritocratic view of schooling and with selection in education. Use of the metaphor 'ladder of opportunity' assumes the existence of different levels of school so that an individual child can climb from one level (e.g. the nineteenth-century or early twentieth-century **elementary school**) to a higher level (the **grammar school**). This view of education is objected to by many educationists of the egalitarian view, since it appears to regard the majority level as inferior. Thus in the early twentieth century many Labour Party educationists as well as those in the TUC proposed instead the 'broad highway' approach to education for all. (*See also* **Bryce Report**, **'eleven plus' examination**, **Secondary Education for All**.)

P. GORDON and D. LAWTON, *Curriculum Change in the Nineteenth and Twentieth Centuries*, Hodder and Stoughton, 1978

laissez-faire

1. The policy of non-interference by government in the activities of business and industry. It was particularly important in the history of elementary education in the UK, since advocates of *laissez-faire* did not believe that the State should provide or interfere in education. Although the doctrine of *laissez-faire* in education was apparently overcome by the middle of the nineteenth century, the attitude still survives particularly in England where many parents who can afford to do so choose to send their children to fee-paying schools. Many politicians of the Right believe this to be a much healthier attitude to education than State provision.

2. The teaching style which allows pupils to work according to their own interests, with a minimum of direction and control.

language across the curriculum
See **Bullock Report**.

language deficit
The theory that some children underachieve at school because their language skills are inadequate. The theory is related to a view of society which suggests that certain kinds of homes – working-class and some ethnic minorities – do not equip children with adequate language skills to cope with the curriculum and other demands of the classroom. (*See also* **Bullock Report, compensatory education, disadvantage, Educational Priority Areas**.)

language laboratory
A specially designed room equipped with electronic equipment for the teaching of languages. The laboratory consists of booths for the students and a console, a large control desk, for the instructor, who communicates through a microphone with one or more students at a time. In more sophisticated installations tape recorders (previously, record players) carrying programmes enable individuals to proceed at their own pace. Language laboratories became popular in the 1960s; though common enough in higher education, they have almost disappeared from maintained secondary schools. (*See also* **direct method**.)

E. M. STACK, *The Language Laboratory and Modern Language Teaching*, Oxford University Press, 2nd edn, 1966

J. D. TURNER, *Introduction to the Language Laboratory*, University of London Press, 1965

late developer
Children develop, physically, emotionally and intellectually, at different rates. Late developers are those who realize their potential in some or all aspects of school work after the majority of their contemporaries.

lateral thinking
A technique of looking at a problem from many different points of view instead of following the one which is most obvious. In some respects, lateral thinking is related to **divergent thinking**. Lateral thinking is particularly associated with the work of Edward de Bono.

E. DE BONO, *Children Solve Problems*, Penguin, 1972

law of education
See **legal aspects of education**.

learned journal

A publication in an **academic discipline** or field of study normally consisting of a collection of articles, written by authoritative figures. In education, for example, all the foundation disciplines have such journals, e.g. *British Journal of Educational Psychology, Journal of Philosophy of Education*. Frequency of publication may vary from journal to journal.

learning

A permanent or lasting change in knowledge, skill or attitude which is the result of experience rather than maturation. (*See also* **active learning, CAL, CAMOL, conditioning, distance learning, individualized learning, learning theory, over-learning, passive learning, precision learning, programmed learning, psychology of education, rote learning**.)

learning theory

Different schools of psychology explain learning in different ways. There are, therefore, many learning theories rather than a single learning theory. Behaviourist psychology explains learning in one way, **Gestalt** psychology quite differently, and there are also different kinds of developmental theories which include learning. (*See also* **psychology of education**.)

R. C. BOLLES, *Learning Theory*, Holt, Rinehart and Winston, 2nd edn, 1979

Leathes Report

Appointed in August 1916, the Committee to enquire into the Position of Modern Languages in Great Britain was one of the earliest of the **Prime Minister's Reports** to be issued, in 1918. Chaired by Stanley Leathes and including in its membership Albert Mansbridge and H. A. L. Fisher, the Committee drew attention to the disadvantage under which modern languages laboured in schools because of their comparatively late appearance in the curriculum. The needs particularly for wider study of modern languages were rehearsed, especially in industry and commerce, scientific institutions, and for the public service as well as in conducting business overseas.

Report of the Committee Appointed by the Prime Minister to Enquire into the Position of Modern Languages in the Educational System of Great Britain, HMSO, 1918, Cd 9036

lecture

Presentation of a topic in oral form by a **lecturer** to students, who take notes. It may be accompanied by visual aids and followed up with a **seminar**. (*See also* **tutorial**.)

D. BLIGH, *What's the Use of Lectures?*, Penguin, 1972

J. MCLEISH, *The Lecture Method*, Cambridge Institute of Education, 1968

lecturer

1. A post associated with higher education institutions. Some retain the assistant lecturer status, which is below the rank of lecturer. Above this are senior and principal lecturer and **reader**.

2. A person who delivers a **lecture**.

legal aspects of education

The law of education is enshrined in **Education Acts**, for instance, those of 1944, 1980 and 1981, and in the delegated powers given under the Act to Ministers. Statutory law is complemented by common law: for example, the teacher is said to be *in loco parentis* and is accountable to the courts if there is a failure to fulfil this responsibility. Examples of law cases concerned with education which have been heard in the courts will be found in this Guide. (*See also* **Cockerton Judgment**, **homework**, **Tameside case**.)

G. R. BARRELL, *Teachers and the Law*, Methuen, 5th edn, 1978

G. TAYLOR and J. B. SAUNDERS, *The Law of Education*, Butterworths, 1980 edn

Leicestershire Plan

A two-tier system of schooling devised by S. C. Mason, then **Director of Education** for Leicestershire, in 1959, for the county, excepting the city of Leicester. Pupils between the ages of 10 and 14 attended **high schools**, formerly **secondary moderns**, and then transferred to **upper schools**, all but one created from former **grammar schools**, which catered for 14- to 18-year-olds. The Plan came into operation in 1969.

A. N. FAIRBURN (ed.), *The Leicestershire Plan*, Heinemann, 1980

S. C. MASON (ed.), *In Our Experience: the changing schools of Leicestershire*, Longman, 1970

lesson

1. A period of time, usually between 35 and 50 minutes, into which the **timetable** is divided for teaching purposes. Traditionally, at secondary school level, some subjects are allocated double periods or more of lesson time, e.g. home economics and technology.

2. The smallest unit of **curriculum planning**, i.e. a single planned learning episode which would normally form part of a sequential scheme of work. (*See also* **syllabus**, **timetabling**.)

Lewis Report

Set up during the First World War, the Departmental Committee on Juvenile Education in Relation to Employment after the War reported in 1917. It particularly concerned itself with young persons who required special training and those who could not find relevant work. The chairman was J. Herbert Lewis, M.P. The report's main recommendations were that the **school leaving age** should be raised to 14 and that **day continuation schools** should be widely available. Although the first recommendation was adopted and was written into the 1918 Education Act, the second was only briefly and partially implemented.

Report of the Departmental Committee on Juvenile Education in Relation to Employment after the War, HMSO, Interim, 1916, Final, 1917, Cd 8374

liberal education

The meaning of 'liberal' in this connection is associated with freedom. Liberal education is that kind of education which broadens and therefore frees the mind from narrow prejudices and preconceptions. Liberal education avoids premature specialization. In England, sixth form studies have attempted to be both specialized and 'liberal' by the strategy of **general studies**. Liberal education is frequently contrasted with vocational training by association with a nineteenth-century upper-class view of the correct form of education for Christian gentlemen. In the nineteenth century, the upper classes were regarded as needing liberal education whereas vocational training was more appropriate for the lower classes. (*See also* **general education, liberal studies**.)

V. A. MCCLELLAND, *The Liberal Education of England's Youth: idea and reality*, University of Hull, 1979

L. TRILLING, *The Liberal Imagination: essays on literature and society*, Penguin, 1970

liberal studies
The curriculum followed by many students in **further education** is narrow and vocational. It was frequently thought that such students needed a liberalizing element in their programme (*see* **liberal education**), and the teaching of liberal studies was a compulsory part of many further education programmes. Liberal studies is derived from the medieval idea of liberal arts which consisted of the **trivium** (grammar, logic and rhetoric) and the **quadrivium** (arithmetic, geometry, music and astronomy). Modern liberal studies are, however, much more likely to be concerned with literature, social studies and possibly appreciation of film and television.

J. WATSON, *Liberal Studies in Further Education: an informal survey*, NFER, 1973

Library Association
The Association was founded in 1877 and received a Royal Charter in 1898. It is concerned with the professional education and with raising the standards and working conditions of its members. The Association actively promotes the improvement of library services. The importance of the links between schools and the library service have long been recognized by the Association. (*See also* **School Library Association**.)

linked course
A course run co-operatively by two or more institutions. Some courses for the 16 to 19 age group are run jointly by secondary schools and by local **colleges of further education**.

literacy
The ability to read and write at a conventionally accepted level. There is no universal standard of literacy, but within any given society it is possible to define '**functional literacy**' and then to arrive at figures for the number of illiterates in that particular society. (*See also* **graphicacy**, **numeracy**, **oracy**.)

local education authority (LEA)
LEAs came into existence with the 1902 Education Act, replacing the **school boards**. Unlike the latter, the new LEAs were also responsible for **voluntary schools**; the county and borough councils were also given responsibility for **secondary** and **technical education**. One important feature of the system is that each LEA must appoint an Education Committee (Section 101, Local Government Act 1972), consisting of elected councillors and co-opted members. Since 1974, when the Local Government Act of 1972 came into operation, there are 97 LEAs in England and 8 in Wales, consisting of 20 Outer London Boroughs, the **ILEA**, 36 metropolitan districts and

40 shire counties (London had already been reorganized in 1964). Education spending accounts for a large part of a local authority's budget, and participation by elected members of the council in the deliberations of the Education Committee is eagerly sought after. The political party gaining a majority at a local election elects from its members a chairman of this Committee. (*See also* **advisers**, **corporate management**, **falling rolls**, **Local Government Acts**, **rate support grant**.)

local education authority inspectors
See **advisers**.

Local Government Acts
Local government legislation from the last quarter of the nineteenth century has had a direct effect on the development of the education service in England. The 1888 Local Government Act set up county and borough councils and provided the administrative unit for education, the **local education authority (LEA)**, under the 1902 Education Act; LEAs received greater powers under the 1944 Act. The system of percentage grants was swept away by the 1958 Local Government Act, to be replaced by a **rate support grant**. There was a shake-up of local educational administration following the 1963 London Government Act, which abolished the London and Middlesex County Councils; these were replaced by the Greater London Council, with education powers exercised by an **Inner London Education Authority (ILEA)** and twenty separate outer London boroughs. The 1972 Local Government Act which came into effect on 1 April 1974, dealt with the remainder of the country. This has resulted in a reduction in the number of LEAs. Large conurbations have been divided into metropolitan districts and some county authorities have disappeared, leaving shire counties responsible for education. An important piece of recent legislation has been the Local Government, Planning and Land (No. 2) Act, 1980. This signalled a shift towards the centre in regard to local government finance with the introduction from April 1981 of the new rate support grant system.

J. MANN, *Education*, Pitman, 1979

Lockwood Report
See **Schools Council**.

log book
The **'payment by results'** Code of 1862 required schools on the Grant List to keep a systematic record of day-to-day happenings. From 1863 surviving logbooks present useful evidence of classroom life in both the past and present centuries.

E. W. GADD, *Victorian Logs*, Brewin Books, 1980

London allowance
An extra sum of money paid to teachers and others, working within the London area, to compensate for the cost of housing and travel. (*See also* **Burnham Committee**.)

London County Council (LCC)
The 1888 Local Government Act enabled the newly created county councils to be directly elected. London was dealt with in a different way from others, becoming an administrative county consisting of those

parts of the Metropolis that were in Middlesex, Kent and Surrey. The LCC's education functions were limited, with the School Board for London (established 1870) continuing to carry out this work. The 1902 Education Act did not apply to London, but a London Education Act two years later transferred the whole range of education services to the LCC. The London Government Act 1963 resulted in the replacement of the LCC by the Greater London Council from 1964, with an **Inner London Education Authority** (ILEA) responsible for the education service.

W. E. JACKSON, *Achievement. A Short History of the London County Council,* Longman, 1965

longitudinal study

A study over a period of time which is concerned with following through changes in a group of individuals, with reference to, for example, health and educational achievement. Three of the best known longitudinal studies are those carried out by the **National Children's Bureau** of 17,000 children born in the same week in 1958; the smaller investigation of J. W. B. Douglas, who followed up the educational progress of 4,000 children, born in March 1946, which is still continuing; and the study directed by Professor Neville Butler of 16,000 children for the cohort born in 1970.

R. DAVIE, N. BUTLER and H. GOLDSTEIN, *From Birth to Seven,* Second report of the National Child Development Study, Longman with National Children's Bureau, 1972

J. W. B. DOUGLAS, *The Home and the School,* MacGibbon and Kee, 1964

Lord President of the Council

After the establishment of the **Committee of the Privy Council on Education** in 1839, the Lord President was one of its key members. He represented the Council, and later the **Education Department**, in the Lords. The Order in Council of 1856 made the Lord President Minister for Education *de jure* with a **Vice-President** the Minister *de facto*. Whilst the Lord President was invariably a member of the Cabinet, his Vice-President was rarely so. The educational aspects of the Lord President's work were transferred to the **President of the Board of Education** from 1900.

lower school

1. Formerly, referred to the first two or three forms of a **public** or **grammar school**, now more commonly to **comprehensive schools** where, for organizational purposes, there is a lower, followed by a **middle** and **upper school**.

2. When Harrow School decided to constitute a separate establishment for local day boys of the borough in 1875, it received the title of the Lower School of John Lyon.

M

Macfarlane Report

A committee chaired by Mr Neil Macfarlane, then Under Secretary for Education, was set up in 1979 to examine the educational provision for the 16 to 19 age group. Its report, issued in January 1981, proved to be a disappointment. No national policy was put forward, though local authorities were urged to review their provision for this age group. It acknowledged the educational and other advantages of a break in schooling at 16 years in favour of **tertiary** or **sixth form colleges**; for financial and demographic reasons, however, such a course was not officially recommended. Meanwhile, the report called for diversity of provision by local authorities and better careers education.

DES, *Education for 16 to 19 Year Olds*, HMSO, 1981

McNair Report

In 1942, a committee, chaired by Sir Arnold McNair, was appointed by the **Board of Education** to consider the supply, recruitment and training of teachers and youth leaders. Its report, published in 1944, recognized that the status of the teaching profession required raising. Better conditions of service, a longer training (three years' full-time study), higher salaries and a wider field of recruitment were four recommendations which the Committee put forward to remedy the situation. On the administration of teacher training, the Committee was divided. One group suggested that a Central Training Council be established, with **university training departments** and **training colleges** retaining their identities and being in direct relation with the Council and the Board of Education. The other group favoured a plan whereby each university established a School of Education, or **Institute of Education**, consisting of a federation of approved training institutions, responsible for the training and assessment of student teachers. On the **Youth Service**, the report laid down similar guidelines to those recommended for teachers – a three-year full-time training or a one-year course for those with suitable previous experience and qualifications, and salaries comparable with those of teachers. It also recommended that transfer between the two services should be encouraged. Not all the Committee's findings were accepted by the Government. The three-year course of teacher training did not come into operation until 1960. The new **Ministry of Education** postponed putting into action the proposals on youth leaders. However, teacher training was reorganized, and Institutes of Education were established and officially recognized as **Area Training Organizations**. (*See also* **Albemarle Report, James Report, Pelham Report, teachers' centres, Thompson Report.**)

Report of a Committee appointed by the President of the Board of Education to consider the Supply, Recruitment and Training of Teachers and Youth Leaders, HMSO, 1944

maintained school

A state school which is maintained by an **LEA**. There are two types –

county schools, which are wholly the responsibility of the LEA, and **voluntary schools**, which are connected with a religious denomination.

maintenance grant

A sum of money awarded to students to meet day-to-day living and accommodation costs, as distinct from fees, for college courses. Many **LEAs** have discretionary schemes for educational maintenance allowances to enable children to stay on at school after 16. (*See also* **discretionary award, Educational Welfare Service, entrance award, mandatory award**.)

Man – A Course of Study (MACOS)

A **curriculum development project** based on the work of Jerome Bruner and developed by Peter Dow. The project included film and course materials for which teachers needed a course of training. It has been used to a limited extent in the UK as a social studies teaching kit. In some parts of Australia and USA it has been highly controversial and even banned for periods.

J. BRUNER, *Towards a Theory of Instruction*, Harvard University Press, 1966

R. M. JONES, *Fantasy and Feeling in Education*, Penguin, 1972

manager

Historically associated with nineteenth-century voluntary elementary education, school managers were responsible for the control of and supervision over school personnel and organization as well as raising funds. After the 1870 Education Act,

school boards appointed managers to their schools. The 1902 Act took away many powers from **voluntary school** managers: at the same time all county council schools were in future to have managers, though this was left optional for borough councils. It was not until the 1944 Act that it was made a requirement for all **primary schools** to have managers, whose powers and terms of office were stated in an instrument of management. Since the 1980 Education Act came into force, the use of the term 'manager' has disappeared, with all schools now having **governors**. (*See also* **instrument of government**.)

P. GORDON, *The Victorian School Manager*, Woburn Press, 1974

mandatory award

LEAs have a duty under law to make grants to full-time students taking advanced courses if they are eligible under national regulations. For example, **first degree** courses and those for initial teacher training fall into this category. The award, covering fees and maintenance during **term** time and Christmas and Easter **vacations**, is means tested. (*See also* **discretionary award, entrance award, maintenance grant**.)

Manpower Services Commission (MSC)

An offshoot of the Department of Employment, the Manpower Services Commission was set up in 1972 'to assist manpower resources to be developed'. The Commission has two main divisions, employment and training. It assists people in finding employment and liaises with employers in order to fill vacancies. The MSC has become increasingly recognized as an educational agency, organizing and funding **Youth Opportunity Programmes** (replaced by the **Youth Training Scheme**) and the **Open Tech**. The MSC's influence on aspects of **further education** and the **youth service** has been criticized recently. (*See also* **careers guidance**, **New Technical and Vocational Education Initiative**, **Training Opportunities Scheme**, **Unified Vocational Preparation**.)

mass media

The large-scale communication network including television, radio, film, press and records. Their influence on forming public attitudes towards a range of political, economic and social issues is a constant source of debate.

M. H. SEIDEN, *Who Controls the Mass Media? Popular Myths and Economic Realities*, Basic Books, New York, USA, 1974

A. WELLS (ed.), *Mass Media and Society*, 2nd edn, Mayfield Publishing Company, Palo Alto, California, USA, 1975

master

1. A male member of the teaching staff of a school who is not a **headteacher**, **deputy** or **senior teacher**: the term for a woman teacher is mistress.

2. A **degree** which may be proceeded to after gaining a Bachelor's degree or equivalent. Examples are Master of Arts (MA), Master of Science (MSc) and Master of Laws (LLM).

3. A head of a **university college**, e.g. Master of Birkbeck College, London.

mastery learning

A theory put forward originally by Benjamin Bloom and some of his colleagues that mastery of any kind of **knowledge** is theoretically possible for any learner given sufficient time and appropriate teaching. Part of the theory is that pupils differ not only in their pace of learning, but also in learning styles. Mastery learning is, therefore, closely associated with **individualized learning**.

J. H. BLOCK, (ed.), *Mastery Learning: Theory and Practice*, Holt, Rinehart and Winston, 1971

B. BLOOM, 'Mastery Learning and its Implications for Curriculum Development', in E. W. EISNER (ed.), *Confronting Curriculum Reform*, Boston, Little, Brown and Co., 1971

matching

A type of item in an objective test where the student has to choose from a set of pictures the one that matches a corresponding word (or vice versa).

matriculation

Candidates who achieved credit grades in five subjects including one at least from each of three groups – humanities, foreign languages, and mathematics and science – at the **School Certificate** examination were given matriculation exemption by the majority of universities. The University of London offered as early as 1858 a Matriculation examination which could be taken by external candidates wishing to go on to higher education. The term originated with the ceremony of signing the roll (*matricula*) on being admitted to a university. (*See also* **degree**.)

UNIVERSITY OF LONDON, *The Historical Record 1836–1912*, 1912

maturation

The physical, mental or moral changes that occur as part of an individual's 'natural' development: maturation is always the result of innate factors, not environmental ones. The work of Piaget is much concerned with the development and thus the maturation of certain innate abilities. (*See also* **Piagetian**.)

mature students

Defined for grant purposes as those students over 25 years of age on 1 September in the year they intend to enter a course of study in **higher education**. But universities and colleges differ in the age they regard students as 'mature', some accepting a lower age of 21 or 23. Mature students are sometimes exempt from normal entry requirements. (*See also* **entry qualification**, **Open Tech**, **Open University**, **university entrance requirements**.)

Mechanics' Institutes

In 1799 Dr George Birkbeck began a series of evening lectures at the Andersonian Institution, Glasgow, on natural and experimental philosophy for local workmen. From this sprang his idea of a course of scientific instruction in the principles of arts and manufactures. In 1823, his *Proposals for a London Mechanics' Institute* was published, and that same year a committee to carry out Birkbeck's plans was formed. The movement rapidly spread: by 1850 there were over 600 Institutes throughout the country. This early experiment in **adult education** lost momentum as an increasing proportion of the middle classes joined the movement. However, Birkbeck's vision prepared the way for the developments in **technical education** later in the century.

T. KELLY, *George Birkbeck: pioneer of adult education*, Liverpool University Press, 1957

M. TYLECOTE, *The Mechanics' Institutes of Lancashire and Yorkshire before 1851*, Manchester University Press, 1957

Media Resources Officer (MRO)

A non-teaching member of school staff in the **ILEA** who is responsible for the preparation, operation and maintenance of **audio-visual aids**, and other **educational technology**. All secondary schools have MROs and they are shared by **primary schools**.

memory

An individual's inner record of his past mental and sensory experience. Memory may be made evident by the individual's ability to recall or recognize. Some psychologists have been interested in the difference between conscious and unconscious memory. Memory span is the technical term indicating the amount of information a person can remember either immediately after, or within a specified time, of having data presented. Some **intelligence tests** involve, for example, the memorization of unrelated digits. Certain psychologists have claimed that the ability to memorize a long series of unrelated digits is a very good indication of general **intelligence**.

OPEN UNIVERSITY, Cognitive Psychology Course Team, *Memory*, Parts 1 and 2, Open University Press, 1978

mental age

See **age: chronological and mental**.

meritocratic education

Meritocracy was a word invented by Michael Young (1961). His book satirized a society in which the status of a person is determined by 'merit' and merit is determined by the simple formula IQ plus effort equals merit. Meritocratic education is that kind of education which concentrates on the identification of talent, preferably by means of **intelligence tests**, and then separating the talented from the less talented by different schools and curricula. Meritocratic education is different from élitist education inasmuch as élitist education depends upon social selection whereas meritocratic education depends on selection by 'ability'. Michael Young's book demonstrated the folly of such a system very convincingly. (*See also* **ladder of ability**.)

M. YOUNG, *The Rise of the Meritocracy 1870–2033; an essay on education and equality*, Penguin, 1961

micro teaching

A system used in some **colleges** and departments of education for developing specific teaching skills. Normally, the student teacher would teach a small group for a limited amount of time, perhaps only ten minutes, concentrating on a specific objective. The **lesson** is then analysed with the help of the **tutor** and other students from a film or video tape recording. A student might then be required to repeat the lesson, making use of the points made by fellow students and tutors. It is a technique which is usually regarded as having a limited value in teacher training, and is rarely used with all students. It is increasingly likely that its use will be confined to those with particular problems or difficulties. (*See also* **competency based teaching**.)

G. BROWN, *Microteaching: a programme of teaching skills*, Methuen, 1975

E. PERROTT, *Effective Teaching*, Longman, 1982

middle school

1. The shift to a **comprehensive school** system in the early 1960s without a stock of adequate buildings gave rise to the setting up of middle schools. The West Riding of Yorkshire submitted plans for 9 to 13 schools in 1963 and in the following year the law was amended to allow transfer ages other than 11. A further impetus to the spread of middle schools followed with DES Circular 10/65 which suggested middle schools as one way of establishing comprehensives. The **Plowden Report** also recommended an extension of the primary mode until 12 or 13. The starting and leaving ages of pupils differ from LEA to LEA, with patterns such as 8–12, 9–13 and 9–14. There were some 1400 middle schools in England and Wales in 1981. However, **falling rolls** and the changing pattern of **sixth form** education has resulted in LEAs returning to 11–16 schools, at the expense of middle schools.

2. Describes the 13- to 14-year-old age range in a comprehensive school between the upper school and the lower school.

J. BURROWS, *The Middle School: High Road or Dead End*, Woburn Press, 1978

M. TAYLOR and Y. GARSON, *Schooling the Middle Years*, Trentham Books, 1982

Ministry of Education
The 1944 Education Act provided for a Minister of Education in place of a President and a corresponding change in the title of the department, from **Board of Education** to Ministry of Education. Whereas the President had been charged with superintending the education system, the new Minister was responsible for promoting education, developing institutions and ensuring that **LEAs**, under his control and direction, carried out a national policy of providing a varied and comprehensive educational service in every area. The Minister was to be advised by the **Central Advisory Councils**. The Ministry was replaced in 1964 by the **DES**. (*See also* **President of the Board of Education**.)

minority group
Refers to a group in any society which can be identified usually by reason of religion, race, nationality or special needs. (*See also* **subculture**.)

mixed ability grouping
The grouping of pupils in such a way that each class in a year group has an equal range of attainment. Allocation of pupils to such groups may be operated on the basis of pupils' scores on tests supplemented by teacher **assessment**, by random sampling or by alphabetical ordering. A survey undertaken by **HMI** and published in a report entitled *Mixed Ability Work in Comprehensive Schools* (1978) stated that only in a very small number of the schools visited were pupils learning at an appropriate level and pace in classes organized in this way. Other criticisms made were that bright pupils were not being extended and

that too much emphasis was put upon social objectives. A third of all **comprehensive schools** in the sample were undertaking some mixed ability work which was found largely in the first three years of the schools. (*See also* **labelling, setting, streaming, unstreaming, workcards**.)

M. I. REID et al., *Mixed Ability Teaching; Problems and Possibilities*, NFER, 1981

E. C. WRAGG (ed.), *Teaching Mixed Ability Groups*, David and Charles, 1976

mock examination
An examination, internally set by an institution, taken by candidates preparing for a formal examination. It is usually of the same standard as the latter and is designed to acclimatize students to the forthcoming examination and/or to ascertain if they are capable of being successful if entered.

'Modern Greats'
The final **honours degree** course at Oxford University in philosophy, politics and economics (PPE).

modern side
Introduced by Dr Arnold at Rugby School about 1830, it consisted of 'modern' subjects in the curriculum such as geography, mathematics and modern languages. Pupils on the modern side did no Greek and less Latin than those on the classical side. The **Taunton Report** recommended that first-grade schools should be encouraged to develop modern sides and include Latin. For many years the modern side was reserved for the less intellectually able pupils. (*See also* **public school**.)

modular course

A departure from the tradition in higher education of studying a single **discipline** in depth, modular courses allow students to choose a **course** consisting of a number of **multi-disciplinary** based units. It is claimed that consumer satisfaction is increased by giving a wider choice and that resources can be used more economically. Most of these courses are based in **polytechnics**, though some university disciplines, such as engineering, employ the modular system. In the University of London, most undergraduate work in science is organized on a modular structure.

mongols, education of

See **Downs Syndrome.**

monitor

Usually denotes a rank inferior to **prefect**. The term has been in use since the sixteenth century. (*See also* **monitorial system**.)

monitorial system

The monitorial or mutual system of education is associated with an Anglican clergyman, Andrew Bell, and a Quaker schoolteacher, Joseph Lancaster, at the beginning of the nineteenth century. Both men arrived at a similar plan for mass education through different routes. By their method, one master, aided by a number of older boys called **monitors**, could supervise a large number of pupils. Such instruction was confined to the **three Rs** and was cheap but mechanical and ignored individual children's needs.

H. C. BARNARD, *A History of English Education from 1760*, University of London Press, 2nd edn, 1961

monitoring

Systematically studying the work of pupils, teachers, schools or even **LEAs** in order to assess levels of performance. During the 1970s, the phrase 'monitoring standards' became commonly used especially in connection with the work of the **Assessment of Performance Unit**.

H. ROSEN, *The Language Monitors*, Bedford Way Papers, 11, 1982

R. SUMNER, (ed.), *Monitoring National Standards of Attainment in Schools*, NFER, 1977

moral development, moral education

Moral development is sometimes confined to the sense of maturation or the innate development of a child's moral thinking; more commonly, it is used to refer to the combination of maturation and experience including moral education. Moral education is the conscious attempt to contribute to a child's moral development. In the UK various attempts have been made to base moral education on sound psychological and philosophical criteria, and to distinguish moral education from **religious education**. See the work of Peter McPhail and the Schools Council's projects on Moral Education and also the Farmington Trust project, which was reported on in a book by J. Wilson, N. Williams and B. Sugarman, *An Introduction to Moral Education*, Penguin, 1968.

R. H. HERSH, J. P. MILLER and G. D. FIELDING, *Models of Moral Education*, Longman, 1980

P. MCPHAIL, *Social and Moral Education,* Blackwell, Oxford, 1982

multi-cultural or multi-ethnic education

The two, somewhat different but overlapping, meanings of both terms can lead to confusion.

1. Refers to the fact that in many areas of the UK there are now sizeable groups of children from ethnic minorities in some schools not all of which provide adequately for all the children, so that some of the groups are classified as 'underachieving'. The problem is then seen as one of adapting the curriculum to make it more suitable for members of those minority groups.

2. Refers to the fact that England is now a multi-cultural or multi-ethnic society, and that even if children live in an area where there are no ethnic minorities, the school still has the duty to include in the curriculum subject matter which will help pupils to understand the concept of **culture** and to appreciate the variety of cultures which now exist in English society. (*See also* **black studies**, **Rampton Report**, **religious education**, **underachiever**.)

A. LITTLE and R. WILLEY, *Multi-ethnic Education, The Way Forward*, Pamphlet 18, Schools Council, 1981

P. WALKING, 'The Idea of a Multi-Cultural Education', *Journal of Philosophy of Education*, Vol. 14, No. 1, 1980

multidisciplinary studies
See **interdisciplinary studies.**

multilateral school

One which catered for all the secondary education of children in a given area and included provision for **grammar**, **technical** and **modern** courses on one site. Unlike children in **comprehensive schools**, those in multilateral schools remained in their separate courses during their secondary school life. This type of school was advocated by the TUC from the 1920s as a first step to breaking down class distinctions in education. (*See also* **Secondary Education for All**, **Spens Report**, **tripartite system**.)

M. PARKINSON, *The Labour Party and the Organization of Secondary Education 1918–65*, Routledge and Kegan Paul, 1970

multiple choice test

A form of **assessment** where the candidate is presented with a number of alternative answers to questions posed. Responses are usually denoted by ticks. Multiple choice tests are now common in many public examination papers in addition to essay type questions. (*See also* **open-ended**.)

CAMBRIDGE TEST DEVELOPMENT AND RESEARCH UNIT, *Multiple Choice Item Writing*, Occasional Publication No. 2, Cambridge, 1975

Munn Report

A Scottish Committee under the chairmanship of Dr James Munn considered the appropriate curriculum for third and fourth year secondary school pupils. It reported in 1977. A **core curriculum** was favoured, based on a 40-period week; 14 'non-core' periods were recommended for two additional optional activities which were available. An important point made by the Committee was that **assessment** should be geared to educational objectives in the curriculum, rather than the curriculum being controlled by the assessment system. This might be achieved by schools making their own assessment on a range of subjects. Further consideration of assessment procedures was undertaken at this time by the **Dunning Committee**. (*See also* **Scottish Education Department**.)

SCOTTISH EDUCATION DEPARTMENT, *The Structure of the Curriculum in the Third and Fourth Years of the Scottish Secondary School*, HMSO, 1977

museum education

The educational value of museums in education has long been recognized, though the appointment of Education Officers in national and some local museums to liaise with schools is a fairly recent innovation. Museums cater for groups of pupils who may be preparing for examinations, engaged on topic work or making a visit in connection with some aspect of the school curriculum. There is now a **CSE** mode 3 examination in museum studies, devised by teachers and the National Portrait Gallery, but which can be used with any museum. Lecturers and workshops may be provided; many museums have loan services to schools. The **DES** has direct responsibility for the Victoria and Albert Museum and the Science Museum.

E. ALEXANDER, *Museums and how to use them*, Batsford, 1974

DES, Education Survey 12, *Museums in Education*, HMSO, 1971

N

N and F levels

A proposal put forward by **Schools Council** in 1973 to replace **GCE A level** examinations with a two-tier five-subject system entitled N (Normal) and F (Further) levels. Occupying the same amount of time as the present A level course, the two-level course was to be organized in such a way that students would take three N levels each equal to half an A level and two F levels each equal to three-quarters of an A. Although there was widespread agreement in schools and colleges on the need for change, the proposal encountered opposition and has now been dropped. (*See also* **examinations: history of**, **Q and F levels**.)

SCHOOLS COUNCIL, Working Paper 66, *Examinations at 18 plus: Report of the N and F Debate*, Methuen Educational, 1980

National Advisory Body (NAB)

The National Advisory Body for Local Authority Higher Education was formed by the Government in December 1981. Its main task is to advise on the present and future provision of **higher education** in the non-university sector at a time when resources available are shrinking. There have been criticisms that the NAB requires more members involved in, and with experience of, higher education, and that the committee of the board, chaired by the Under Secretary of State for Higher Education and with a membership of **DES** officials, local authority officers and representatives of the **Council of Local Education Authorities**, has more power than the NAB itself. (*See also* **Oakes Report**, **University Grants Committee**.)

J. S. BEVAN, *The National Advisory Body for Local Authority Higher Education*, Association of Colleges for Further and Higher Education, Sheffield, 1982

National Advisory Council on Education for Industry and Commerce (NACEIC)

Established in 1948 following the recommendations of the **Percy Report**. During its 29 years, the NACEIC issued a series of important reports. Its first, *The Future Development of Higher Technological Education* (1950), led to the setting up of the National Council of Technological Awards, later the **Council for National Academic Awards**, and others dealt with such areas as business studies, **sandwich courses** and **day release**. The Council was disbanded in 1977. (*See also* **business education**, **Haslegrave Report**.)

National Advisory Council on the Training and Supply of Teachers (NACTST)

Set up in 1949 to advise the **Minister of Education** on national policy regarding the training, qualifications, recruitment and distribution of teachers. The Council represented most shades of educational opinion, consisting of some 58 members at the time of its demise. By 1965, the Council was proving to be an embarrassment to the **DES**, as it was making recommendations which trespassed on the Department's policy-making functions. There were also disagreements on issues of national policy within the Council itself. Nevertheless, the nine reports issued by NACTST were an important focus on issues in teacher training. It was later revived in 1973 under the title Advisory Committee for the Supply and Training of Teachers (ACSTT) and was succeeded in 1980 by the **Advisory Committee for the Supply and Education of Teachers** (ACSET).

D. HICKS, 'The National Advisory Council on the Training and Supply of Teachers', *British Journal of Educational Studies*, Vol. 22, No. 3, 1974

National Association for Gifted Children (NAGC)

The aim of the Association, which was founded in 1966, is to enable gifted children to achieve their full potential at home and school. There are over 4,000 members, the majority of whom are parents. A full-time education officer maintains contact with the **DES**, **LEAs** and schools. The Association mounts courses at Easter and in summer in a number of centres where a range of interests can be developed. Many local branches run Saturday clubs. (*See also* **giftedness**.)

National Association for Multiracial Education (NAME)

Begun in 1965 under the name of ATEPO (Association for the Teaching of English to Pupils from Overseas), this Association aims at bringing about changes in the education system in order to achieve a more just multiracial society. As a **pressure group**, it lobbies the **DES** and teachers' unions and presents evidence to appropriate committees. Local branches have produced a large amount of teaching material suitable for the classroom. (*See also* **multicultural and multi-ethnic education**.)

National Association for the Promotion of Social Science (NAPSS)

A reforming body founded in 1856, the Association was divided into five sections, Art, Economy and Trade, Health, Jurisprudence and the Amendment of the Law and Education. Papers were given by leading figures in each field at the Association's annual meetings and were published in its *Transactions*. Twenty-eight volumes appeared during the existence of the NAPSS, which came to an end in 1886.

R. ALDRICH, 'Association of Ideas: The National Association for the Promotion of Social Science', *History of Education Society Bulletin*, No. 16, 1975

National Association for the Promotion of Technical and Secondary Education (NAPTE)

The Association, set up in 1886, had three objectives: to develop dexterity of hand and eye among the young with a view to their future employment, to disseminate knowledge of the principles of science and art underlying industrial work and to encourage better instruction generally, which would include more effective teaching of foreign languages and science. It was hoped that industrial education would be available for both boys and girls. A. H. D. Acland and Sir Henry Roscoe were general secretaries and H. Llewellyn Smith was the secretary. From 1891, the Association issued a bi-monthly journal, *The Record of Technical and Secondary Education*.

National Association of Governors and Managers (NAGM)

Launched in 1970, this pressure group was constituted for the purpose of reforming governing bodies by involving parents, pupils, teachers, the local community and the local authority. This philosophy was later endorsed by the **Taylor Committee** in its Report. The Association, which is non-political, is attempting to obtain training for **governors**.

NAGM, *Planning a Training Course for Governors: a brief guide*, Paper No. 6, Liverpool, 1978

National Association of Head Teachers (NAHT)

A body established in 1897 with a membership of over 20,000, which represents the interests of heads in both primary and secondary sectors in England and Wales. More than 75 per cent of primary heads and over 60 per cent of secondary heads are members. (*See also* **headteacher**, **teachers' associations**, **Secondary Heads Association**.)

National Association of Schoolmasters/Union of Women Teachers (NAS/UWT)

The second largest teachers' union since the amalgamation of the two separate bodies in 1976. At the present time there are more than 125,000 members, with twice as many men as women. It is now the largest teachers' union in Northern Ireland and is the only British union represented on the Scottish national negotiating body. (*See also* **teachers' associations**.)

National Association of Teachers in Further and Higher Education (NATFHE)

Formed in 1975 from the Association of Teachers in Colleges and Departments of Education (ATCDE) and the Association of Teachers in Technical Institutions (ATTI), this body, of some 75,000 members, represents 85% of teachers working in this sector. It has 12 representatives on the **Burnham Committee**. (*See also* **teachers' associations**.)

National Campaign for Nursery Education (NCNE)

A **pressure group**, formed in 1965 as an offshoot of the National Assembly of Women. Concern was expressed at **Ministry of Education** Circular 8/60 in 1960 which halted the expansion of **nursery education**. Less militant than some other pressure groups, the NCNE is remembered for its first demonstration in 1968 when 500 women and babies marched to Westminster. Later the **Secretary of State for Education**, Edward Short, relaxed the nursery education provision ban. (*See also* **Plowden Report**.)

National Children's Bureau

Founded in 1962 as the National Bureau for Co-operation in Child Care, with Dr Mia Kellmer Pringle as its director, it has addressed itself to research into the care, development and education of children. The Bureau membership ranges from local and health authorities and professional and voluntary organizations to universities and other teaching bodies. It is perhaps best known for the National Child Development Study, a **longitudinal study** based on subjects born in one week in March 1958 and followed up by the Bureau when they were aged 7, 11 and 16 years. Since its inception, the Bureau has undertaken over 70 research projects.

National Confederation of Parent-Teacher Associations (NCPTA)

Parent-teacher associations (PTAs) exist in many schools and are mainly concerned with local issues. The NCPTA, formed in 1954, provides a national organization to which PTAs can affiliate. A non-political body, it holds annual conferences and raises issues of concern with government departments. (*See also* **Home and School Council**, **pressure group**.)

National Council for Educational Standards (NCES)

Founded in 1972 'because it was felt that rising expenditure on education was not leading to any proportionate improvement in standards'. The Council aims at influencing and alerting public opinion through its conferences and twice yearly *Bulletin*. Many of the contributors to the latter have also written for the **Black Papers**. (*See also* **pressure groups**, **standards**.)

national criteria

The Government's proposal for a single system of examining at 16+, announced in February 1980, recommended that national criteria should be established for **syllabuses** and **assessment** procedures 'to ensure that all syllabuses with the same subject title have sufficient content in common, and that all boards apply the same performance standards to the award of grades'. The **GCE** and

CSE examination boards themselves were invited to draft the criteria for some 20 subjects. They subsequently formed a Joint Council representing all the boards with observers from **Schools Council** and **HM Inspectorate**. The **Secretary of State for Education** provided guidelines for the work and stated the nature of the target group. The Government requested that the boards should report back by early 1983. Not every subject is to be investigated by working parties; nor will there be time to look at **interdisciplinary studies**. (*See also* **sixteen plus examination**.)

DES, *Examinations at 16+: a statement of policy*, 1982, HMSO

National Education League

A Nonconformist **pressure group** established in 1869. Its aim was to ensure that State education should be secular, free and compulsory. One of the governing principles was that local authorities should provide school accommodation; all schools aided by the rates were to be unsectarian. The League originated in Birmingham: George Dixon was chairman, Joseph Chamberlain was vice-chairman and Jesse Collings secretary. Some of the aims of the League were achieved by the 1870 and 1876 Education Acts and it therefore disbanded in 1877. (*See also* **free education, National Education Union, school board**.)

National Education Union

The Union was formed in the same month as the **National Education League** (1869) by supporters of the **voluntary schools** in order to counteract the League's activities. The first President was the second Earl of Harrowby and the Union was based at Manchester. It promoted denominational teaching in schools. The endeavours of the Union were rewarded in the 1870 Act which admitted for the first time the principle of a **dual system**. (*See also* **school board**).

National Foundation for Educational Research (NFER)

Established in 1946 by **LEAs**, with the co-operation of the **Ministry of Education** and others, the NFER's task was to investigate such 'practical problems arising within the public system of education as are amenable to scientific investigation'. Its research programme ranges from the pre-school stage to higher education. The Foundation is publicly funded but seeks individual sponsors for its projects. For example, in the current **APU** monitoring programme initiated by the **DES**, the NFER is concerned with the standards of performance in mathematics, English language and foreign languages. Other recent work includes **special educational needs** in ordinary schools, an examination of **mixed ability teaching**, the teaching of study and information skills and an evaluation of **TEC** programmes. It also produces a range of tests in the basic subjects for classroom use by teachers. (*See also* **research project**.)

National Institute of Adult Continuing Education (NIACE)

A national centre for co-operation, enquiry, information and consultation in the field of **continuing education** for adults, founded in 1949. It receives support and finance from **LEAs**, universities, residential colleges and the **DES**. The Institute carries out surveys in such areas as **mature students**, open learning systems and the training of **tutors**. The **Adult Literacy and Basic Skills Unit** (ALBSU) is an agency of the Institute and is grant-aided by the DES.

National Nursery Examination Board (NNEB)

The Board offers a two-year course mainly for girls of 16 to 19, leading to a certificate which qualifies the holder to work in hospitals, schools and **day nurseries**. A sizeable proportion, about a quarter, become private nannies. In 1980, a committee set up by the NNEB to examine its future recommended that the age of entry to courses should be raised from 17 to 18 and that the Board should negotiate with the **Technician Education Council** for validation of **in-service** courses.

NNEB, *A Future for Nursery Nursing*, London, 1980

National schools
See **National Society**.

National Society

The National Society for Promoting the Education of the Poor in the Principles of the Established Church was founded in 1811 as a result of the success of the non-sectarian **British Society** in this field. Its connection with the Church of England ensured the rapid provision of both schools and teachers. Teaching in National schools was based on the Madras system of monitorial instruction under the auspices of Dr Andrew Bell. National Society **training colleges** included St Mark's, Chelsea,

and St John's, Battersea, for masters and Whitelands for mistresses. (*See also* **monitorial system**.)

National Union of School Students (NUSS)

In the late 1960s and early 1970s, secondary school pupils began to demand rights such as places on governing bodies of schools. The NUSS was launched in 1971 and affiliated to the **NUS**. NUSS started with moderate left-wing leadership, but by 1978 it was dominated by the SWP (Socialist Workers' Party) and had published the magazine *BLOT* which combined extremist policies with obscene language. NUS in 1981 withdrew its support; numbers continued to decline.

National Union of Students (NUS)

Founded in 1922, NUS was initially intended for university students only, but now includes most institutions in further and higher education in the UK. The NUS is a federation of the autonomous students' unions which each send delegates to the twice annual conference. There is an elected executive body which carries out the decisions of the conference. The main aim of the union is to promote and maintain the educational, social and general interests of students.

National Union of Teachers (NUT)

The largest of the **teachers' associations** with a membership of over 260,000. Originally called the National Union of Elementary Teachers when it was founded in 1870, it dropped 'Elementary' from its title in 1889. The 560 local associations elect delegates to the annual Conference, where policy matters are debated.

A. TROPP, *The School Teachers. The Growth of the Teaching Profession in England and Wales from 1900 to the Present Day*, Heinemann, 1957

natural wastage

The process of achieving a smaller teaching staff either in schools or in universities and other institutions of higher education by allowing members of staff to leave either on retirement or by resignation without their being replaced. Many institutions preferred to pursue the policy of 'natural wastage' in the 1970s and 1980s rather than invoke redundancy. The problem of such policies was, however, that this frequently resulted in a very unbalanced staffing and a patchy curriculum since retirements and resignations tended to be completely haphazard rather than falling equally across all subject areas. (*See also* **falling rolls**.)

W. TAYLOR, 'Contraction in Context', in B. SIMON and W. TAYLOR (eds), *Education in the Eighties*, Batsford, 1981

nature–nurture controversy

For a number of years psychologists, sociologists and others have debated, sometimes bitterly, whether aspects of an individual's personality are mainly inherited genetically or are due to environment and, in particular, to learning. The argument has been pursued on both sides of the Atlantic. In England, advocates of the genetic point of view have included Cyril Burt (whose work has been partly discredited) and Professor H. Eysenck; in the USA the best

known advocate of hereditarianism was Professor Jensen, who felt that there was evidence to suggest that black children and working class children were genetically inferior in terms of intelligence scores.

C. BURT, 'The Genetic Determination of Differences in Intelligence: A Study of Monozygotic Twins Reared Together and Apart', *British Journal of Psychology*, No. 57, 1966

L. KAMIN, *The Science and Politics of IQ*, Penguin, 1977

neighbourhood school

1. A school which draws its pupils from a clearly identifiable 'neighbourhood' in the sense of a **catchment area** which is both homogeneous and compact.

2. The view that schools should identify closely with neighbourhood people and neighbourhood interests. Some **comprehensive schools** would be classified as neighbourhood schools, whereas **grammar schools** drew their pupils from a much wider area. (*See also* **community school/ college**.)

Newbolt Report

One of the **Prime Minister's Reports**. The Departmental Committee on the position of English in the English educational system was appointed in May 1919. Its brief was unusually wide, taking in both English language and literature in schools, universities and other institutions of higher education and the needs of business, the professions and public services. The Committee attracted many of the leading literary figures of the time. Besides the chairman, Sir Henry Newbolt, it included Sir Arthur Quiller-Couch,

Caroline Spurgeon, J. Dover Wilson and George Sampson. The report itself, published in 1921, marked an advance in the centrality of English in schools, advocating the modern-sounding doctrine that 'every teacher is a teacher of English'. It also drew attention to the use of literature as 'a possession and a source of delight, a personal intimacy and a gaining of personal experience, an end in itself and, at the same time, an equipment for the understanding of life'. (*see* **Bullock Report**.)

The Report of the Departmental Committee appointed by the President of the Board of Education to Inquire into the position of English in the Educational System of England: The Teaching of English in England, HMSO, 1921, reprinted 1935

Newcastle Report

Apart from the investigations of three **Select Committees** in the first half of the nineteenth century into the provision of education for the working classes, little official attention had been directed to this end. The Newcastle Commission, appointed in 1858, was set up 'to inquire into the present state of Popular Education in England, and to consider and report what Measures, if any, are required for the extension of sound and cheap elementary instruction to all classes of people'. The chairman, the Duke of Newcastle, reluctantly agreed to undertake this task and insisted upon greater representation from Voluntaryist interests and fewer Church members on the Commission. Previously, progress in introducing a general system of education had foundered on the denominational issue. The report, issued in 1861, was a comprehensive survey of all types of education available for the poor in England as well as its provision in Continental countries. Although it made no recommendations to change Church control in education matters, the report supported the notion of establishing county and borough education boards with power to levy rates, examining secular instruction and paying grants. It also drew attention to the unsatisfactory state of the **curriculum** offered and the low standard of achievement in the basic subjects. The report noted that undue emphasis was being placed on the instruction of older scholars at the expense of the younger. Only half of the pupils were under any sort of inspection. The remedy suggested 'a revealing examination by competent authority of every child in every school to which grants are to be paid, with the view of ascertaining whether these indispensable elements of knowledge [i.e. the **three Rs**] are thoroughly acquired, and to make the prospects and position of the teacher dependent, to a considerable extent, on the results of this examination'. This was the only recommendation of the Commission to be adopted. Cheap and efficient education was to be obtained by the system of **payment by results** introduced under the Revised Code of 1862 by the **Vice-President of the Council**, Robert Lowe.

Report of the Commissioners appointed to inquire into the state of Popular Education in England, P.P. 1861, xxi

New Education Fellowship (NEF)

An organization designed to promote various aspects of progressive, non-authoritarian education in schools. It was launched by Mrs Beatrice Ensor at the Calais Conference in 1921. The journal, *The New Era*, was part of the early work of NEF and is still published. In 1966, the NEF became The World Education Fellowship. (*See also* **New Educationists**, **progressive education**, **progressive schools**.)

M. D. LAWSON, 'The New Education Fellowship: The Formative Years', *Journal of Educational Administration and History*, Vol.13, No.3, 1981

New Educationists

The name given to reformers active from the end of the last century who were opposed to the traditional, instrumental education of the time. There was no conscious school united under one banner and the views of individual reformers often differed widely. One group, the practical educationists, advocated manual training as a means of promoting educational values. Another, the social reformers, placed more emphasis on ways of improving the physical well-being of children. The naturalists expounded the theories of Froebel and Pestalozzi whilst others looked to Herbart's teachings. There were also the scientific educationists who based their work largely on psychological research as well as those who looked to moral education as a replacement for religious instruction. The ideas of the New Educationists helped to provide a basis for the later progressive education movement. (*See also* **progressive education**, **progressive schools**, **New Education Fellowship**.)

R. J. W. SELLECK, *The New Education*, Pitman, 1968

new information technology

In contrast to old information technology, such as the press, postal service and books, the new information technology relies much less on mechanical means. It is essentially electronic and relies heavily on three complex technologies which have converged: computing, microelectronics and telecommunications. Schools now use some of this technology, for example, microcomputers, videotext such as Prestel and calculators. (*See also* **CAL**, **CAMOL**, **computers in schools**, **educational technology**.)

D. G. HAWKRIDGE, *New Information Technology in Education*, Croom Helm, 1983

G. HUBBARD, 'Education and the new technologies', *Proceedings of the Royal Society of Arts*, Vol. 129, No. 5297, April 1981

Newsom Report

The **Central Advisory Council for Education**, under its chairman John Newsom, was asked in 1961 by the **Minister of Education** 'to consider the education between the ages of 13 and 16 of pupils of average or less than average ability who are or will be following full-time courses either at schools or in establishments of further education. The term education shall be understood to include extra-curricular activities.' The Council's report, published in 1963, was entitled *Half Our Future*, a reminder of the fact that the pupils within the terms of reference of the Council accounted for half the population of secondary schools. One of its main recommendations, which the Council had already made in the **Crowther Report**, was that the school leaving age should be raised to 16. Many changes in the curriculum were suggested. Schools were urged to provide a range of courses broadly related to occupational interests for fourth and fifth year pupils; equally, attention was to be paid both to imaginative experience through the arts and to the personal and social development of the pupils. The Newsom Report also recommended that the Ministry of Education should institute a programme of research in teaching techniques designed to help those with environmental and linguistic handicaps. Teacher training was to be geared to the new demands. **In-service courses** for teachers were to be provided and initial training was to take into account the new demands which would be made by the **raising of the school leaving age**. External pressures to extend public examinations to pupils for whom they were inappropriate were to be resisted: instead, schools were asked to devise an internal assessment with a general school record. Links with the adult world – the youth employment service, further education, the youth service and adult organizations – all needed strengthening. One interesting recommendation was that the school day should be extended for pupils aged 14 to 16 to include 'extra-curricular activities.' The report drew on a mass of valuable factual information to support its recommendations. It should be noted that there is no discussion in the report of the relative merits of the different forms of secondary school organization. (*See also* **extended day**, **school day**.)

Report of the Central Advisory Council for Education (England): Half Our Future, HMSO, 1963

Newsom Report (on Public Schools)

In 1965, following the issue of Circular 10/65, a Public Schools Commission, chaired by Sir John Newsom, was established to explore ways in which **public schools** could be integrated into a system of **comprehensive schooling**. Some of the Commission's proposals, which were published in 1968, were far-reaching. Whilst there would be a limited number of public schools which would be involved in the scheme, these schools would allocate at least half of their places to pupils from the maintained sector, representing a wider academic range than was normally found in public schools. The criteria for boarding were to be widened, being based on social or academic grounds. The cost of the proposals amounted to over £18 million. In the year that the report appeared, the Commission was reconstituted. (*See also* **Assisted Place Scheme**, **Donnison Report**, **Fleming Report**.)

PUBLIC SCHOOLS COMMISSION, *First Report, Vol. 1, Report*, HMSO, 1968

New Technical and Vocational Education Initiative

A project, under the auspices of the **Manpower Services Commission**, announced in 1982, to reintroduce specialized vocational and technical education for those between 14 and 18. The courses are full-time and are intended for a wide range of ability. Although the first two years of the course are envisaged as being for general **vocational preparation**, it may be possible to concentrate on specific occupational studies from the beginning. Much of the cost is provided by the Manpower Services Commission. **Pilot schemes**, which started in 1983, are expected to continue for five years in volunteer **LEA**s. It is now referred to as **TVEI**.

New Training Initiative
See **Youth Training Scheme**.

Normal college
The Normal schools of France, Switzerland and Prussia, where teachers were trained on the lines laid down by a reformer, Philipp von Fellenberg, were much admired in England during the early part of the nineteenth century. When Dr Kay was appointed as first Secretary of the **Committee of the Privy Council on Education** in 1839, he gave priority to the foundation of 'Normal Training Colleges', model schools where candidates could learn the art of teaching. A rector was to be appointed to give lectures on pedagogy to the students. The title still survives, in the instance of Bangor Normal College. (*See also* **training college**.)

normal curve
A bell-shaped curve on a graph that shows the distribution which is expected to occur when the number of people obtaining each score follows the distribution which occurs for height in the adult population. There are very few people who are very tall and very few who are extremely short, but the curve rises to the highest point midway between the two extremes, showing that the majority are around the average or mean height (hence the bell-shaped curve).

Psychologists involved in constructing **intelligence tests** make the assumption that **intelligence** follows the normal distribution and therefore construct tests so that a normal population will have that same kind of distribution. Not all social scientists accept this assumption. (*See also* **Gaussian curve**.)

norm-referenced test
A test in which a pupil's performance is compared with the performance of other pupils; the pupil's grade is therefore dependent on the average performance of the candidates as a whole. Norm-referenced tests are contrasted with **criterion-referenced tests**.

Norwood Report
A Committee of the **Secondary School Examinations Council** was appointed in 1941 'to consider suggested changes in the secondary school curriculum and the question of school examinations in relation thereto'. Under the chairmanship of Sir Cyril Norwood, the Committee issued its report in 1943. Like the earlier **Spens Report**, it supported the notion of a **tripartite** division of secondary education into **grammar**, **technical** and **modern schools**: each should have its own type of curriculum corresponding to the 'needs' of the pupils. The 1944 **Education Act**, whilst not specifying a particular type of secondary organization, was interpreted very much in the Norwood spirit. The report also recommended that the existing group examination, the **School Certificate Examination**, should be ended and be replaced by a single subject examination; this recommendation was acted upon

when the **General Certificate of Education** replaced the former in 1951. A school leaving examination for 18-year-old leavers which would be acceptable for universities and employers was also recommended: the **Higher School Certificate** was replaced by the **General Certificate of Education A level examination**.

Report of the Secondary School Examinations Council on Curriculum and Examinations in Secondary Schools, HMSO, 1943

Nuffield Science

In 1962, it was announced that the Nuffield Foundation, a body concerned with making available funds for research in academic subjects, intended to encourage the development of curricula in school science. Since then, more than 20 projects in science and mathematics have been produced and published. These include **GCE O** and **A level** Chemistry, Physics and Biology schemes, Nuffield Science 13–16, an integrated course, combined science for 11- to 13-year-olds, and themes for the middle years, 9–13. The innovative approaches adopted by Nuffield, reflected in methods of examining, have influenced science teaching in British schools. In 1979, the Nuffield Foundation Teaching Project was transferred to a new body, the Nuffield-Chelsea Curriculum Trust, jointly established by the Foundation and Chelsea College, University of London. (*See also* **curriculum development project**, **heurism/ heuristic method**.)

M. WARING, *Social Pressures and Curriculum Innovation: a study of the Nuffield Foundation Science Teaching Project*, Methuen, 1979

numeracy

The **Crowther Report** (1959) first introduced the concept of numeracy, defining a well-educated man as one who was both literate and numerate (para. 401). Numeracy includes the need to think quantitatively and have an understanding of the scientific approach to the study of phenomena – observation, hypothesis, experiment and verification. Some twenty years later, the **Cockcroft Report** proposed a more modest approach: that the individual should be sufficiently familiar with mathematical skills to cope with everyday life and have some understanding of information presented in mathematical terms, such as graphs, charts or tables (paras. 35–9). (*See also* **graphicacy**, **literacy**, **oracy**.)

nursery classes

For children between the ages of 2 and 5, these classes form part of an infant primary school, unlike **nursery schools**, which are freestanding institutions. (*See also* **playgroups**, **pre-school education**.)

nursery school

Caters for children of pre-school age, usually between the ages of 2 and 5. There are both State and private schools, though the former invariably have qualified staff. State schools have a recommended staff-:child ratio of 1:13. The school day usually begins at 9 a.m. and ends at 3.30 p.m. (*See also* **National Campaign for Nursery Education**, **nursery classes**, **playgroups**, **Plowden Report**, **positive discrimination**, **pre-school education**.)

D. DEASEY, *Education under Six*, Croom Helm, 1978

M. HUGHES et al., *Nurseries Now*, Penguin, 1980

O

Oakes Report

In 1978, the Labour Government set up a Working Group on the Management of Higher Education in the Maintained Sector, chaired by Gordon Oakes, Minister of State at the **DES**. Its report, published in the same year (Cmnd 7130), promoted the notion of a central body, though based on the assumption of expansion. In 1981, a Conservative Government **Green Paper**, *Higher Education in England outside the Universities: policy, funding and management*, stated that the funding and management of public sector higher education was no longer acceptable and outlined two alternative schemes for a national body, parallel to the **University Grants Committee**, to take charge. This led to the setting up of the **National Advisory Body**.

objectives

There are a number of different interpretations of this word in an educational context. **Behavioural objectives** are concerned with the desirable changes in behaviour of pupils to be brought about by formulating specific objectives at the beginning of a course. Such an approach is criticized on the grounds that it is too deterministic, the outcomes may be trivial and it is not applicable to the arts and humanities. One writer, Elliot Eisner, therefore suggested the need for **expressive objectives** as well, where the predicted terminal behaviour is not fixed in advance, in some aspects of the curriculum. It is important, too, for teachers to distinguish between the *short-term* and the *long-term* objectives they wish to achieve. (*See also* **aims**, **objectives teaching**.)

E. EISNER, 'Instructional and Expressive Educational Objectives: Their Formulation and Use in the Curriculum' in W. J. POPHAM et al. (eds.), *Instructional Objectives, AERA Monograph Series on Curriculum Evaluation 3*, Rand McNally and Co., Chicago, 1969

SCHOOLS COUNCIL, Science 5–13 Curriculum Project, *With Objectives in Mind*, Macdonald, 1972

objectives teaching

The **objectives** model of teaching seeks to evaluate pupil performance in any curriculum area against an agreed list of teacher or pupil curriculum objectives. It implies that the teacher has already formulated, clarified and written down objectives which he or she wishes to attain and is the medium through which the recording and evaluation of pupil performance takes place. In this sense it is sometimes known as 'precision learning'. It is a model which originated in America and has aroused a great deal of interest among educational psychologists.

M. AINSCOW and D. A. TWEDDLE, *Preventing Classroom Failure: An Objectives Approach*, Wiley, 1979

object lessons

Stemming from Pestalozzi's teaching that the educator must work in accordance with natural laws which are discoverable by observation, object lessons consisted of lessons where objects were analysed, under such headings as qualities, parts and uses, by first-hand examination. This system was popularized in England by the publication of a series of textbooks by a disciple of Pestalozzi, Elizabeth Mayo, entitled *Lessons on Objects* in 1830. Object lessons remained popular in **elementary schools** for the rest of the century and were often badly taught.

K. SILBER, *Pestalozzi, The Man and his Work*, Routledge and Kegan Paul, 1960

Office of Special Inquiries and Reports

The Office, a section of the **Education Department**, later the **Board of Education**, was established in 1895, with Michael Sadler as its Director (until 1903) and Robert Morant as his assistant. It was charged with the task of keeping a systematic record of educational work and experiments in Britain and abroad. It also provided research and information for politicians, Civil Servants and inspectors of the Board. Between 1895 and 1914, twenty-eight volumes of the Office's investigations, under the title *Special Reports on Educational Subjects*, were published, ranging from the place of boys' preparatory schools in English education to an assessment of **training colleges** in France, Germany, Switzerland and the USA.

J. E. VAUGHAN, 'Board of Education Special Reports: index of authors and translators', *History of Education Society Bulletin*, No. 26, 1968

old boy/old girl

Refers to pupils previously at a school. It is common to find Old Boys' and Old Girls' Associations which support school causes, participate in sport and hold social gatherings. In Scotland, the term 'former pupils' is used.

O level (Ordinary level examination)

The General Certificate of Education Ordinary level examination was intended, when it replaced the **School Certificate Examination** in 1951, as a test for bright pupils who had completed a **secondary school** course up to the age of 16. The minimum age limit was abandoned in 1953 and it is clear from the number of candidates who attempt the examination each year that it is not entirely appropriate for many. The pass level is equivalent to the credit grade of the former School Certificate Examination. It was originally designed for potential higher education students and those entering the professions and business, though O levels have been widely demanded by employers. Unlike the School Certificate, it is a single-subject examination and is offered by eight different examining boards. Candidates are awarded one of five grades, A to E, with E being the lowest standard for recording. The introduction of the **Certificate of Secondary Education** in 1965 for the ability range below those capable of achieving O level raised questions of comparability between the two examinations – for example, a CSE Grade 1 is accepted as equivalent to

O level grade C or better. It was because of these and other difficulties that moves were made to establish a common system of examining at 16+. (*See also* **A level, examinations: history of, General Certificate of Education, Schools Council, sixteen plus examination**.)

open admission

The policy of allowing students into a university (or other institution) irrespective of their possession of normal **entry qualifications**. In the USA, a few universities operate open admission systems (or open access, open enrolment or open-door policies); in the UK, the **Open University** is the only institution of higher education which operates on this basis, although some conventional universities have admission systems for **mature students** which are more permissive but not completely open – in other words, access would be by means of alternative methods of **assessment** such as interview or essay writing rather than **A level** results. (*See also* **Open College, Open Tech, Universities Central Council on Admissions**.)

open-air school

The open-air movement, which started in England at the beginning of the present century, arose out of the concern of the medical profession for school hygiene. From 1907, open-air schools were built by **LEAs**, mainly for delicate children in need of a healthy environment. The 1931 **Hadow Report** on the Primary School commended the design of these schools as a model for ordinary primary schools because of the freedom of movement which such buildings allowed. (*See also* **School Health Service**.)

M. SEABORNE and R. LOWE, *The English School, its architecture and organization, 1870–1970*, Routledge and Kegan Paul, 1977

Open College

An alternative method for adults without **A levels** who are interested in entering **higher education**. Students attend a local college and take two introductory units, in study techniques and methods of inquiry, and two others from a range of subjects. The pioneering work was started in the north-west of England, where further education colleges were linked to Lancaster University and Preston Polytechnic. In some ways, the scheme is similar to the **Open Tech**. (*See also* **open admission, Open University, university entry requirements**.)

open day

An occasion when a school or college opens its doors for visitors to view aspects of its work. There are usually displays of students' efforts and demonstrations of activities.

open-ended

An item on a test where the candidate is encouraged to answer the question in his own words, and where a variety of responses is possible. This is a very different technique from a **multiple choice** item in which only one of the alternatives is correct. Open-ended questions avoid the danger of guessing and enable the candidate to express himself or herself more fully; the disadvantage is in the difficulty of marking and scoring such items.

open plan school

A shift away from conventional school architecture, which divided pupils into separate classrooms, open planning recognizes the link between progressive educational methods and the need to break down the class or form into several working groups. This flexibility is achieved in a number of different ways and there is no one standard pattern. Ten per cent of all **primary schools** are of open plan design with a much smaller number in the secondary sector. (*See also* **Architects and Building Branch**, **(DES)**, **progressive education**.)

N. BENNETT, J. ANDREAE, P. HEGARTY, B. WADE, *Open Plan Schools; Teaching, Curriculum, Design*, NFER, 1980

K. A. P. RINTOUL and K. P. C. THORNE, *Open Plan Organization in the Primary School*, Ward Lock Educational, 1975

Open Tech

A Government-sponsored body, set up in 1981 by the **Manpower Services Commission** and involving both the Department of Employment and the **DES**. It consists of 14 members from industry and education and is charged with the task of creating a system to help people of different ages to study technology and to enable adults to retrain for different jobs. Full and part-time courses in colleges and individual firms are mounted to increase the supply of technicians. (*See also* **Open College**.)

MANPOWER SERVICES COMMISSION, *Open Tech Task Group Report*, June 1982

Open University

A university established at Milton Keynes in 1969 to provide degree courses for students, 21 years old and over, operating an **open admissions** policy – that is, not insisting on normal entrance qualifications such as two **GCE A levels**. The University arose out of the idea of a 'University of the Air' much favoured by Harold Wilson when he was Prime Minister. However, the courses now provided are normally much more like well-planned **correspondence courses** with supplementary tuition by means of television and radio. Tutorial advice on a local basis is usually available. Students pursue their courses at home for about twelve to fifteen hours a week, thirty weeks in each year. Only about one-half of the 90,000 students are following undergraduate courses; the rest are involved in special short courses or various forms of **continuing education**. Each undergraduate course is planned as a year's (part-time) study; an ordinary degree is awarded after successful completion of six courses, an honours degree after passing eight courses of suitable standard. Courses are available in arts (humanities), social sciences, mathematics, science and technology, as well as education. Professional qualifications in law and medicine are not available. (*See also* **academic year**, **developmental testing**, **foundation course**, **PICKUP**, **universities: history of**.)

W. PERRY, *Open University: a personal account by the first Vice-Chancellor*, Open University Press, 1976

options

Many courses at school and university are designed on the core plus options system. This means that a certain amount of the learning required is laid down as compulsory, but beyond that a student is free to choose from a number of alternatives; for example, a student involved in a B.A. in English literature might be required to study a core course of Chaucer, Shakespeare and seventeenth-century literature, but after that be free to choose from a number of specialist courses. In English secondary schools, most pupils have a core or common course for the first three years, but in the fourth and fifth years, options schemes tend to operate (with or without a core). This system has been much criticized by **HMI** and others as a poor substitute for curriculum planning which tends to result in very unbalanced curricula. (*See also* **curriculum: core curriculum.**)

DES, *Curriculum 11–16*, Working Papers by HM Inspectorate, HMSO, 1977

ORACLE

A project funded by the **SSRC** and carried out by members of the University of Leicester School of Education on primary school children's behaviour and progress when working with different types of teachers. The conclusion of the ORACLE project (Observational, Research and Classroom Learning Evaluation) was that **teaching styles** had a large effect on achievement.

M. GALTON and B. SIMON, *Progress and Performance in the Primary Classroom*, and *Inside the Primary Classroom*, both Routledge and Kegan Paul, 1980

B. SIMON and J. WILLCOCKS (eds), *Research and Practice in the Primary Classroom*, Routledge and Kegan Paul, 1981

oracy

A term invented to indicate the importance of speech as well as reading and writing. **Literacy** is the ability to read and write adequately; oracy is the ability to understand and communicate fluently in speech. (*See also* **graphicacy**, **literacy**, **numeracy**.)

A. WILKINSON, *Language and Education*, Oxford University Press, 1975

oral examination

A form of examination in which the candidate is assessed on her/his performance in response to an examiner's questioning. For example, examinations in modern languages often contain an oral component. (*See also* **viva**.)

Order in Council

An Order made by the Queen 'by and with the advice of Her Majesty's Privy Council' for the carrying on of Government business. The Order may be either by virtue of the Royal Prerogative, such as declaring war, or under statutory authority. The latter category, often termed subordinate legislation, is widely used by governments to give force to administrative regulations. (*See also* **statutory instrument**.)

Ordinary National Certificate (ONC)

A post-school vocational award, sponsored by the **DES** and the professional institution concerned (in Scotland, most courses are administered by the Scottish Technical Education Council). The two-year part-time course, of approximately **A level** standard, is still offered in a limited range of subjects, but is being replaced by **BEC** and **TEC** certificates. (*See also* **Higher National Certificate**.)

Ordinary National Diploma (OND)

A post-school vocational course, either two years' full time or on a **sandwich** basis, sponsored by the **DES** and the professional institution concerned. The entry requirements are normally four **GCE O levels** but they may be lower. The Diploma is being replaced by **BEC** and **TEC** qualifications. (*See also* **Higher National Diploma**.)

Organization for Economic Co-operation and Development (OECD)

Established in Paris in 1961 as successor to the Organization for European Economic Co-operation (OEEC), OECD aims to promote economic and social welfare by assisting its member governments in the formulation of such policies. As a result, co-ordination of policies might be achieved. There is worldwide membership, consisting of 24 countries. The Council consists of one representative of each country and decisions and recommendations are adopted by mutual agreement of all members. There are more than a hundred specialized committees and working parties including one on education. Much of the educational work is carried out by the **Centre for Educational Research and Innovation** (CERI). OECD publishes reviews of national policies for education of its member countries.

organized games

Activities, involving teams or classes, such as rugby, cricket, hockey and netball, which are timetabled as a regular feature of the school curriculum.

organized science school

The term given by the **Science and Art Department** to schools and colleges which from 1872 organized science classes, on either a day or an evening basis, and presented candidates for the Department's examinations. Courses lasted for three years. In return, these institutions received a grant.

orienteering

An outdoor activity which combines cross-country running, map reading, and locating check points with the assistance of map and compass. Orienteering is sometimes organized as a race in which contestants follow a pre-planned course in much the same way as drivers in a car rally. The educational merits of orienteering are considered to be the development of map-reading skills, enjoyment of the environment and practical application of physical fitness.

out-of-school activities

Activities which take place out of normal school hours and do not form a regular part of the school **curriculum**; these often involve supervision by members of staff. Inter-school sporting events would be an example. (*See also* **school day**.)

G. HAIGH, *Out-of-School Activities*, Pitman, 1974

outreach

Originally a USA term, but one which is increasingly being used to describe certain programmes in the UK, where it is felt necessary to encourage staff to go out into the community rather than wait for members of the community to come into the college or university. In some projects, outreach workers are now employed to make contact with the kind of young person not otherwise attracted to **further education**. Outreach staff are employed by the **Youth Service** and in adult education.

over-learning

A technical term in psychology to indicate not that too much **learning** has taken place, but that learning continues in the process of practising a skill or piece of **knowledge** which is already superficially learned. The theory behind over-learning is that short-term retention of knowledge or skill may be possible after a certain period, but if the need to recall the knowledge or recover the skill is required over a longer period, then it will be necessary to continue practising beyond the time when apparently the skill has been acquired.

overpressure in education

The New Code of 1882, which attempted to raise the **standards** of education in **elementary schools**, resulted in a national debate on its social and educational consequences. Teachers claimed that the new system resulted in overpressure on pupils, leading in many cases to mental and physical strain, and even death from brain disease. On the basis of some visits to London schools, Dr J. Crichton-Browne, Superintendent of the West Riding Lunatic Asylum, stated that the health of children was being affected by the pressure of work, though he admitted that malnutrition was also an important factor. Crichton-Browne's evidence was challenged by J. G. Fitch, an **HMI**, who accompanied the former on many of his school visits. Their respective reports were published as a **Parliamentary Paper** in 1884. (*See also* **homework**, **three Rs**, **standards**.)

S.   BUXTON,   *Overpressure   and Elementary Education*, Swann, Sonnenschein, 1885

Report of Dr Crichton-Browne upon the alleged Overpressure. Memorandum relating to Dr Crichton-Browne's Report by Mr J. G. Fitch HMI, P.P. 1884, lxi

Oxbridge

A term denoting the universities of Oxford and/or Cambridge.

P

pacing

It is sometimes suggested that a good teacher carefully matches the rate of material presentation with the pupil's abilities and attention span; he paces his teaching carefully.

paracurriculum

See **curriculum: paracurriculum**.

paradigm

In 1970 the American writer on the philosophy of science, Thomas Kuhn, wrote a book *The Structure of Scientific Revolutions* which suggested that science did not develop in a linear fashion, but by a series of revolutions in which the dominant paradigm was replaced by a new paradigm. Since then, the word paradigm has been much used in the sociology of knowledge to indicate a set of perspectives or assumptions which may be dominant at one time, but which is eventually replaced suddenly by a new paradigm. In the **sociology of education**, the traditional paradigm which took for granted official statistics and positivist methodology was replaced by the new wave sociology described by Michael Young in his book *Knowledge and Control* (1971). Kuhn's view of the development of science and the application of that view of social sciences has been challenged a good deal during the 1970s and 1980s. The use of the word paradigm has been particularly criticized for its ambiguity.

B. DAVIES, *Social Control and Education*, Methuen, 1976

R. L. ROSNOW, *Paradigms in Transition: the methodology of social inquiry*, Oxford University Press, 1981

parametric statistics

Statistical procedures based on the assumption that a sample is appropriate because the parent population was 'normal', that is, had a normal distribution. If that assumption cannot be made safely, then nonparametric statistics are recommended. In statistics, parameters can be estimated from a sample, and the resulting distribution may be tested to see if it fits the sample information. If the sample distribution is a reasonably close fit to the expected normal distribution, assumptions may then be made about the parent population. Difficulties exist in educational experiments in terms of whether a population can be regarded as falling into a normal curve or not. (*See also* **Gaussian curve**, **normal curve**.)

S. SIEGEL, *Nonparametric Statistics for the Behavioural Sciences*, McGraw-Hill, 1956

parents and education

The 1944 Education Act stated that pupils were to be educated in accordance with the wishes of their parents, subject to public expenditure and so far as it was compatible with the provision of efficient instruction and training. However, before the **Taylor Report** (1977), parents had limited rights to involvement in curriculum policy-making in schools. The 1980 Education Act, called 'the parents' charter', required **LEAs** and **governors** to publish information on their schools to help parents to decide where to send their children. Though parents are able to make such decisions, they are subject to an appeals procedure. The 1981 Education Act provides for parents' being consulted when decisions on the provision for meeting the **special educational needs** of their children are being made. Various agencies, particularly **ACE**, **CASE** and the **NCPTA**, have urged, since **Plowden**, the closer involvement of parents in education. **Parent-teacher associations** and parent governors are two examples of participation, though a research project (Lynch and Pimlott, 1976) showed that the majority of parents have little desire to interfere with the present running of schooling. (*See also* **'Great Debate'**, **parent-teacher association**, **school records**, **school report**, **Warnock Report**.)

J. LYNCH and J. PIMLOTT, *Parents and Teachers*, Macmillan, 1976

P. WILBY, *Parents' Rights*, Franklin Watts, 1980

Parents' National Education Union (PNEU)

This Union was founded by Charlotte Mason in 1890 with several objectives: to create wider interest in the training of children and to gather information on this subject; to inform parents on the best principles of education and enlist their help in the school process; and to secure greater co-operation between home and school. 'The House of Education', where teachers and parents could participate in residential courses, was opened at Ambleside, Westmorland, in 1891. Besides founding its own schools, the Union was able to introduce its liberal curriculum into **elementary schools** in Yorkshire and Gloucestershire during the second decade of this century. (*See also* **parents and education**.)

E. CHOLMONDELEY, *The Story of Charlotte Mason 1842–1923*, Dent, 1960

parent-teacher association (PTA)

An association, consisting of members of staff and parents of pupils in a particular school, for discussing educational issues, raising funds for the school and organizing social functions which lessen the division between home and school. Much of the success of such an association depends on the enthusiasm or otherwise of the **headteacher**. There is a **National Confederation of Parent-Teacher Associations** which puts forward policies reflecting the views of its membership. (*See also* **Home and School Council**, parents and teachers, pressure group**.)

R. CYSTER, P. S. CLIFT and S. BATTLE, *Parental Involvement in Primary Schools*, NFER, 1980

R. GIBSON, *Parent-Teacher Communication*, Cambridge Institute of Education, 1980

Parliamentary Papers

All documents delivered to the House of Commons for the information of MPs. The papers are ordered to be laid on the Table and many are subsequently printed by Her Majesty's Stationery Office (HMSO). They include reports of **Royal Commissions**, **Select Committees**, **Departmental Committees**, **Blue Books**, **White Papers** and **Green Papers** as well as **Orders in Council**, which include **statutory instruments**. Before 1921, all important official reports and documents were issued as Parliamentary Papers.

participant observation

Research in the field of social psychology in which the researcher takes part as a member of the group being observed and records the behaviour of the group. See, for example, Ervin Goffman's field work on the social world of the hospital inmate, published as *Asylums*, Penguin, 1968. (*See also* **case study**, **triangulation**.)

J. P. SPRADLEY, *Participation Observation*, Holt, Rinehart and Winston, 1980

participation rate.

See **age participation rate**.

passive learning

Some eduational psychologists and other educationists make a distinction between active learning and passive learning. In a passive learning situation, a pupil is given no opportunity to make any contribution and is simply expected to learn predigested information which is presented to him by the teacher or lecturer. (*See also* **learning**.)

passive vocabulary

Words which an individual can recognize and understand when used by others, although they may not be part of that individual's **active vocabulary** (i.e. the vocabulary which he actually uses himself). Active and passive vocabulary may be confined to speech or may also be measured in terms of reading and writing.

pass mark

The grade or numbered mark fixed by examiners which examinees are required to obtain to be successful.

pass rate

The ratio or proportion of candidates who are successful in an examination or **assignment**.

pastoral system

During the 1960s it became common in some local authorities for **comprehensive schools** to divide responsibilities of teachers into academic and 'pastoral care'. In such schools there were two hierarchies of teachers and senior staff, one academic, the other pastoral. This system of separating academic from pastoral was sometimes referred to as the 'pastoral system'. Pastoral care is seen to have a dual role: on the one hand it serves as a support system to pupils in academic aspects of the school's work, and on the other serves as a 'pastoralizing agent' for those pupils who do not appear to benefit from what the school offers. Marland (1974) points out that the pastoral care system exists to help the school achieve its objectives, not as a welfare system dealing with crises the causes of which lie outside the school. Pastoral systems tend to be structured into Year or House Groupings, with **tutors** attached, responsible to a pastoral leader, called Head of House or Head of Year, for the guidance of a number of pupils. (*See also* **counselling**.)

M. MARLAND, *Pastoral Care*, Heinemann Educational, 1974

R. BEST, P. RIBBINS, C. JARVIS and D. ODDY, *Education and Care*, Heinemann Educational, 1983

'payment by results'

The **Newcastle Report**, published in 1861, was concerned with the cost of extending sound and cheap instruction to all classes. As a result, Robert Lowe, then **Vice-President of the Council**, introduced a Revised Code in the following year. Grants hitherto payable to certificated teachers were abolished. A school's finances were dependent on the annual examination of children by **HMI** in the **three Rs** with plain needlework for girls ('payment by results') , coupled with the fulfilment of a minimum number of attendances. The **grant** earned by the school was paid direct to the **managers**. Opposition to the Revised Code delayed its introduction until 1863, but its effects on elementary schools were felt until after the close of the century. (*See also* **homework**, **log book**.)

D. W. SYLVESTER, *Robert Lowe and Education*, Cambridge University Press, 1974

pedagogy

Defined by Simon (1981) as 'a science of teaching embodying both curriculum and methodology.' Unlike their continental counterparts, British schools have tended to shy away from evolving a pedagogical method, focusing instead on the 'needs' of the individual child.

B. SIMON, 'Why no pedagogy in England?' in B. SIMON and W. TAYLOR (eds), *Education in the Eighties*, Batsford, 1981

Pelham Report

Following the recommendations of the **McNair Report** that **training colleges** after the Second World War should recruit well-qualified staff, a committee on staff salary scales was appointed and reported in 1945. The report, signed by its acting chairman, Sir Henry Pelham, a former Civil Servant, suggested an enhanced scale. This was accepted and remained in operation until superseded by the **Houghton Report**'s findings in 1975. (*See also* **Burnham Report**, **Clegg Report**.)

Committee on Scales of Salaries for the Teaching Staffs of Colleges of Education, HMSO, 1945

percentile

A statistical term used for many educational tests. A percentile indicates the point in a set of scores or marks that exceeds a given percentage. For example, the fortieth percentile is the mark below which 40% of all the candidates score. The term percentile rank is used to indicate the relationship between an individual score and its relationship to all other scores. Thus a person might score 59% on a test, but if that score was better than 70% of all other candidates, he would be said to have the percentile rank of 70.

Percy Report

A Special Committee set up by the **Minister of Education** 'to consider the needs of higher technological education in England and Wales and the respective contributions made thereto by universities and technical colleges.' In its report published in 1945, the Committee envisaged a complete reshaping of higher technological education. Universities were to play a much larger part in producing scientists. The status of technical education was to be raised by the creation of colleges of technology. All courses should contain a **sandwich** element. A National Council of Technology was essential to co-ordinate provision and grant qualifications, called either a B. Tech. degree or Dip.Tech. **Regional Advisory Councils** would be formed to bring together universities, colleges of technology and **technical colleges** in an area to ensure adequate provision. The Minister of Education accepted the report and many of the Committee's main recommendations were implemented. The Percy Report was important in casting the mould for post-war technical education in this country. (*See also* **Colleges of Advanced Technology**, **Robbins Report**.)

Report of the Special Committee on Higher Technological Education appointed by the Minister of Education, HMSO, 1945

performance contracting

During the accountability debate in the USA in the 1970s, some States employed commercial organizations to provide instructional services to a school district on the basis of fees being determined by success rates measured by performance of students on criterion tests. Such schemes were closely scrutinized by teachers' professional organizations, who were delighted to report those occasions when the organizations failed, or where maladministration amounting to fraud was reported. No such experiments have been undertaken in the UK, although some observers feared that the **APU** might take education in that direction.

J. P. STUCKER and G. R. HALL, *The Performance Contracting Concept in Education*, Rand Corporation, California, USA, 1971

performance test

1. The kind of test in which the candidate is required to demonstrate a practical skill rather than write about it.
2. A test which requires a candidate to perform certain tasks specified as a means of selection.
3. A test of actual ability and/or attainment rather than an indication of possible future potential. (*See also* **aptitude test**, **attainment test**.)

peripatetic teacher

A teacher, usually in subjects such as languages and music, who is not attached to any one particular school, but visits various schools in an **LEA** for a number of sessions with pupils.

permanent education (l'éducation permanente)

A term more frequently used on the continent of Europe than in England, but one which is gaining ground. Permanent education is an ideal which aims for the availability of education throughout an individual's life, not ending with the completion of compulsory schooling or a further period of **higher education** or **further education**. The **Council of Europe** has committed itself to the ideal of permanent education and has produced a large number of reports on this subject. Permanent education overlaps but is not identical with either **recurrent education** or **continuing education**. (*See also* **adult education**.)

COUNCIL OF EUROPE, *Permanent Education: the basis and essentials*, Strasbourg, 1973

phenomenology

A term which became very important in the **sociology of education** in the 1970s, but which had its roots in earlier discussions in philosophy and psychology.

1. In philosophy, phenomenology referred to the method of enquiry developed by Brentano and later his student, Husserl. The method begins from a careful inspection of one's own conscious, intellectual processes. All assumptions about the wider and external causes and consequences of these internal processes have to be 'bracketed' (that is, excluded); according to Husserl, this was not an empirical technique but an **a priori** investigation of essences or meanings. Husserl's pupil, Heidegger, developed this into existentialism.

2. In the psychology of perception, phenomenology indicates a doctrine which states that the significant role of sense data consists in what is

perceived, however distorted, by the individual, not in the object itself. M. Merleau-Ponty, *The Phenomenology of Perception*, Routledge and Kegan Paul, 1962.

3. In sociology, the key figure is Alfred Schutz, who adapted Husserl's method in order to investigate everyday social life. In the sociology of knowledge Schutz and others have concentrated on the relationship between commonsense knowledge and social action. For Schutz, all facts are 'interpretations', a selection from the world made by a conscious being. Because reality is infinite there are limitless possible interrelationships, but we have somehow to make sense of reality; we do this by 'freezing' consciousness in a limited way, not arbitrarily, but by making use of a set of assumptions referred to as 'commonsense'. This is a necessary process (if we are to make sense of the world at all) but one which has to be questioned. The method of questioning is the method originated by Husserl and developed by Schutz. (*See also* **ethnology, ethnomethodology**.)

P. L. BERGER and T. LUCKMAN, *The Social Construction of Reality*, Penguin, 1967

A. SCHUTZ, *The Phenomenology of the Social World*, Heinemann Educational, 1972

philosophy of education
The combination of philosophy and education has a long history: many philosophers have shown a considerable interest in education; ever since education has been studied as a subject its philosophical implications have featured as an important aspect of the subject. At the beginning of the twentieth century, the major source of philosophical inspiration in education was Plato's idealism and its nineteenth-century reinterpretation. Courses on philosophy of education sometimes took the form of the history of philosophical ideas in education – such as those of Plato, Aristotle, Rousseau, Dewey. A major change occurred in the 1950s and 1960s, in England, particularly associated with the work of R. S. Peters. Peters applied to philosophy of education the techniques of analytical philosophy – that is, he attempted to clarify the meaning of basic concepts in education and to use them consistently. For example, he and his colleagues examined such key terms as teaching, training, conditioning, indoctrination, worthwhile, authority and so on. Probably the best introduction to this approach is still R. S. Peters, *Ethics and Education*, Allen and Unwin, 1966. By the 1970s, some philosophers and educationists were suggesting that the work of the analytical philosophers having been accomplished it was now time to think again about other kinds of philosophical approaches to education.

phonic method
A technique used in the teaching of reading. It is based on the sounds of letters rather than the names of letters. (*See also* **Gestalt**.)

P. J. CONGDON, *Phonic Skills and their Measurement*, Blackwell, Oxford, 1974

Piagetian
The adjective referring to the work of Piaget, in particular the stages of development approach. Piaget's

theory was that children, by a process of **maturation**, progress through four stages of development: (1) the sensory motor stage; (2) pre-operational; (3) concrete operations and (4) formal operations. (*See also* **enactive**.)

PICKUP

Acronym for the Government's scheme announced in 1982, Professional Industrial and Commercial Updating, an information system sponsored by the **Further Education Unit**, which stores details of courses available at colleges for updating the skills of workers in industry. Colleges are being encouraged to devise short and part-time courses which meet the needs of local industry and which will be self-financing, paid for either by employers or the trainees themselves. **Distance learning** packages are also being developed for the scheme by the **Open University**. The schemes are regionally operated with agents appointed to liaise between education and industry. (*See also* **recurrent education**.)

pilot scheme, pilot study

Many curriculum development projects involve a 'pilot stage'. This usually involves trying out experimental materials in a small number of 'pilot' schools. The object is either to improve the materials at this stage or possibly to reject them completely as inappropriate. In more general terms a pilot study is one which precedes a main study. (*See also* **feasibility study**, **induction scheme**.)

play centre

Offers a range of leisure activities for children of **primary school** age, after school in term time and full-time for an extended age range in the school holidays. Play centres are situated in schools near to the children's homes and may be staffed by either teachers or outside helpers.

playground

An area normally within the precincts of a school where pupils may play either before, during or after school hours. The official morning and afternoon breaks in the primary school day are often called 'playtime'. The playground is also frequently used for outdoor physical education and games. It is regarded as much more important in England than elsewhere.

playgroups

Begun in 1960 after the refusal of the **Ministry of Education** to give preference in State **nursery schools** to young children of teachers. A playgroup has a minimum of six children aged between 3 and 5 supervised by leaders who do not have to hold teaching qualifications. Sessions usually last for a morning or an afternoon in premises which have been passed by the Social Services Department. There is a national body which looks after the interests of its members, the Pre-School Playgroups Association. (*See also* **pre-school education**.)

B. CROWE, *The Playgroup Movement*, Allen and Unwin, 2nd edn 1983

HENDERSON, A. and J. LUCAS, *Pre-School Playgroups. A Handbook*, Allen and Unwin, 1981

Plowden Report

The Report of the **Central Advis-**

ory **Council** (England) entitled *Children and their Primary Schools* was published in 1967. The Council's terms of reference were 'to considei primary education in all its aspects, and the transition to secondary education'. This aspect of schooling had not been examined since the two **Hadow Committees** in the 1930s. Under the chairmanship of Lady Plowden, the Council made a number of important recommendations for the amelioration of social **disadvantage. Positive discrimination**, in the form of **educational priority areas** (EPAs) where extra staffing and resources could be allocated, was suggested. Better **nursery education** provision was needed nationally, but especially for EPAs. The structure of **primary education** was to be changed. Instead of the existing pattern of **infant** (5 to 7) and **junior** (7 to 11), there should be a **first school** (5 to 8) and then a **middle school** (8 to 12). The starting age for children was to be more flexible. Continuity between the stages, including the secondary stage, was recommended. The report also stressed the need for more co-operation between home and school: as the focus of the community, the school should welcome **parents** to participate in school activities. Many of the recommendations, if implemented, would have been costly, though EPAs were established and in 1968 the **DES** and **SSRC** gave a grant for three years' action research in this area. The form of the report itself is of interest as it was published in two volumes, the second consisting of research and surveys, some of which were commissioned. The Plowden Report was the last of those produced by the Central Advisory Council. (*See also* **community college/school**, **parents and education**, **transition primary to secondary school**.)

R. S. PETERS (ed.), *Perspectives on Plowden*, Routledge and Kegan Paul, 1969

Report of the Central Advisory Council for Education (England): Children and their Primary Schools, Vol. 1 Report, HMSO, 1967

politics of education
In this context 'politics' does not necessarily refer to 'party politics', but to questions of influence and control. When changes in educational policy take place (or fail to take place), who are the decision-makers? Major changes in education such as **raising of the school leaving age** require legislation (and therefore involve party politics), but most changes are not of this kind. Two major issues have been discussed under the heading of politics of education: first, the extent to which power lies in the hands of Civil Servants rather than their 'political masters'; *see* Maurice Kogan, *The Politics of Education*, Penguin, 1971: second, the extent to which important changes in education (such as the move towards **comprehensive schools**) is dependent on the consent of **pressure groups** such as the **National Union of Teachers** and other professional organizations; *see* R. Bell and W. Prescott (eds), *The Schools Council: A Second Look*, Ward Lock, 1975, especially the chapter by R. A. Manzer.

D. LAWTON, *The Politics of the School Curriculum*, Routledge and Kegan Paul, 1981

polytechnics
The first polytechnic to be opened in England, that in Regent Street, London, catered for working-class young men and women in advancing their general knowledge and industrial skill on a part-time or full-time basis. Quintin Hogg, its founder, persuaded the **Charity Commissioners** to endow a number of similar institutions in London and by 1904 there were altogether 12 in the capital. Sidney Webb as chairman of the Technical Education Board encouraged the polytechnics to offer **degree** courses and considered these institutions as complementary to the universities. From 1965, when the then Secretary of State for Education, Anthony Crosland, made his famous Woolwich speech on the **binary system**, their role has changed. The 1966 White Paper *A Plan for the Polytechnics and Other Colleges* (Cmnd 3006) described the polytechnics as regional centres of higher education linking with industry and business. University validation was to be largely replaced by the **Council for National Academic Awards** (CNAA); the institutions would continue to be financed by local authorities. In 1969, 8 polytechnics were established in England and Wales and there are now 30. After 1973, a number of **colleges of education** were absorbed into the existing polytechnics, bringing with them additional expertise in the arts and humanities. In 1981 there were 127,000 **full-time equivalent** students in these institutions, two-thirds of whom were in full-time attendance. Out of the total 85,000 were taking degrees. One interesting feature is that a third of the courses have a **sandwich** element. With the recent cuts in university admissions resulting from Government policy, the number of well-qualified applicants applying to polytechnics is rising. (*See also* **polyversity**, **validation**.)

A. MATTERSON, *Polytechnics and Colleges*, Longman, 1981

J. PRATT and T. BURGESS, *Polytechnics: A Report*, Pitman Publishing, 1974

polyversity
Name given to a comprehensive-type university which combines both university and polytechnic institutions, with departments from different **faculties** on each of the main sites, thus blurring the existing **binary system** of higher education. Plans for the first polyversity, that of the New University of Ulster and Ulster Polytechnic, were announced in March 1982. It is headed by a **Vice-Chancellor**.

positive discrimination
The provision of resources to mitigate educational or other **disadvantage** caused by social and/or economic deprivation. This is often known as **compensatory education**. The **Plowden Report** recommended the identification of inner city districts which were to be recognized as **Educational Priority Areas** (EPA) for this purpose. Much of the emphasis is on pre-school facilities, **nursery schools**, the involvement of the **parents** with teachers and the development of **community education**. The issue is a political one and there are different views on the causes of inequality. As a result, the **Plowden** philosophy has not been fully translated into resources. (*See also* **Head Start**.)

EQUAL OPPORTUNITIES COMMISSION, *Positive Sex Discrimination in Training Schemes*, EOC, Manchester, 1981

A. H. HALSEY, 'Whatever happened to positive discrimination?', *Times Educational Supplement*, 21 January, 1977

postgraduate

A person studying for an award above that of a **first**, i.e. Bachelor's, **degree**. This might take the form of a **diploma** or a **higher degree**, either at the Master's or doctorate levels. (*See also* **dissertation**, **graduate**, **thesis**, **undergraduate**, **university department of education**.)

Postgraduate Certificate of Education (PGCE)

A certificate taken by **graduates**, either immediately after their **first degree** course or (increasingly frequently) a few years later after some work experience. It is a one-year full-time course of educational studies; a minimum number of days of practical teaching in schools under supervision is normally prescribed. During the 1950s it would have been true, as a generalization, to have said that the PGCE course was the route for teachers destined for **secondary schools**, whereas **primary school** teachers were trained either by a non-graduate certificate or, later, by the **B.Ed**. In the 1970s and 80s, however, it became increasingly common for primary school teachers to enter the profession by a suitable degree and a PGCE course. Applications for the PGCE are made through the **Graduate Teacher Training Registry** (GTTR). (*See also* **diploma**, **qualified teacher status**, **teaching practice**.)

post of responsibility

A teaching post, in schools or institutions of further and higher education, which involves responsibility for some aspects of teaching or other aspect of the institution's activities. The post usually carries with it extra salary. (*See also* **head of department**, **scale post**.)

praxis

A term used by many Marxist educationists, but especially Paulo Freire (1972). For Freire, real education is an individual's interaction with his environment. The task of a teacher is not to pass on a package of **knowledge** (the banking concept of education), but to go with the pupil and explore the relationship between experience and knowledge in a practical way. Praxis is, therefore, more than the opposite of theory. It is the exploration by an individual (or a group) of the environment in a way which produces 'real' knowledge rather than theoretical or second-hand knowledge.

P. FREIRE, *Education as Cultural Action*, Penguin, 1972

precision learning
See **objectives teaching**.

prefects

Pupils, usually chosen from the upper forms, who occupy posts of special responsibility in a school. They assist the smooth running of the school in various ways. The term itself dates back only to 1865 in this sense. An earlier equivalent term traceable to the sixteenth century is *praepostor*. One of the *praepostor*'s duties was to register the names of offenders. (*See also* **curriculum:**

hidden curriculum, head boy/ girl, monitor.)

preparatory schools

Often abbreviated to 'prep schools', these are private schools, either of the day or boarding type, which prepare their pupils for either the **Common Entrance examination** at 13 plus or, where it still exists, the **11 plus examination**. Some **public schools** retain their own preparatory schools, but most are independent of them. Where the target is the Common Entrance examination, the curriculum includes Latin and French. (*See also* **Incorporated Association of Preparatory Schools, registration of independent schools**.)

pre-school education

All education provision for children below the statutory school-starting age of 5, whether organized by local authorities or voluntary organizations. It includes **nursery classes, nursery schools** and **playgroups**.

S. H. SHINMAN, *A Chance for Every Child? Access and response to pre-school provision*, Tavistock, 1981

President of the Board of Education

The Board of Education Act (1899) created a single body charged with the superintendence of educational development in England and Wales. At its head was a President, a post filled by a Government minister. Although its holder was normally a member of the Cabinet, the presidency was regarded as a step to higher office. Nineteen politicians held this office between 1900 and 1944 when it became the **Ministry of Education**. Among its more dis-

tinguished holders were C. P. Trevelyan and R. A. Butler. (*See also* **Board of Education, Lord President of the Council, Vice-President of the Committee of Council**.)

pressure group

Like-minded people who band together to press their claims on a particular issue or a set of issues to affect or modify the behaviour or actions of a body holding power. Since the 1960s they have become a familiar part of the education scene. An early example was in the field of **pre-school education**, i.e. the National Campaign for Nursery Education, formed in 1965, which succeeded in persuading the Government to make wider provision available. Some pressure groups have a national organization but rely on local branches to provide the momentum, such as the Campaign for Comprehensive Education and the **National Confederation of Parent-Teacher Associations**. Cuts in education have caused new pressure groups to spring up alongside older-established ones.

M. LOCKE, *Power and Politics in the School System*, Routledge and Kegan Paul, 1974

C. ST JOHN-BROOKS, 'The Education Watchers', *New Society*, 11 June, 1981

pre-test (and post-test)

In some experimental situations used in education a test is given to a student before starting a course on using experimental materials and, again, at the end of such a course. The pre-test results are then compared with the post-test and an estimate made of the effectiveness of the course or teaching programme or materials involved. The procedure seems to be a plausible one, but in practice all sorts of contaminating influences work to the detriment of simple interpretations of results.

primary school

Prior to the reorganization following the **Hadow Report of 1926**, most **elementary schools** were divided into two parts – infant, taking in children from 5 to 7, and then boys' and girls' departments, from 7 to 14. The Hadow Report's suggestion, that 11 years of age was a more suitable time for the transition to secondary education, produced a distinctive unit, the primary school, consisting of an **infant department**, as in pre-Hadow times, and a **junior department**, with children of 7 to 11. As a result of the Education Act of 1944, the elementary school finally disappeared and was officially replaced by the primary school. This system still exists in most **LEAs**, except where **middle schools** have come into existence. (*See also* **integrated day**.)

DES, *Primary Education in England*, HMSO, 1978

C. RICHARDS (ed.), *Primary Education: issues for the eighties*, Black, 1980

Prime Minister's Reports

Early in 1916, H. H. Asquith, then Prime Minister, had presided over a Reconstruction Committee, consisting of seven Cabinet colleagues, which later decided to investigate questions of public interest such as the neglect of science and the place of modern languages in education. The political upheaval caused by the accession of Lloyd George in place of

Asquith in December 1916 led to the removal of responsibility from the Reconstruction Committee to *ad hoc* bodies, thus lessening the impact of their recommendations. Nevertheless, the four reports issued between 1918 and 1921 – the **Thompson Report on Natural Science** (1918), the **Leathes Report on Modern Languages** (1918), the **Newbolt Report on English** (1921) and the **Crewe Report on Classics** (1921) – are impressive documents. Each report is described in this Guide under the name of its chairman.

J. M. LLOYD, 'The Asquith Reconstruction Committee and Educational Reform', *Journal of Educational Administration and History*, Vol. 8, No. 2, 1976

primer

Originally having a religious connotation, a 'book of prime' (or hours), the word now covers any book which deals with the elements of a subject. (*See also* **reader**.)

Principal

Holder of the post of chief officer of a university, college or school. The title of the office varies from one university to another. In London the post is largely administrative, as there is also a **Vice-Chancellor**. (*See also* **Committee of Vice-Chancellors and Principals**.)

private school

See **independent school**.

probation

To obtain **qualified teacher status**, trained teachers are required by the **DES** to complete successfully one year's teaching in a maintained education institution. **LEAs**, through their inspectors or **advisers**, are responsible for approving the majority of the probationers. They also provide courses and other assistance to support the new teacher, but the quality and amount varies from LEA to LEA. The 1982 Commons Select Committee on Education recommended that the probationary period should be extended to the first three years of teaching, with an efficiency bar before reaching the next grade on the salary scale. Probation is normally required for new staff in further and higher education institutions. (*See also* **security of tenure**.)

DES, HMI Matters for Discussion 15, *The New Teacher in School*, HMSO, 1982

problem-solving

A style of teaching or learning where the aim is to encourage pupils to acquire **knowledge** and **skills** in the process of solving problems rather than simply learning about how other people have solved such problems. (*See also* **child-centred**, **convergent thinking**, **Dalton Plan**, **divergent thinking**, **project**.)

Professional Association of Teachers (PAT)

This association, which has over 22,000 members, is best known for the pledge of its members never to go on strike. It also seeks a professional code of conduct for teachers. The Association claims to be non-party-political. It is recognized by almost a quarter of **LEAs** and was recently given a seat on the **Burnham Committee**. (*See also* **teachers' associations**.)

professor

The highest ranking teacher in a field of learning at a university. A professor can either hold an established post, carrying with it a named chair, i.e. professor in a particular named **faculty**, or a personal title, awarded on the basis of the holder's academic standing. A professor is often a **head of department**, though this is not universal. The use of the term 'professor' can be traced back to the sixteenth century. Since 1969, **polytechnics** have created professorships for senior staff. Specialist institutions, such as the Royal College of Surgeons and Cranfield, have their own professorships. (*See also* **inaugural lecture**, **Regius professor**, **universities: history of**.)

H. PERKIN, *Key Profession*, Routledge and Kegan Paul, 1969

profile

An attempt to provide an alternative form of **assessment** to **school reports** for pupils. Whereas the conventional report concentrates on performance in particular subjects, profiles assess a range of pupils' qualities, attitudes and behaviour, so that a much fuller picture of each individual may be given. It is claimed that they are particularly appropriate in the **upper secondary school** for potential employers. Criticisms are directed at the ethical and technical difficulties of profiles, the place of teachers' value judgements in assessments, and their value if confined only to those who achieve few examination successes. Some schemes, such as those of the **Further Education Unit** and the **City and Guilds Institute**, have been piloted in schools. The adoption of profiling is not yet widespread. It should be noted that profile schemes can be pupil-controlled as an alternative to teacher-based judgements: this involves the pupils in recording their experiences and achievements. (*See also* **school records**, **school report**, **vocational preparation**.)

J. BALOGH, *Profile Reports for School Leavers*, Longman for Schools Council, 1982

FURTHER EDUCATION CURRICULUM REVIEW AND DEVELOPMENT UNIT, *Profiles: a review of issues and practice*, HMSO, 1982

programmed learning

Programmed learning is based upon **self-instructional** materials. They are designed to allow the pupil to progress at his own pace, step by step, through a carefully structured sequence. The programmes may be either linear or branching or a mixture of the two. They are normally presented in the form of a programmed text or in a teaching machine. More recently, programmed learning has been associated with computer assisted instruction or **computer assisted learning** (CAL). Some programmed learning is associated with the **behavioural objectives** school and/or the work of B. F. Skinner. (*See also* **individualized learning**, **Skinnerian**.)

J. LEEDHAM and D. UNWIN, *Programmed Learning in the Schools*, 2nd edn, Longman, 1971

Programme for Reform in Secondary Education (PRISE)

A **pressure group** formed in 1975 which called for a fully comprehensive system of schooling and the abolition of selection. It was also concerned to improve the quality of education and to involve parents and the community in the everyday life of the school.

progressive education

One of the most ambiguous terms in the whole of educational literature. For some, 'progressive' meant no more than a reaction against the harsh nineteenth-century discipline and unimaginative teaching methods. The reaction (at the end of the nineteenth century and more particularly at the beginning of the twentieth) usually took the form of schools which did not use corporal punishment, which treated children as individuals and which moved away from rote learning as the main system of acquiring knowledge. After the 1944 Education Act, however, the word 'progressive' began to be used by those who supported **comprehensive schools** rather than the traditional **tripartite** schools. Comprehensive school supporters were described as progressive; those who wished to retain the **grammar schools** would be labelled traditional. This was particularly confusing since one strand in the English progressive education movement was the group of independent schools associated with the **New Education Fellowship**. In the late 1960s and early 1970s, progressivism in education was attacked in the **Black Papers**. This attack was on so-called progressive school methods in **primary schools**, which usually consisted of an integrated approach to the curriculum rather than a subject-based timetable; in secondary schools, a more **child-centred** approach was attacked; in primary and secondary schools, the alleged lack of 'discipline' was deplored. The abolition of the **'eleven plus'** system in primary schools and the liberalizing of examinations at 16+ in secondary schools were also criticized by the writers of the Black Papers. In the 1980s these are probably still the major issues separating 'progressives' from traditionalists, but the label is sometimes applied indiscriminately. For example, an educationist might be a strong advocate of comprehensive schools, but wish to retain traditional examinations. 'Progressive' is a term now best avoided unless carefully defined. (*See also* **New Education, open plan school, progressive schools**.)

progressive schools

First pioneered by Cecil Reddie at Abbotsholme in 1889, the English progressive school movement was based on the notion of social reform through education. **Independent schools**, many of which are mainly **boarding** in character, represented miniature societies; Reddie and others looked to a reformed and enlightened system of schooling which eliminated **corporal punishment**, furthered team spirit rather than individualism, and was co-educational in composition and democratic in its day-to-day running. This movement received a second impulse after the First World War and again in the 1930s. Well-known schools associated with the movement include Bedales, Dartington Hall, King Alfred School and Summerhill. (*See also* **New Education, progressive education**.)

R. SKIDELSKY, *English Progressive Schools*, Penguin, 1969

W. A. C. STEWART, *The Educational Innovators, Progressive Schools 1881–1967*, Macmillan, 1968

project

1. An educational activity based on pupils' interests, centred on a particular problem or issue. This method emphasized co-operative learning between pupils and teachers. W. H. Kilpatrick, a colleague of John Dewey in the USA, was instrumental in popularizing this approach after the First World War. (*See also* **assignment, problem-solving, team teaching, topic work**.)

2. Name given to a small- or large-scale research programme, carried out by one or more persons, in some aspect of education. A good example would be the **Schools Council** Projects which investigated various aspects of the **curriculum**. (*See also* **curriculum development project**.)

D. WATERS, *Primary School Projects: Planning and Development*, Heinemann Educational, 1982

proprietary school

A type of joint-stock company **public school** which became popular with the middle classes from the earlier part of the nineteenth century. They were the result of local pride and effort, with profit as a secondary motive. Some of the early ones, such as University College School, London, and the Liverpool Institute, founded in the 1820s, were essentially **day schools** with a broad curriculum but without religious teaching. Later, with the coming of the railways, **boarding schools** became common, and resulted in a growth of such schools as Marlborough (1842),

Wellington (1859), Clifton (1860) and Malvern (1862). The Church of England proprietary schools started by Nathaniel Woodard are dealt with separately. (*See also* **Woodard Schools**.)

psychology of education

'Psychology' is itself not easy to define: 'the study of the mind' was once useful, but many psychologists – especially behaviourists – objected to the use of the word 'mind', and would prefer to define psychology as a study of human behaviour, or the study of human beings interacting with their environment. With that last definition, it might however be argued that the whole of psychology is relevant to the study of education. Nevertheless, the psychology of education normally focuses on a limited number of ideas and controversies which have particular relevance to the process of teaching and learning. A central issue is the fact that human beings probably differ in their abilities, and certainly in their achievements. Part of the psychology of education is concerned with identifying and attempting to measure such differences (the special field of psychometrics and **intelligence testing**); another field (developmental psychology) is concerned with the growth and development of children, the extent to which **learning** depends on maturational factors rather than teaching, and so on; a final, but comparatively neglected, field is the study of how to improve techniques of teaching and learning – including motivation, teaching and learning styles, and theories of learning. (*See also* **child development**, **learning theory**.)

D. CHILD, *Psychology and the Teacher*, Holt, Rinehart and Winston, 1973

public school

In England, an independent fee-paying school, of which there are about 200, most of whose heads are members of the **Headmasters' Conference**. The majority of them are **boarding schools**. The origins of this type of school are complex and varied. Many were the result of the endowment of pious founders and were indistinguishable from **grammar** schools. Eton, Winchester and Westminster are typical examples. One characteristic of many public schools is that their intake is not restricted to their immediate locality: from the sixteenth century charity schools such as Christ's Hospital drew their pupils from a wider catchment area. By the eighteenth century, a number of 'Great Schools' had emerged, including Harrow, Rugby, Sherborne, Canterbury and Shrewsbury. The **Clarendon Commission** of 1861 named nine public schools as the object of its investigations and thus marked off these institutions from other endowed schools. During the nineteenth century, many more purpose-built **proprietary schools** such as Cheltenham, Marlborough and Malvern were established. Some have close links with universities under the terms of their founders, for example Henry VI established King's College, Cambridge for Eton scholars, and similarly William of Wykeham, founder of Winchester, endowed New College, Oxford. (*See also* **Donnison Report, Fleming Report, house system, modern side, Newsom Report on Public Schools, Remove, upper school**.)

J. R. DE S. HONEY, *Tom Brown's Universe: The Development of Public Schools in the 19th Century*, Millington, 1977

J. RAE, *The Public School Revolution: Britain's independent schools, 1964– 1979*, Faber, 1981

Public Schools Commission
See **Donnison Report**, **Newsom Report**.

punishment: corporal punishment
Though once common in schools as a means of maintaining control and dealing with infringement of rules, the administration of corporal punishment has declined in recent years. Other forms of punishment, such as detention and, for more serious cases, expulsion are employed. At the present time 16 **LEAs**, including the **ILEA**, have abolished corporal punishment. The number of authorities committed to abolition in the near future is also growing. In February 1982, an important case was brought by two Scottish parents to the European Court of Human Rights on this issue. The judges decided that the European Convention on Human Rights had been breached in that parents have the right to have their children educated according to their own philosophical or religious views. This included the right to refuse to allow their children to be given corporal punishment. (*See also* **discipline**, **punishment: philosophy and psychology of**, **STOPP**.)

punishment: psychology and philosophy of
A good deal of work has been done by educationists on both the psychol-ogy of punishment and the philosophy of punishment. Much of the work on the psychology of punishment has been carried out from a behaviourist point of view and sees punishment as a way of discouraging certain kinds of behaviour and encouraging alternative preferred behaviour. In the philosophy of punishment, distinction is made between punishment as a deterrent, punishment as retribution and punishment as a means of reform. (*See also* **behaviourism**, **corporal punishment**, **STOPP**.)

R. S. PETERS, *Ethics and Education*, Allen and Unwin, 1966

B. F. SKINNER, *The Technology of Teaching*, Appleton Century Crofts, 1968

pupil
See **student**.

pupil : teacher ratio (PTR)
The majority of **LEAs** approach the allocation of teaching staff to schools at all levels by the use of a pupil-teacher ratio (PTR). At the **primary** level, schools are staffed on the basis of numbers of children and size of school; at the **secondary** level, LEAs have moved from a single PTR for all pupils to age-specific PTRs which take account of the higher staffing demands imposed by older pupils; special factors are increasingly taken into account as schools face the difficulty of adjusting to cuts and falling numbers. The latter is designed to protect the **curriculum** and to this end may be regarded as curriculum-based staffing. (*See also* **falling rolls**.) In Scotland, basic staffing levels are set out in SED Circular 1029 for primary, and staff

complements based on scales set out in SED Report *Secondary School Staffing* (1973), for secondary schools. (See also **staff : student ratio**.)

DES, Report on Education 98, *Teacher Numbers – looking ahead to 1995*, HMSO, 1983

pupil teacher system

In 1846, the **Committee of the Privy Council on Education** allowed one or more clever scholars between the ages of 13 and 18 in a school under Government inspection to be apprenticed to a headteacher for five years. Pupil teachers received a stipend and were examined annually. If they completed their apprenticeship successfully, they were allowed to enter for Queen's Scholarships which would admit them to a **training college** for a further three years. To improve the system, from 1875 pupil teacher centres were established where apprentices received further instruction outside their schools in the evenings (they were later released to attend during the day). A Departmental Committee reported in 1898 on the system. It recommended that more recruits should come from secondary schools and indeed suggested that the better centres should become secondary schools. Regulations issued in 1903 and 1907 raised entry requirements – a good secondary schooling until 16 or 17 with a two-year apprenticeship. At the same time, parents of apprentices could not afford to keep their children at school until this age. The system continued, with a diminishing number of entrants, until after the Second World War. (*See also* **workhouse school**.)

Pygmalion effect

See **self-fulfilling prophecy**.

Q

Q and F levels

In 1969, the Standing Conference on University Entrance and the **Schools Council** put forward proposals to replace **A level examinations**. This consisted of two stages: a Q or Qualifying Examination, based on one year's study of five subjects beyond **O level**, and an F or Further Examination, corresponding to one year's work beyond the Qualifying Examination in not more than three subjects. These proposals were not adopted. (*See also* **N and F levels**.)

STANDING CONFERENCE ON UNIVERSITY ENTRANCE AND THE SCHOOLS COUNCIL JOINT WORKING PARTY ON SIXTH FORM CURRICULUM AND EXAMINATIONS AND THE SCHOOLS COUNCIL'S SECOND WORKING PARTY ON THE SIXTH FORM CURRICULUM AND EXAMINATIONS, *Proposals for the curriculum and examinations in the sixth form*, 1969

quadrivium

The school curriculum in the Middle Ages consisted of the so-called seven liberal arts. The first three – grammar, logic and rhetoric – formed the **trivium** and the other four – music, arithmetic, geometry and astronomy – made up the quadrivium. The whole made a course of seven years' duration. The term 'quadrivium' dates back as far as Boethius (AD 480–524). (*See also* **liberal studies**.)

qualified teacher status (QT status)

Granted by the **Secretary of State for Education and Science** under regulations which set out different categories of qualifications which are acceptable for all teachers in publicly maintained schools. The most common ones are the possession of a **B.Ed**. degree or a degree of a UK university with a **Postgraduate Certificate of Education** or Diploma in Education. All qualified teachers must serve a probationary period. In England and Wales (but not Scotland) QT status is general, i.e. a qualified teacher may teach any subject to any age group. In 1982, the desirability of this 'flexibility' was questioned by the Secretary of State. The Government White Paper, *Teacher Quality*, issued in March 1983 declared that Teacher Regulations were to be amended to encourage **LEAs** to have regard to formal qualifications of teachers in order to ensure that school teaching staffs are suitable. (*See also* **General Training Council, Institutes of Education, probation**.)

White Paper, *Teacher Quality*, HMSO, 1983, Cmnd 8836

quango (quasi-autonomous non-governmental organization)

A term developed in the 1970s to describe a particular kind of bureaucratic structure. Some quangos were educational organizations, and included, for example, the **Schools Council** and the **University Grants Committee**. The overall number of quangos was reduced in the early 1980s and a number of educational organizations disappeared.

A. BARKER, *Quangos in Britain*, Macmillan, 1982

Queen's Scholarships
See **pupil teacher system**.

quota system
A scheme operated by the **DES** until 1975, whereby **LEAs** were allocated a quota of teachers as a means of ensuring fairness during a period of teacher shortage.

R

ragged schools
Schools, aimed at street children, which were pioneered by John Pounds (1766–1839), a Portsmouth cobbler. The Ragged School Union which was formed in 1844 under the presidency of Lord Shaftesbury provided schools for the very poor.

Religious teaching figured prominently in the curriculum. Ragged schools developed various agencies for employment, the best known being the Shoeblack Brigade.

raising of the school leaving age
See **ROSLA**.

Rampton Report
One of the results of the discussions

during the 1970s about the under-achievement of certain ethnic minorities was that a Committee of Enquiry was set up under the chairmanship of Mr Anthony Rampton in March 1979. Its report was published in 1981 and became very controversial. One of the major findings was that children of West Indian parents underachieved in schools whereas Asian minorities performed as well as, or almost as well as, native born children. The explanation of this seemed to be the conscious or unconscious racism of some teachers in English primary and secondary schools. Soon after the publication of the Interim Report, Anthony Rampton was replaced as chairman by Sir Michael Swann. (*See also* **multicultural or multi-ethnic education**.)

West Indian Children in Our Schools: Interim Report of the Committee of Enquiry into the Education of Children from Minority Ethnic Groups ,HMSO, 1981, Cmnd 8273

rank, ranking, rank order

Ranking is the process of arranging individuals in order of achievement (e.g. reading ability, intelligence or performance on arithmetic test). The highest rank is given to the person with the highest score and this person is numbered 1, the second highest 2, and so on. (In the USA, ranking is sometimes reversed so that 1 is the lowest rank.) If a list of marks is published in this way (rather than alphabetically) the list may be described as a rank order.

rate support grant (RSG)

A grant from central government towards the cost of services for which a local authority is responsible. Over half of all local authority spending is on education and 60 per cent of net approved expenditure for education in England and Wales comes from this source: the balance is made up mainly by rates which are levied locally. RSG is a block grant, which means that no part of it is specifically allotted to services provided by a local authority. The RSG is fixed as a result of complicated negotiations between the Government and local authorities. From April 1981, a new RSG system was introduced whereby an authority's grant is governed by its grant related expenditure (GRE), that is, what the Government assesses that local authorities should spend to provide a standard level of service. Local authorities have expressed their opposition to these assessments for the separate services which are provided, for it is claimed that GRE restricts councils' freedom to distribute the block grant as they see fit.

A. CRISPIN, 'State Schools in England and Wales – Finance Aspects', in T. HUSEN and N. POSTLETHWAITE (eds), *International Encyclopaedia of Education*, Pergamon, 1984

readability

Since it is important that material presented to young pupils is not too 'difficult' for them, a number of educationists have attempted to develop measures of 'readability' which indicate the ease with which a passage or even a whole text may be read. Sometimes **reading ages** are assigned to texts in this way. The measures most frequently employed are length of words and sentences, but the familiarity of the language used and the style are also important. It is rarely possible to give an exact indication because two other factors are also very important and they are much more difficult to measure: the first is the number of abstract words and examples given; the second is the author's ability to motivate the child. It has been found that children can read 'above their reading age' if they find the subject matter sufficiently interesting.

L. J. CHAPMAN (ed.), *The Reader and the Text*, United Kingdom Reading Association, Annual Conference Proceedings, 1980, Heinemann Educational, 1981

reader

1. A volume consisting of extracts of the works of various authors on a particular theme. (*See also* **primer**.)
2. A university title, in status between that of senior lecturer and **professor**.

readiness

A concept described by Jerome Bruner as a 'mischievous half truth'. The idea of readiness is that a pupil should not be forced to learn certain **skills** (particularly reading) until he has reached a certain maturational stage, and is ready to embark upon that particular learning skill. Critics of the concept point out that it might encourage some teachers to avoid teaching children until they were 'ready', when they ought to be making them ready by teaching them the prerequisite abilities.

J. BRUNER, *Towards a Theory of Instruction*, Harvard University Press, 1966

reading age

A pupil's competence in reading measured against the average competence of children for his age. An 8-year-old pupil who was advanced in his reading ability might have a reading age of 10, whereas a less advanced 8-year-old might only have a reading age of 6 or 7. (*See also* **dyslexia**, **Gestalt**, **i.t.a.**, **mental age**, **readability**.)

reception class

The class reserved for 5-year-old new entrants into the **infant** section of a **primary school**.

recognized as efficient

See **registration of independent schools**.

recurrent education

A policy based on the view that compulsory education should be regarded as the first stage in the educational process, followed, if not by **further education** or **higher education**, by a series of returns to courses of education throughout the period of adult life. Recurrent education could be vocational, professional or entirely non-vocational, but there tends to be an association of recurrent education with the idea of updating professional skills. (*See also* **adult education**, **continuing education**, **in-service education of teachers**, **permanent education**, **PICKUP**.)

K. RUBENSON, *Developments in Recurrent Education*, Centre for Educational Research and Innovation, 1977

'redbrick' university

Name coined by Bruce Truscot (pseudonym of F. Allison Peers) in his book *Redbrick University*, Faber,

1943, to describe the characteristics of seven of the English **civic universities** established in the late nineteenth and early twentieth centuries. The term has now passed into general usage and is contrasted with **Oxbridge**. (*See also* **universities: history of**.)

redeployment

Voluntary or compulsory transfer of staff to another teaching post in another school. Because of **falling rolls** in schools, this practice has become widespread. Most of those redeployed are young teachers on Scale 1 with no special responsibilities. (*See also* **scale post**.)

reductionism

A belief held by some psychologists and others that it is possible to explain a complex phenomenon by breaking it down into smaller parts and explaining the individual constituents. Behaviourist psychology is said to be reductionist because it claims to explain the whole of human behaviour in terms of the two concepts stimulus and response. Similarly, the behavioural objectives approach to curriculum planning is said to be reductionist because it reduces the learning process to a series of behavioural changes which can be measured. In psychology, an opposite point of view is held by **Gestalt** psychologists. In curriculum studies, the opposite point of view would be taken by those describing themselves as humanistic. (*See also* **behaviourism**, **objectives**.)

reformatory school

By the early 1850s, it was clear that the punishment of juvenile offenders by imprisonment was not having the desired effect. Accordingly, an Act of 1854 'for the better Care and Reformation of Youthful Offenders in Great Britain' attempted to deal with the problem by sending such offenders to reformatory schools for periods ranging from two to five years. Between 1854 and 1875, 61 reformatories were certified, 51 being provided by Protestant and 10 by Catholic authorities. No money was provided by Government for their construction.

J. A. STACK, 'Interests and Ideas in Nineteenth Centry Social Policy: The Mid-Victorian Reformatory School', *Journal of Educational Administration and History*, Vol. 14, No. 1, 1982

Regional Advisory Councils (RAC)

These Councils were established in 1946, following the **Percy Report**, with the aim of co-ordinating further education and bringing education and industry closer together. There are ten Regional Advisory Councils in England and one in Wales. Each Council, numbering between 60 and 100 members, consists of representatives of **LEAs**, college staffs, universities, employers, officials from the main government departments concerned with further education, the **DES** and the Department of Employment One of their important functions is to render advice on the rationalization of advanced courses, though final approval or otherwise is delegated to a senior **HMI**, who is a regional staff inspector. Most of the Council's work is done by its 12 subject advisory committees.

Registrar

A senior post in a college or university whose holder is responsible for student enrolment, student records, examinations, academic administration and the oversight of committees. Some institutions have both an Academic Registrar (concerned with enrolment) and a Registrar with more general responsibilities. (*See also* **Bursar**.)

registration of independent schools

Since the 1944 Education Act, all **independent schools** have been obliged to register with the **DES** or **Welsh Office** and are open to inspection by **HMI**. To be registered, a school must demonstrate that the standards of accommodation are satisfactory. At a higher level, schools could apply to be 'recognized as efficient'; this involved an inspection of the school, and proven evidence of good academic standards and of a suitably qualified staff. In 1977, the Government announced that, as an economy measure, independent schools could no longer apply to be recognized as efficient.

Regius professor

Holders of university chairs which were endowed by the Crown. The first, at Oxford in 1497, was the professorship in divinity. There followed other chairs at Oxford and Cambridge in divinity, law, physic, Hebrew, Greek and other fields. These chairs are confined to **Oxbridge** and Scottish universities. Although the Crown may nominate candidates for these chairs appointments are in fact made on the advice of the Prime Minister or the Secretary of State for Scotland. (*See also* **professor**.)

regression

1. A term derived from psychoanalysis which has become common in educational and counselling circles. Regression occurs when an individual returns (regresses) to behaviour typical of an earlier stage of his emotional or intellectual development. Regression is said to tend to occur when an individual encounters a situation which is extremely painful.

2. Regression is a statistical technique for analysing relationships between two or more variables in order to predict or estimate values. (*See also* **regression to the mean**.)

regression to the mean

A phrase which is often found in discussions of **intelligence** and other desirable qualities. Where parents are tall (or intelligent) there is a tendency for children of those parents to be tall (or intelligent) but not as tall or intelligent as the parents – in other words, there is a tendency for offspring to be somewhere between the parents' score and the average score. This is, of course, a tendency and not a general rule. The same process applies with unintelligent parents: their children are likely to be below average, but closer to the average than their parents. (*See also* **regression**.)

reification

A term much used in **sociology of education**. It refers to the tendency of individuals, including social scientists, to treat ideas as if they existed as things. For example, the class structure is 'man-made' or socially constructed, but it is often referred to as if it had an independent existence.

More controversially, some sociologists have suggested that knowledge is reified and that subject barriers are taken for granted when they ought to be questioned.

reliability

A technical term which must be distinguished from **validity**. Reliability means the extent to which a test or an individual test item will give the same result on different occasions. For example, an individual test of intelligence should give the same result for a given individual on a number of separate occasions. If it does that it could be said to be a 'reliable test' even if there were some doubts about whether or not it was measuring real intelligence – that is a question of the validity of the test. (*See also* **intelligence test**.)

religious education

The only subject which must, according to the 1944 Education Act, appear as part of the curriculum for all UK schools, both **primary** and **secondary**. Yet the subject is not clearly defined and the legal requirement is often ignored or paid little more than lip-service by schools. When the 1944 Act was passed it was, presumably, envisaged that religious education meant Christian (but non-denominational) education. Since then, the UK has become much more of a multi-cultural society and the tendency in recent years has been for religious education to cover both **moral** and social education on the one hand, and comparative religion on the other. In both areas, many teachers are not really well equipped to teach the subject. (*See also* **Agreed Syllabus**, **Butler Act**, **multi-cultural or multi-ethnic educa-**

tion, **special agreement school**, **voluntary aided school**, **voluntary controlled school**, **voluntary school**.)

E. COX, *Problems and Possibilities for Religious Education*, Hodder and Stoughton, 1983

remedial education

Gulliford (1971) stated that such education tends to be of relatively short duration and limited to specific **objectives**, particularly remedying failures or difficulty in learning some school subjects, especially in basic education. Schools differ in their method of providing such education. In the **Warnock** conception of a range of alternative forms of special provision in ordinary schools, the remedial teacher would be part of a school's response to children with **special educational needs**.

R. GULLIFORD, *Special Educational Needs*, Routledge and Kegan Paul, 1971

M. HINSON and M. HUGHES, *Planning and Implementing the Curriculum for Children with Learning Difficulties*, Hulton Educational with National Association for Remedial Education, Amersham, 1982

Remove

A school **form**, usually found in **public** and **grammar schools**, between the ordinary yearly stages. For example there might be a Remove between the third and fourth forms, possibly for those needing more time to reach examination standards.

research and development (R and D)

A style of research activity which focuses on practical issues and where the intention is to produce results of a practical-improvement kind as part of the research programme. It is closely related to the style of research described as **action research**. In curriculum studies, one style of innovation is described as R, D and D (research, development and dissemination). This is based on a concentric model of **dissemination** with an expert at the centre doing the research, pilot schools carrying out the development and, finally, the good news being disseminated to other schools. The model is now regarded as generally too simple to be of practical use in curriculum development programmes. (*See also* **curriculum development project, pilot study**.)

A. HARRIS, M. LAWN and W. PRESCOTT, *Curriculum Innovation*, Open University Press/Croom Helm, 1975

OECD, *Research and Development in Education: a survey*, OECD, Paris, 1974

Research Fellow
An individual, holding a post in an institution of higher education for a specific period of time, who is employed to investigate a particular topic or range of topics. Many of these posts are sponsored by bodies outside the institution. (*See also* **Fellow, Science Research Council, Social Science Research Council**.)

research grant
A sum of money made available to an individual or an institution in order to carry out research into a topic. The outcome is usually presented in the form of a report. (*See also* **research and development (R and D)**.)

research project
A systematic inquiry of some kind, of limited duration, designed to produce new knowledge or test new materials or methods, or in some other way engage in scientific discovery or **problem-solving**. The **Schools Council** has funded many research projects in the field of education. The **National Foundation for Educational Research** (NFER) also engages in a series of such projects. (*See also* **curriculum development project**.)

resource centre
The information explosion has been reflected in the wide range of learning materials now available in schools, particularly at the secondary stage. Resource centres have been established in many schools and serve a number of different purposes. They store book and non-book material and audio-visual software. Ideally, resource centres should have facilities for manufacturing learning materials, including a reprographic workshop and a recording studio. The complex of rooms making up the resource centre should be in a central position in the school. In 1970, the **Library Association** recommended that centres should be large enough to accommodate one-tenth of the school's pupils at any one time. Resource centres are also located in further and higher education institutions. (*See also* **ERIC, information retrieval, teachers' centres, SATROs**.)

N. BESWICK, *Resource-based Learning*, Heinemann Educational, 1977

R. THORNBURY, et al., *Resource Organization in Secondary Schools: report of an investigation*, Council for Educational Technology, 1979

Revised Code
See '**payment by results**'.

'rising fives'
By law, parents are obliged to send their children to school at the beginning of term after reaching the age of 5. **LEAs** may admit them to schools if there is sufficient accommodation before the statutory age. Such pupils are called 'rising fives'. (*See also* **infant school**.)

Risinghill School
A new **comprehensive school**, Risinghill, was opened in Islington in March 1960. The school, under its head, Michael Duane, soon attracted public attention because of its alleged libertarian attitudes and the abolition of corporal punishment. Five years later, in 1965, the **Inner London Education Authority** closed the school.

L. BERG, *Risinghill. Death of a Comprehensive School*, Penguin Books, 1968

Robbins Report
A committee on **higher education** chaired by Lord Robbins was appointed by the Prime Minister to review the existing patterns of higher education in Great Britain and to advise whether there should be any changes in that pattern and whether any new types of institution were desirable. The enquiry stemmed from the growing numbers of sixth formers who were eligible for advanced education. The committee's report, published in 1963, assumed as an axiom ('the Robbins Principle') that courses 'should be available for all those who are qualified by ability and attainment to pursue them and wished to do so'. Several important recommendations were made. University **first degree** courses should be broadened and increased in length to four years, and more provision should be made for research and advanced courses. A radical change in the status of teacher **training colleges** was to be effected by closer links with universities and the introduction of an appropriate degree. The report recommended that they should be renamed **colleges of education**. The need to attract a higher proportion of first-class talent to technology was to be recognized by an expansion of **postgraduate** research and training. A new type of technological institution, called Special Institution of Scientific and Technological Education and Research (SISTER), comparable in size and standing with those in Europe and America, should be established and **Colleges of Advanced Technology** were to be granted charters as technological universities. With a calculated 560,000 student population in 1980, it was necessary to take immediate steps to ensure sufficient places. The universities' share of entrants to higher education was to be increased from 55 per cent in 1962 to 60 per cent in 1980. The report therefore recommended the immediate foundation of six new universities, of which at least one was to be in Scotland, and the advancement of university status of ten other colleges. It is worth noting that Robbins did not conceive of a university education for all who were qualified, stating that some of the pressure for places 'may well be reduced by the extension of facilities for obtaining

degrees in other institutions'. The Government immediately accepted the report, making £650m. available for capital expenditure, advancing Colleges of Advanced Technology to university status and creating some technological universities. (*See also* **Percy Report**, **universities: history of**.)

Report of the Committee on Higher Education appointed by the Prime Minister, Vol. 1, Report, HMSO, 1963

ROSLA (raising of the school leaving age)

During the academic year 1972–3 the statutory minimum leaving age was raised from 15 to 16, as was envisaged in the 1944 Education Act and specifically recommended by the **Newsom Report** (1963). The 'extra year' caused many secondary schools to rethink what they were doing and to mount in some cases special courses for pupils who had previously left at age 15. To some observers it seemed that schools could be divided into two categories: those which regarded the extra year as a challenge and an opportunity to provide a full course of secondary education for all their pupils; and those schools which regarded the extra year as a problem and began talking of courses for 'ROSLA pupils'. (*See also* **school leaving age**.)

J. W. TIBBLE (ed.), *The Extra Year*, Routledge and Kegan Paul, 1970

rote learning

Learning facts mechanically, 'by heart', by a process of practice and repetition. A style of teaching which indulges in a good deal of rote learning without any attempt at understanding the material will now be criticized as old-fashioned. (*See also* **learning**.)

Royal Commissions

All Royal Commissions are appointed by the Queen in Council and are charged with the duty of investigating and reporting on public issues. Members of either of the Houses of Parliament or both and persons representing other interests are invited for their knowledge of the topic to be investigated. The evidence collected and the Commission's report are published as a **Blue Book**. Their recommendations usually form the basis for legislation. The great age of Royal Commissions in education was the second half of the nineteenth century. Before this time, **Select Committees** were the chosen instrument, as for example, **Brougham**'s Committees of 1816 and 1818 on the education of the poor. It was not until 1850 that the first important Royal Commission on education was appointed, that which inquired into the Universities of Oxford, Cambridge and Dublin. There followed investigations into the endowed schools, **Clarendon**, 1864 and **Taunton**, 1868; elementary schools, **Newcastle**, 1861 and **Cross**, 1888; and technical education, **Samuelson**, 1884. With the **Bryce Commission** on secondary education in 1895, the series came to an end. From the founding of the **Board of Education** in 1900, the work of the Commission was given first to **Consultative Committees** and later still to **Central Advisory Committees**. (*See also* **Parliamentary Papers**.)

Royal Society of Arts (RSA)

Founded in 1753 'for the encouragement of the Arts, Manufactures and Commerce of the Country' (and incorporated by Royal Charter in 1847), the Society, an independent and self-financing body, carries out a number of educational functions. It offers examinations in a range of business and commercial studies for older school pupils and further education students. The single-subject examinations form the greater part of the candidate entry. Each can be taken in three grades. Recently, a number of basic level schemes in literacy and numeracy have been introduced for the 16–19 age group. The Society acts as a liaison between the practical arts and sciences and is involved in lectures on educational topics, such as education for capability.

D. HUDSON and K. W. LUCKHURST, *The Royal Society of Arts, 1754–1954*, John Murray, 1954

Ruskin College

An adult education college established in Oxford in 1899, offering full-time courses up to two years in length. Many of the students are actively involved in trades unions. At a ceremony to mark the opening of a hall of residence in October 1976, the then Prime Minister, James Callaghan, launched the **Great Debate** on education.

Russell Report

A Committee of Inquiry under the chairmanship of Sir Lionel Russell was appointed in 1969 to review the provision of non-vocational **adult education** in England and Wales and to consider the appropriateness of existing educational, administrative and financial policies. Its report,

issued in 1973 and entitled *Adult Education: A Plan for Development*, was an ambitious one. It recommended the commitment of central government funds to assist local authority financing of adult education and assumed a doubling of student numbers between 1973 and 1978. With the change of government in 1970, when Mrs Thatcher became Secretary of State at the **DES**, the recommendations were not implemented.

Adult Education, a Plan for Development. A report by a Committee of Inquiry appointed by the Secretary of State for Education and Science, HMSO, 1973

Rutter Report

A study, following a comparative survey of 10-year-olds in London and the Isle of Wight, of 12 inner London non-selective secondary schools which attempted to measure success by reference to pupils' behaviour both in and out of school, their academic achievements and attendance rates. The team of researchers led by Professor Michael Rutter published in 1979 their findings in a book called *Fifteen Thousand Hours*, the number of hours at school spent by a child during the period of compulsory schooling. The report concluded that schools could significantly affect children's achievements, compared with home and other influences. Schools with good attendance tend to have well-behaved pupils who perform well in examinations. The ethos of the school was found to be an important factor. Where the teachers set good standards, provide good models of behaviour, praise pupils and give them responsibility, and where lessons are well prepared and organized, all these were indicators of a good school. Criticisms of the report's findings have been made on a number of grounds. It is claimed that the schools selected were untypical, that some of the statistics were wrongly analysed and that it overestimated the extent to which schools can overcome social influences. Nevertheless, the study raises a number of important issues, especially on the relationship between life in schools and factors affecting achievement.

A. HEATH and P. CLIFFORD, 'Seventy Thousand Hours that Rutter Left Out', *Oxford Review of Education*, Vol. 6, No. 1, 1980

M. RUTTER et al., *Fifteen Thousand Hours*, Open Books, 1979

S

sabbatical

A period of paid leave for private study or research, varying from one term to one year. In the original sense of the term, a sabbatical year should occur once every seven years, but institutions differ widely in their practices. Sabbatical leave is commonly available in higher education institutions but much less so in schools. (*See also* **study leave, unpaid leave**.)

Samuelson Report

The terms of reference of the Royal Commission on Technical Instruction chaired by an industrialist, Bernhard Samuelson, were 'to inquire into the instruction of the industrial classes of certain foreign countries in technical and other subjects for the purpose of comparison with that of the corresponding classes in this country; and into the influence of such instruction on manufacturing and other industries at home and abroad'. The Commission was appointed in 1881. Its second report in 1884 outlined a programme for developing **technical education**. In elementary schools, drawing was to be incorporated with writing as a single subject and to be subject to inspection. Proficiency in the use of tools for working in wood and iron would attract a grant, although the work was to be done outside school hours. In secondary schools, it was recommended that departments of natural science, drawing and mathematics might replace Latin and Greek, and local authorities should be empowered to apply endowments to support this work. In addition, local authorities should be empowered to establish and maintain secondary and technical schools and colleges. Many of these recommendations were implemented after the passing of the **Technical Instruction Act 1889** and a Local Taxation Act in the following year. (*See also* **Devonshire Commission**.)

M. ARGLES, 'The Royal Commission on Technical Instruction, 1881–4', *Vocational Aspects of Secondary and Further Education*, Vol. 9, No. 23, 1959

Reports of the Royal Commission on Technical Instruction, 1882–4, P.P. 1882, xxvii; P.P., 1884, xxix–xxxi

sandwich course

A course consisting of full-time studies and a period of full-time work. Many **CNAA** and some university degree courses combine these two elements in such areas as engineering and business studies. The sandwich element can be either 'thick', with full-time employment for a year, or 'thin', consisting of two or three periods of time each lasting up to half a year.

DES, *A Review of the Provision of Sandwich Courses in Higher Education*, 1982

A. G. SMITHERS, *Sandwich Courses. An Integrated Education?*, NFER, 1976

SATROs

Science and Technology Regional Organizations (SATROs) are a national network of organizations, sponsored by the Department of Industry, for encouraging links between school and industry. At present there are about 30 SATROs, based in universities, polytechnics, **LEAs** and industry. Much of the work is carried on with teachers, offering assistance in organizing visits, developing **resource centres** and providing information on **curriculum development** which takes account of industry. (*See also* **industry: links with schools**.)

scale post

Pay scales for **assistant teachers** which are nationally agreed. The scales are from 1 to 4, with new entrants usually beginning at Scale 1. (*See also* **post of responsibility**.)

schema

A technical term used by Piaget and other developmental psychologists to refer to those conceptual structures which are used to interpret information in the external world which is perceived by the senses. A schema is, therefore, a kind of hypothesis set up by the brain to make sense of reality. When the child (or the adult) encounters a new situation which does not fit in with the existing schema, the individual will either be puzzled or adapt the schema or schemata (plural) to make better sense of reality.

M. DONALDSON, *Children's Minds*, Fontana, 1978

scholarship

1. Refers to erudition in an academic field.

2. An **entrance award**, carrying with it a sum of money, for candidates who are successful at **Oxbridge** colleges' entrance examination.

3. Name formerly widely given to the examination for entry to a secondary school, often called the **'eleven plus'**.

school

1. Most commonly refers to buildings where children of school age are taught.

2. At Oxford, may describe a course of study leading to an examination for a first degree, e.g. Philosophy, Politics and Economics, or more widely to describe all persons working in a subject, e.g. Chemistry School. It also appears as part of a title of a college in other universities, e.g. the London School of Economics and Social Science. In the University of London, a school is a semi-autonomous college, as distinct from a Senate institute.

school attendance committee

The Elementary Education Act of 1876 established machinery for closing the loopholes of the 1870 Act concerning compulsory attendance. **School boards** adopted by-laws requiring attendance, but where there were no boards, school attendance committees were to carry out this function. The committees appointed annually by Boards of Guardians or sanitary authorities consisted of between 6 and 12 members. The Act had some success, increasing the attendance of children living in by-law areas from about half of their number in 1876 to almost three-quarters four years later. (*See also* **compulsory education**.)

P. GORDON, 'Lord Sandon and the Century of Compulsory Education', *History of Education Bulletin*, No. 18, 1976

school board

The 1870 Education Act had two aims – to induce children to attend schools and to provide good schools throughout the country. This latter aim was to be achieved by filling up the gaps in the voluntary system then prevailing. Where there was a deficiency in the accommodation provided by voluntary effort, a school board was elected by the district. The board's duty was to build new schools from rate aid or help existing ones. Normally, school fees were required where parents could pay and boards were empowered to frame by-laws for compulsory attendance for children between 5 and 13 years of age. The Act contained a **conscience clause** for board schools, individual boards determining the form of religious instruction given. The Act proved to be a success, with some 300 boards being formed by the end of 1871. This system of elementary education, together with those from denominational organizations, continued until they were abolished by the 1902 Education Act. (*See also* **free education**, **National Education League**, **National Education Union**, **School Attendance Committee**.)

J. S. HURT, *Elementary Schooling and the Working Classes 1860–1918*, Routledge and Kegan Paul, 1979

F. SMITH, *A History of English Elementary Education 1760–1902*, University of London Press, 1931

School Certificate

Introduced by the **Secondary School Examinations Council** in 1917, the School Certificate was an examination taken by pupils at the end of a four-year secondary school course of study, usually at 16 years of age. No certificate was awarded unless passes in five subjects were obtained. Credits in five subjects bestowed **matriculation** exemption on successful candidates. It was replaced by the **GCE O level** examination in 1951. (*See also* **General Certificate of Education**, **Higher School Certificate**.)

O. BANKS, *Parity and Prestige in English Secondary Education*, Routledge and Kegan Paul, 1955

school closure
See **Section 12 notice**.

school council
A council of pupils who are either elected or nominated within a school.

It expresses views on school matters, though its terms of reference are normally laid down by the **head-teacher** and staff. Such councils do not exist in all schools.

school day

The length of time during which the school is open for pupils. Usually the morning session is of about three hours' duration with a slightly shorter time in the afternoon. Some schools are now experimenting with a more flexible approach which allows for more pupil choice of activities. For example, where closer links with the community are reflected in the curriculum, a school may start as early as 8.30 a.m. so that the majority of 'normal' lessons are fitted into the morning session: with a shortened midday break, the rest of the time is available for activities, both within and outside the school, which may require longer periods of time than can be accommodated in the more traditional school day. (*See also* **extended day**, **Newsom Report**, **out-of-school activities**.)

School Health Service

Three official reports at the beginning of this century – those of the Royal Commission on Physical Training in Scotland (1903), the Interdepartmental Committee on Physical Deterioration (1904), and the Interdepartmental Committee on Medical Inspection and the Feeding of School Children (1905) – revealed the extent of ill-health and malnutrition amongst school children. As a result, in 1907 the Government established a School Medical Service (renamed School Health Service in 1945). The 1907 Education (Administrative Provisions) Act made **LEAs** responsible for providing for the medical inspection of pupils in **elementary schools**. In the same year, a Medical Branch of the Board of Education was formed under Dr George Newman, who reported in 1910 'that in spite of all the difficulties, limitations and adverse conditions, a national system of medical inspection and supervision of school children has been established throughout England and Wales'. The 1944 Education Act requested LEAs to provide for medical inspection of children from time to time on school premises. By the National Health Service Reorganization Act 1973, which came into force on 1 April 1974, responsibility for the School Health Service passed from LEAs to the Secretary of State for Social Services, though LEAs still have some responsibility under the 1944 Education Act. (*See also* **open-air school**, **school meals service**.)

P. HENDERSON, *The School Health Service 1908–1974*, HMSO, 1975

school leaving age

Under the 1870 Education Act, the newly formed **school boards** were required to draw up by-laws for the purpose of securing attendance of pupils between the ages of 5 and 13. The 1880 Act required unconditional attendance between 5 and 10 years of age with exemption on the grounds of proven proficiency for those between 10 and 13. In 1893, the minimum leaving age was raised to 11 and in 1899 to 12 years of age. The 1918 Education Act raised the leaving age to 14; it was further raised to 15 in 1947 and to 16 in the academic year 1972/3. (*See also* **compulsory education**, **ROSLA**, **school** attendance committee, **Spens Report, vocational preparation**.)

School Library Association (SLA)

The Association promotes the development of school libraries and the use of books and other resources. It was founded in 1937 and its members include representatives of all levels of education, as well as publishers and public libraries. A joint board comprising representatives of the School Library Association and the **Library Association** validates courses for the Certificate in School Library Studies. Only about 3 per cent of professional librarians work in schools.

School Meals Service

The poor physical condition of potential recruits for the Boer War led to the setting up of an Inter-Departmental Committee on Physical Deterioration in 1904. Amongst its recommendations were the feeding of necessitous children and the establishment of school medical inspection. Accordingly, another Inter-Departmental Committee the following year, headed by the President of the Board of Education, Lord Londonderry, examined these two aspects with special reference to the elementary school. In its report, the committee asked for better co-ordination of existing organizations providing food. However, in 1906 an Education (Provision of Meals) Act went further in stating that the **LEAs**, not voluntary societies, should be responsible for provision. LEAs were empowered to levy a rate of ½d. in the pound for this purpose. Both World Wars increased the demand for such a service. The 1944 Education Act made it obligatory for

LEAs to provide a school meals service. The 1980 Education Act removed this obligation, though the need for provision for pupils whose parents were in receipt of supplementary benefit or family income supplement was acknowledged. (*See also* **School Health Service**.)

L. ANDREWS, 'The School Meals Service', *British Journal of Educational Studies*, Vol. 30, No. 1, 1972

HOUSE OF COMMONS, Education, Science and Arts Committee Report, 1981–2. 7th Report, *School Meals*, HMSO, 1982, Cmnd 8740

School of Education

See **university department of education**.

school of industry

A type of school for pauper children advocated by John Locke in 1697 so that they would be kept 'in much better order, be better provided for, and from infancy be inured to work, which is of no small consequence to the making of them sober and industrious all their lives after.' Children worked up to 12 hours a day at, for example, spinning, winding and knitting or straw-plaiting, and received payment. Reading and writing lessons were given at a charge. The products of such schools usually found work in factories or became domestic servants. (*See also* **factory school, industrial school**.)

school phobia

Some children develop strong anxieties about attending school to the extent that they cannot leave their homes. It is seldom the case that the child can pinpoint some problem at school that worries her/him and the condition is seen as a neurotic fear of separation from and being away from the mother. These children should not be confused with truants who are absent from school with or without the knowledge of their parents. Truants have no anxiety about leaving home; some will sign on at school and then truant, others spend their time away from school and home. Occasionally parents actively encourage their children to absent themselves from school to help with shopping and housework. Truancy, therefore, can be a form of social maladjustment. (*See also* **truant school**.)

J. H. KAHN, J. P. NURSTEN and H. C. CARROLL, *Unwillingly to School: school phobia or school refusal – a psychosocial problem*, Pergamon, Oxford, 3rd edn, 1981

school psychological service

Educational psychologists are employed by **LEAs** to provide psychological support services to ordinary schools, **special schools** and units, to other agencies like Health and Social Service Assessment Centres, and to parents. Psychologists have recognized initial and **postgraduate** qualifications in psychology and many are experienced teachers. Psychologists specialize in areas of treatment like family therapy or behaviour modification, and may act in consultative and advisory roles. They are mainly occupied with children with learning problems and maladjustment in ordinary schools and they work closely with remedial services and **child guidance clinics**. (*See also* **diagnosis**.)

J. C. QUICKE, *The Cautious Expert*, Open University Press, 1983

school records

The compiling of school records of a pupil during her/his school career has become a matter for some controversy in recent years. The **Green Paper** following the **Great Debate** called for good record-keeping which can be clearly understood. It also drew attention to the rights of parents, teachers and pupils to know what the records contain and recommend, and called for consistency of practice between different **LEAs**. A Schools Council Survey, *Record Keeping in Primary Schools* (1981), showed that teachers regarded the records as secret, and that they were not on the whole systematically or methodically kept. The uses to which such records are put has been questioned; LEAs differ widely on the question of parental access. (*See also* **parents and education**, **profiles**, **school report**, **underachiever**.)

P. CLIFT, G. WEINER and E. WILSON, *Record Keeping in Primary Schools*, Macmillan Education, 1981

L. HODGES, *Out in the Open? The school records debate*, Writers and Readers, 1981

school report

An **assessment** of pupils' progress in written form, usually subject by subject, for the information of parents. Reports may be issued on a termly, half-yearly or yearly basis. The traditional report has been under attack recently mainly on the grounds that it does not give a rounded picture of a pupil, concentrating too much on academic achievement. **Profiles** have been suggested as an alternative. (*See also* **parents and education**, **school records**.)

L. KEATING, *The School Report*, Kenneth Mason, 1969

Schools Council

In 1962, the **Minister of Education** established a Curriculum Study Group, consisting of officials, **HMIs** and a university educationist to give urgent advice on the school curriculum. Because of hostility from **LEAs** and teachers' unions, a Working Party on Schools' Curricula and Examinations chaired by Sir John Lockwood was asked to discuss the need for new co-operative machinery in these fields. The Lockwood Report in 1964 reaffirmed the importance of the principle that schools should retain the responsibility for their own work, but that a Schools Council for the Curriculum and Examinations was necessary for research and development. The Council, which should be an independent body, was to consist of teachers, LEAs and the **Secretary of State for Education**. It also took over the functions of the Curriculum Studies Group and the **Secondary School Examinations Council**. Between 1964 and 1978, the Council funded 172 **curriculum development projects** dealing with several aspects of school work, and generated much material. Most of the projects were based on universities or colleges. In addition, the Council has published many working papers and research studies for discussion. During this time, the Council carried out its responsibility for examinations in a number of ways. It originally approved new subjects and new syllabuses for **A and O level examinations**, though since 1966, for O levels, only new subjects had to be submitted. It was an early proponent of a common examination at 16+ and was actively involved in the introduction of the **CEE**, as well as attempts to reform **sixth form** curriculum. Criticism of the functioning of the Council, especially the apparent lack of impact of the curriculum development programmes on schools, led to a reassessment of the Council's work. In July 1979, it produced a document *Principles and Programmes* which identified its future role in the curriculum field. Rather than fund large-scale projects, the Council hoped to support LEA and school initiative and work closely with **advisers** and **in-service** trainers in disseminating better practice. It also acted as a **clearing house** for information on curriculum developments funded by other agencies. Except for the Examinations Committee, the majority of committee members were nominated by **teachers' associations**. The Chairman of the Schools Council, normally a distinguished educationist, was also chairman of the three main committees and the Publications Committee. The Council had a full-time Secretary. In March 1981, the Secretary of State for Education and Science announced that Mrs Nancy Trenaman, Principal of St Anne's College, Oxford, had been invited to review the functions, constitution and methods of work of the Schools Council and to make recommendations. Her report, issued in October 1981, stated that the Council was too political, too complicated and overstretched, but concluded that it should continue with its present functions. It outlined a number of changes which should be made and also recommended that the Council should not be the subject of any further review for the next five years. However in April 1982, the Secretary of State announced his intention to disband the Council and put in its place two separate bodies, a Secondary Examinations Council (SEC) of about 15 members and a School Curriculum Development Committee (SCDC) of about 20 members; the appointments were to be made by the Secretary of State. The SEC was given much greater resources than the SCDC. The separation of curriculum and examinations has been criticized as being a retrograde step, signifying governmental determination to assume control of the examination system. (*See also* **teachers' centres**.)

DES, *Review of the Schools Council* (Trenaman Report), 1982

D. LAWTON, *The End of the 'Secret Garden'? A Study in the Politics of the Curriculum*, University of London Institute of Education, 1982 edn

school uniform
See **uniform**, **school**.

Science and Art Department
The Department was created after the Great Exhibition of 1851 in order to encourage industrial skills. In 1852 a Department of Practical Art was established and in the following year a Science Division was added. The Department, situated at South Kensington, administered parliamentary grants in the field of science and art. By the 1890s it had assumed the role of a central authority for **technical education**. The Department was eventually absorbed into the new **Board of Education** at the end of the century. (*See also* **organized science school**, **technical college**.)

M. ARGLES, *South Kensington to Robbins: an account of technical and scientific education since 1851*, Longman, 1964

H. BUTTERWORTH, 'The Department of Science and Art (1853–1900) and the Development of Secondary Education', *History of Education Society Bulletin*, No. 6, 1970

Science Research Council (SRC)
A council set up by the **DES** to allocate funds for approved scientific research. Members of the Council are appointed by the Secretary of State for Education and meet regularly to scrutinize research proposals and to allocate funds to what they consider to be the most deserving projects.

Scottish Education Department (SED)
The SED was established at the time of the 1872 Education (Scotland) Act, which transferred the administration of schools from church to lay authorities, through locally elected school boards. The SED was set up as a central controlling and co-ordinating body for education. A Secretary (since 1926, Secretary of State) for Scotland was appointed in 1885 and since then has been responsible for the development of the system. The Department's functions are the same as the **DES**, except that universities are administered by the **University Grants Committee** for the whole of Great Britain. (*See also* **Dunning Report**, **Munn Report**.)

SCOTTISH EDUCATION DEPARTMENT, *Public Education in Scotland*, HMSO, 1972

Secondary Education For All

The title of a Labour Party policy document, issued in 1922, largely the work of R. H. Tawney. It advocated a wider curriculum for all pupils at the secondary school stage. This sentiment was echoed in the **Hadow Report** (1926) and provided for in the 1944 Education Act (Sections 7 and 8). (*See also* **Butler Act**, **comprehensive school**, **'eleven plus' examination**, **ladder of ability**.)

J. R. BROOKS, ' "Secondary Education For All" Reconsidered', *Durham Research Review*, Vol. 8, 1977

R. H. TAWNEY (ed.), *Secondary Education For All: a policy for Labour*, Education Advisory Committee of the Labour Party, Allen and Unwin, 1922

Secondary Heads Association (SHA)

Set up in 1976, from the former **Headmasters' Association** and the **Association of Headmistresses**, the Association's membership includes heads and **deputy heads** from both the **maintained** and the **independent** sectors. All the major **public schools** are represented. The Association makes pronouncements of common concern to both sectors, such as examinations and curriculum, and is non-political in character. It is the only body on the **Burnham Committee** which speaks solely for secondary heads. At the present time its membership is over 3,000. (*See also* **headteacher**, **National Association of Head Teachers**, **teachers' associations**.)

secondary modern school

The **Hadow Report** on *The Education of the Adolescent* (1926) recommended the division of secondary education into two types: the **grammar school**, for the most intellectually able pupils, and the secondary modern school, which would cater for most adolescents between the ages of 11 and 15. The curriculum to be offered in the latter was to concentrate initially on offering a good broad education, but in the later years of schooling a more practical bias was to be introduced into the **curriculum**. With the blessing of the **Board of Education**, this new type of secondary school came into existence. The White Paper on Educational Reconstruction in 1943, which set the pattern for tripartitism, recommended three types of school, grammar, **technical** and modern, corresponding to supposed psychological categories of pupils. After the 1944 Education Act the secondary modern school flourished. A Ministry pamphlet, *The New Secondary Education* (1947), claimed that it was 'impracticable to combine a system of external examinations . . . with the fundamental conception of modern school education', and teachers were encouraged 'to plan the curriculum of the school on purely educational lines.' Despite this, modern schools developed sixth forms and entered pupils in growing numbers for the **GCE** examinations; the **Certificate of Secondary Education** examinations were introduced in 1965 for the bulk of the modern school's population. Dissatisfaction with the status of the school was increasingly voiced by teachers, parents and politicians. National variations in the provision of grammar school places, the questioning of the validity of **intelligence tests** as a basis of selection and the lack of progress towards the 1944 Education Act's promise of equality of opportunity led to the reorganization of secondary schooling on **comprehensive** lines. From 1964, the numbers of secondary modern schools has diminished and they now survive only in the few **LEAs** which have yet to implement plans for reorganization. (*See also* **Secondary Education for All**, **tripartite system**.)

R. M. T. KNEEBONE, *I Work in a Secondary Modern School*, Routledge and Kegan Paul, 1957

W. TAYLOR, *The Secondary Modern School*, Faber, 1963

secondary school

Normally, a school providing education for children from the age of 11 years. Since the advent of comprehensive reorganization, there are **middle schools** which span the traditional primary and secondary age ranges.

Secondary School Examinations Council (SSEC)

The Council was established in 1917 as a result of the introduction of **School Certificate** examinations that year. The **Board of Education** wished to co-ordinate the work of the different university **examining boards** and to ensure parity of standards. There were 21 members of the SSEC, consisting of ten from examining boards, six teacher representatives and five from LEAs. In 1936, the representation was changed to give each constituency one-third. Following the **Norwood Report**, which recommended the ending of the School Certificate, the Council was once more changed. It was increased to 31 members but examining boards no longer had direct representation. For the first time the **Ministry of Education** had a direct voice on the Council with five members, teachers had eleven, **LEAs** eight, and universities seven. The exclusion of examining bodies from the SSEC made for difficulties in its deliberations. In 1964 the Council's functions were transferred to the **Schools Council**.

J. L. BRERETON, *The Case for Examinations*, Cambridge University Press, 1944

G. BRUCE, *Secondary School Examinations*, Pergamon, Oxford, 1969

second master or mistress

A teacher so designated in a mixed school in Group 7, i.e. 400–500 pupils, or more. The post holder is on the same salary scale as a **deputy head** but is not equal in status. (*See also* **teachers' salaries**.)

secondment

The allocation of a teacher, on a temporary basis, to a course or another post away from his or her normal place of employment.

Secretary of State for Education and Science

The **Robbins Report** recommended that there should be changes in the machinery of ministerial responsibility – that the **Minister of Education** should be replaced by a Minister for Arts and Science. Whilst agreeing to the need for changes, the Government's solution was for a single **Department of Education and Science**, the enlarged ministry to have a Secretary of State as its head. The Secretary of State has overall responsibility for the work of the

Department and the formulation of general policy. He is also a member of the Cabinet. He is assisted by two Parliamentary Under-Secretaries of State who deal respectively with schools and higher education. (*See also* **Ministry of Education**.)

w. PILE, *The Department of Education and Science*, Allen and Unwin, 1979

Section 12 notice

When an **LEA** intends to close a county school or change its character to a significant extent, it issues a public notice for two months for objections in accordance with Section 12 of the 1980 Education Act. Circular 2/80 states that LEAs should give parents at least one term to make alternative arrangements and allow at least a full 12 months between the publication of closure proposals and the date on which they come into effect. The **Secretary of State for Education** has, under the Act, to approve Section 12 notices. It should be noted that the establishment and alteration of **voluntary schools** are covered by Section 13 of the same Act. (*See also* **falling rolls**.)

secular school

A movement begun in the 1830s by radicals and Nonconformists, alarmed at the Church of England's growing hold on the provision of elementary education. In London, William Ellis, the educationist, pioneered secular schools, opening seven Birkbeck schools, with curricula which had a large social science content. Manchester was the other centre of activity. The National Public School Association campaigned from 1850 for a national system of free, secular, rate-aided education and opened a model secular school in 1854. The movement never became widespread and faded later in the century.

D. K. JONES, *The Making of the Education System, 1851–81*, Routledge and Kegan Paul, 1977

security of tenure

The contractual right of an academic (particularly in universities) to retain full-time employment until a specified retirement date. An academic with such a 'tenured post' would not be able to be dismissed except for 'good cause', which in many cases does not include financial difficulties on the part of the educational institution. Security of tenure was normally granted only after satisfactory completion of a probationary period, often three years. In the early 1980s, the privileged position of academics with security of tenure was questioned by the Conservative Secretary of State for Education, Sir Keith Joseph, and others. (*See also* **probation**.)

Select Committee

This Committee is made up of named members of either House of Parliament with the purpose of taking evidence on a subject and reporting its findings back to the House which appointed the Committee. It has power to summon witnesses to attend, give evidence and produce documents. Examples are the **Brougham** Select Committee on the Education of the Lower Orders, 1816 and 1818, and that on Education, Science and Art Administration, 1884. (*See also* **Parliamentary Papers**.)

selection
See **'eleven plus' examination**.

self-concept, self-image
An individual's self-concept is the way he sees himself. Some research has been based on the hypothesis that children with a negative self-image tend to be **underachievers** at school. It has also been suggested that children from certain ethnic minorities have a negative self-image, and that this accounts for their under-achievement in school. The evidence for this is not conclusive. (*See also* **multi-cultural or multi-ethnic education**.)

R. B. BURNS, *Self-Concept Development and Education*, Holt, Rinehart and Winston, 1982

M. STONE, *The Education of the Immigrant Child in Britain*, Fontana, 1980

self-fulfilling prophecy
A term, originally used in sociology, which has increasingly become a feature of some experimental work in schools and of some organizational practices, such as **streaming**. In education, it is often associated with the term **'labelling'**. If a pupil is believed by his teacher to be bright, that pupil is likely to improve; if a pupil or group of pupils is thought to be dull, he or they will become dull. This is sometimes also known as the Pygmalion effect.

D. A. PIDGEON, *Expectation and Pupil Performance,* NFER, 1970

R. ROSENTHAL and L. JACOBSON, *Pygmalion in the Classroom: Teacher Expectation and Pupils' Intellectual Development*, Holt, Rinehart and Winston, 1968

self-instruction
A method of learning in which students use **programmed learning** or other materials in order to teach themselves. No direct help would be given by a teacher although the course would normally be laid out with very specific goals. A **correspondence course** is not, strictly speaking, a self-instructional course, because normally students submit work which has to be marked and commented on by a **tutor**. Some correspondence courses might, however, include self-instructional materials or units. Some textbooks have been written on a self-instructional basis, that is, the content is so devised as to provide answers for the student and alternative routes should the student make mistakes.

semester
Whereas English schools and universities have academic years which are divided into three periods of work (**terms**) plus **vacations**, North American universities tend to divide the **academic year** into two working periods called semesters usually lasting at least fifteen weeks, with longer breaks in between. Thus many courses in American universities are organized in terms of a semester rather than a whole year. (*See also* **half term**.)

seminar
A meeting of students in a group with a **tutor** sometimes for the purpose of following up a **lecture**. Members of the group may present a paper at the seminar to stimulate discussion or raise further issues. (*See also* **tutorial**.)

senior teacher

A grade of teacher recognized for salary purposes between **assistant master** and **mistress** and **deputy head**. In the largest schools (Group 14), up to five such posts are allowed. The post originated in 1972 with the intention of rewarding those who had contributed to the work of the school and to encourage stability of staffing at a time of rapid turnover. These posts are now often used to attract good candidates in scarcity subject areas.

Service children's schools

Schools provided for children of members of the Armed Forces in service garrisons and bases located in Europe, the Mediterranean and the Far East. Teachers are mainly drawn from Britain to staff the schools. The Service Children's Education Authority (SCEA), within the Ministry of Defence, is responsible for providing the schools overseas.

setting

In the early days of **comprehensive schools** most **headteachers** organized the school on the basis of **streaming**, that is, they allocated pupils to classes in terms of their supposed ability and the pupils remained in those streamed classes for all, or most, subjects. For various reasons, this was found to be far too rigid a selection process, and a frequently adopted compromise was the process of setting, which might leave pupils in mixed ability groups for most of their subjects, but allocate them to **ability groupings** for certain subjects where more homogeneous classes were thought to be necessary. Setting is most common in such subjects as modern languages and mathematics. It is a more flexible system than streaming and a pupil might find himself in a mixed ability group for several subjects, in the top set for mathematics, but in a low set for French.

seventeen plus examinations

During the 1960s and 1970s there was much discussion about the 'new sixth former', that is, a student who stayed on in a **comprehensive school** after completing the five-year course, but without sufficient academic success to undertake **GCE A level** courses. Many such students simply retook **O level** examinations which they had earlier failed or even retook **CSE** in order to obtain improved grades. This practice was generally thought to be very undesirable and various proposals for an alternative and better examination were put forward. One of these was the **Certificate for Extended Education (CEE)** which was discussed in the **Keohane Report**. Other suggestions involved even more directly **vocational preparation** and courses designed by the **City and Guilds**. By the 1980s it was regarded as necessary to have some kind of unified policy for these one-year sixth-form courses and examinations, and they were generally referred to as the 'seventeen plus examinations'. (*See also* **sixteen plus examinations**.)

J. DEAN and A. STEEDS, *17+: The New Sixth Forms in Schools and FE*, NFER, 1981

P. SCOTT, 'Silence is Golden?' *Times Educational Supplement*, 12 November 1982

sixteen plus examinations

As long ago as 1970, the Schools

Council recommended a merger of **GCE O level** and **CSE** examinations. Eight years later, the **Waddell Report** concluded that such a system was feasible. In February 1980 a modified scheme was announced by the Conservative Government, with loose grouping of boards, strong **national criteria** and a GCE board veto on the highest grades. Four groups of **examination boards** have been established in England. Examination boards were asked to draw up criteria for every subject and a Joint Council for establishing 16+ national criteria was established by the GCE and CSE boards. The Joint Councils' proposals have to be approved by the **Secretary of State for Education**. Both board-based and school-based examinations are likely to be offered. Details of the marking and administration of the examination and the date for the introduction of the new scheme have yet to be settled. This examination is aimed at the top 60 per cent of the secondary school population. (*See also* **seventeen plus examinations**.)

DES, *Examinations at 16 plus: A Statement of Policy*, HMSO, 1982

H. MACINTOSH, 'Down with 16 plus', *Times Educational Supplement*, 11 February 1983

sixth form

Traditionally, the highest classes in a secondary school, which pupils joined after gaining a group of **GCE O levels**. Courses in the sixth form normally lasted two years, being divided into a Lower and Upper Sixth, followed in some cases by a seventh term for those attempting **Oxbridge** entrance examinations. Since the development of **compre-** **hensive schools**, the 'new' sixth forms offer a wide range of courses, from repeats of **CSE** and **GCE O levels** to **A levels** as well as those of a pre-vocational nature. Pupils may, at this stage, alternatively opt to attend a local **sixth form college** or a **college of further education** to pursue their studies. In some **LEAs**, **tertiary colleges** provide all courses at this level. (*See also* **Dainton Report**, **seventeen plus examinations**.)

W. REID and J. FILBY, *The Sixth: An Essay in Education and Democracy*, Falmer Press, Sussex, 1982

R. WATKINS (ed.), *The New Sixth Form*, Ward Lock Educational, 1974

sixth form college

Unlike the **tertiary college** which caters for all students of 16 years and over in an area, the sixth form college accommodates both the traditional **sixth form** intake and those requiring somewhat less academic courses. Many of the students aim to go on to further and higher education, and the college offers a range of examinations. There are now more than 100 of these colleges in England and Wales. (*See also* **college of further education**, **Macfarlane Report**.)

E. MACFARLANE, *Sixth Form Colleges. The 16–19 Comprehensives*, Heinemann Educational, 1978

P. WATKINS, *The Sixth Form College in Practice*, Edward Arnold, 1982

skill

A physical, social or mental ability learned mainly through practice and repetition. Skill is frequently contrasted with **knowledge**, but this is an over-simplification. It may be convenient to divide educational **objectives** into knowledge, skills and attitudes, but it should always be recognized that these are overlapping categories. (*See also* **social skills**.)

Skinnerian

An adjective describing the work of B. F. Skinner, an American psychologist. One meaning of Skinnerian applies to the behaviourist theory of learning and its particular application in schools; a more limited use of Skinnerian applies particularly to Skinner's work on **programmed learning**, and in this sense a Skinnerian programme is a linear programme (to be contrasted with a branching programme). (*See also* **behaviourism**.)

S level

An examination which may be taken by above average **GCE A level** candidates who wish to go on to **higher education**. There are three grades: 1. Distinction, 2. Merit and 3. Unclassified. (*See also* **General Certificate of Education**.)

Sloyd (or Slöjd)

A system of manual training originating in Sweden which became popular in England by the end of the nineteenth century. It differed from the more mechanical form of training both in the character of the objects produced and in the manner of work and tools used. Its aims were to develop the exercise of judgement and manual dexterity and so by a series of progressive exercises to produce workmanship of a high order in schools.

E. CHAPMAN, 'Slöjd', in LORD BRABA-ZON (ed.), *Some National and Board School Reforms*, Longmans Green, 1887

Social Science Research Council (SSRC)

The Council was set up in 1965 by Royal Charter to encourage research, provide advice and disseminate knowledge concerning the social sciences. It also allocated funds for **postgraduate** students and finances high quality research proposals from the universities. In September 1981, the Council announced that changes needed to be made to encourage a more multidisciplinary approach to problems which are seen to be important in policy formulation. At the same time, the many Standing Committees and ad hoc panels were to be replaced by six Standing Committees – Social Affairs, Education and Human Development, Industry and Employment, Economic Affairs, Environment and Planning and Government and Law. The SSRC suffered a cut of about 20% in real resources between 1978 and 1982. In October 1982 the **Secretary of State** decided, following the recommendation of the Rothschild Report on the SSRC, to continue the Council for at least the next three years. Its title has since been changed to 'Economic and Social Research Council' (ESRC). (*See also* **Science Research Council**.)

social skills

The ability to communicate effectively with people in social and work situations. Many schools and colleges offer courses in this area, for example, preparation for job interviews. In a wider context, it may be seen as one aspect of personal and social education (PSE), an umbrella term covering a number of curriculum areas concerned with values and personal developmental processes. (*See also* **skill**.)

K. DAVID, *Personal and Social Education in Secondary Schools*, Longman, 1983

S. SPENCE, *Social Skills Training with Children and Adolescents*, NFER, 1980

Society of Education Officers (SEO)

A professional association for educational administrators of local authorities in England, Wales and Northern Ireland, formed in 1971. The Scottish counterpart is the Association of Directors of Education in Scotland. Its main objects are to confer on matters relating to education for the benefit of members and through them of their authorities and to make representations to Government departments and other bodies. The Society does not now deal with salaries, conditions of service and other union affairs of education officers. Since 1978, this responsibility has been taken over by a related organization, the Association of Education Officers, membership of which is open to members of the Society.

Society of Teachers Opposed to Physical Punishment (STOPP)

A **pressure group**, as its title clearly indicates, to abolish the use of physical punishment in schools. Since its foundation in 1968 it has attempted, so far without success, to persuade Parliament to pass legislation on this point. The Society, which is controlled by teachers but with parental membership, has, however, made some headway, as a

number of **LEAs** have banned **corporal punishment** in their schools. (*See also* **discipline**.)

sociology of education

Sociology has been defined as the study of man in society, though it has often been pointed out that much depends on whether the emphasis is placed on man or society: in other words, some sociological perspectives (the more optimistic and humanistic) stress the importance of human freedom which is potentially constrained by imperfect social institutions; others (more pessimistic and positivist) stress the innate selfishness of human beings and the need for this egotism to be moderated and controlled by society. Both these extreme views, and the range in between, are represented in the sociology of education. Many of the most famous sociologists have been particularly concerned with education: Emile Durkheim (1858–1917), for example, lectured and wrote about education throughout his career (as in his *Education and Society*; *Moral Education*; *The Evolution of Educational Thought*.) Education is not just another area which sociologists can take or leave as they wish (almost any topic *could* be treated by sociologists – even the sociology of stamp collecting). Education is an important social institution which cannot be ignored by sociologists. In England, one of the dominant concerns of the sociology of education was the influence of social class on educational opportunity; this stemmed from work on 'political arithmetic' in the 1930s, and continued wtih the post-war studies of social mobility (*see* Jean Floud et al., *Social Class and Educational Opportunity*,

Heinemann, 1956). By the 1970s, a more radical sociology of education was beginning to emerge (*see* M. F. D. Young, *Knowledge and Control*, Collier Macmillan, 1971). This 'new wave' sociology of education criticized traditional sociologists for 'taking' problems rather than 'making' them; for example, assuming that the problem of working-class underachievement was a problem located in their background, rather than one caused by the way teachers and schools defined **knowledge** and constructed **curriculum**. (*See also* **labelling**, **paradigm**, **phenomenology**, **reification**, **self-fulfilling prophecy**.)

P. ROBINSON, *Perspectives on the Sociology of Education: An Introduction*, Routledge and Kegan Paul, 1981

spatial ability

The kind of reasoning which manifests itself as the ability to see relationships between objects in space or occupying space. Individuals possessing high spatial ability will find it easier to read maps, find their way in unfamiliar territory, or do jigsaw puzzles and other manipulative tasks. Spatial ability is measured in some tests of general intelligence; there are also specific tests of spatial ability sometimes used for **vocational guidance**. (*See also* **intelligence**, **intelligence tests**, **verbal reasoning**.)

I. P. HOWARD, *Human Visual Orientation*, Wiley, Chichester, 1982

special agreement school

A type of **voluntary school**, usually secondary, where the **LEA** pays, by special agreement with a denominational interest, from a half to three-quarters of the cost of building a school or enlarging an existing one. Two-thirds of the **governors** are appointed by the voluntary body, the remainder by the LEA. The LEAs control the teaching staff and the governors are responsible for religious instruction in the school. (*See also* **religious education**, **voluntary aided school**, **voluntary controlled school**.)

special educational needs

The concept of special educational needs has developed since the 1944 Education Act's definition of 'disability of mind or body'. It has come to be recognized that special educational needs should be based on educational and developmental considerations rather than on purely medical ones. In 1978, the **Warnock Report** concluded that special educational need was a relative concept, a sentiment echoed in the 1981 Education Act: 'a child has "special educational needs" if he has a learning difficulty which calls for special educational provision to be made for him.' The Act recommended that **assessment** should include educational, psychological and medical components. Duties were placed on LEAs and schools to identify a secure provision for a wide range of special educational needs. Parents were also to be consulted when decisions about their children's special needs were being taken and on the choice of provision to meet these needs. (*See also* **exceptional children**, **giftedness**, **integration**, **parents and education**, **special school**.)

L. CLUNIES-ROSS and S. WIMHURST, *The Right Balance. Provision for Slow Learners in Secondary Schools*, NFER-Nelson, 1983

J. WELTON et al., *Meeting Special Educational Needs. The 1981 Education Act and its Implications*, Bedford Way Papers 12, Institute of Education, London, 1982

Special Place system

Because of the economic situation prevailing, Lord Irwin, then **President of the Board of Education**, issued Circular 1421 in September 1932 which introduced a means test for all entrants to secondary schools. Remission of fees was to be available according to family circumstances. Open competition replaced the existing condition that candidates should have been previously in attendance at a **public elementary school**. The name of the award was changed from **Free Place** to Special Place. This system continued until the time of the 1944 Education Act when all places at maintained secondary schools became free. (*See also* **'eleven plus' examination**.)

P. B. BALLARD, 'The Special Place Examination', in M. SADLER (ed.), *International Institute Examinations Enquiry. Essays on Examinations*, Macmillan, 1936

special school

Special schools are provided by **LEAs** and voluntary organizations for groups of children who have **special educational needs** where ordinary schools have not developed resources for meeting these needs. Some schools are boarding placements and others provide education on a daytime only basis. Until the 1981 Education Act, children were classified into categories and special schools made a response to one type of categorized child. The size of

teaching group, **pupil teacher ratios** and curriculum styles are some of the special requirements prescribed for the management of special schools as outlined in Regulations and **Circulars** from the **DES**. (*See also* **assessment**, **educationally subnormal**, **school psychological service**.)

W. SWANN, *The Practice of Special Education*, Blackwell and Open University Press, 1981

S. TOMLINSON, *Educational Subnormality*, Routledge and Kegan Paul, 1981

Spens Report

The Report of the Consultative Committee of the Board of Education on Secondary Education with special reference to Grammar Schools and Technical High Schools, issued in 1938, dealt with their reorganization and interrelation. Basing its findings on psychological evidence then available, the Committee stated that the **tripartite** division of secondary education into **grammar**, **technical** and **modern schools** corresponded to pupils' abilities and aptitudes and that expansion should take place on this basis. Transfer of pupils as well as parity of esteem between the schools was recommended. The **multilateral school** was not favoured. The report considered the **curriculum** appropriate for such a tripartite system and also recommended that the **school leaving age** should be raised to 16. (*See also* **Norwood Report**, **Secondary Education For All**.)

Report of the Consultative Committee of the Board of Education on Secondary Education with Special Reference to Grammar Schools and Technical High Schools, HMSO, 1938

J. SIMON, 'On the Shaping of the Spens Report on Secondary Education, 1933–38: An Inside View', *British Journal of Educational Studies*, Part 1, Vol. 25, No. 1, 1977; Part 2, Vol. 25, No. 2, 1977

spiral curriculum
See **curriculum: spiral curriculum**.

split site
A school or college which is situated on more than one site. Such an arrangement causes many problems, both organizationally and educationally, for staff and students. (*See also* **campus**.)

staff meeting
A meeting of the staff or department of an educational institution to discuss matters concerned with the activities of the department or institution, such as **curriculum planning** and **timetabling**. The frequency of such meetings and the length of the agenda varies from place to place. (*See also* **head of department**.)

staff : student ratio (SSR)
The ratio between the number of teachers and the number of students in a university, college or school. In **higher education** the average SSR is one teacher to ten students, but the range is very wide from one subject to another and from one institution to another. (*See also* **pupil : teacher ratio**.)

standard deviation
A term used in statistics to indicate the measure of variability among the values of a frequency distribution. For example, when indicating the range or the scatter of scores from the mean or average, it is sometimes convenient to express the extent of scatter in terms of standard deviations. When discussing a range of scores it is rarely sufficient to know only the average or mean score; it is also important to know what the standard deviation or 'scatter' of marks is. (*See also* **standardized**, **Z scores**.)

standardized
1. Standardized marks or scores in a test would mean that they had been adjusted in such a way as to make them comparable with scores from a different test, perhaps by reference to a given mean and **standard deviation**, or by use of **Z scores**.

2. A standardized test is one that has been systematically piloted and then modified in order to ensure that it is both **valid** and **reliable**. Standardized tests would have norms which have been carefully established. It would also be standardized in the sense of having unambiguous written procedures.

T. KELLAGHAN, G. F. MADAUS and P. W. AIRASIAN, *The Effects of Standardized Testing*, Nijhoff, Kluwer Academic Publishers Group, London, 1982

W. A. MEHRENS and I. J. LEHMAN, *Standardized Tests in Education,* Holt, Rinehart and Winston, 1980

standards
1. The late-nineteenth-century term referring to stages in the **elementary school**. After the Revised Code of 1862, the work of **elementary schools** was divided into six Standards. Pupils began Standard 1 roughly at the age of six and, given normal attainment, passed through

the other five Standards year by year. Before progressing from Standard 1 to Standard 2, pupils would be tested (on a very narrow and rigid curriculum) to ensure that the required knowledge had been satisfactorily mastered. Later, in 1882, Standard 7 was introduced.

2. All educational institutions have 'standards' in the sense of a level of quality of work below which they do not wish to fall, and would probably wish to raise. In secondary schools, standards are said to be maintained by means of external or public examinations. National standards are thus imposed upon individual institutions. In universities, standards are maintained by a combination of examinations (local not national) which are moderated in terms of standards by the system of **external examiners**. One of the debates about standards in the 1970s and 1980s concerned reading in primary schools and the lower forms of secondary schools. It was partly with this in view that the **Assessment of Performance Unit** was instituted. (*See also* **National Council for Educational Standards, Yellow Book**.)

A. FINCH and P. SCRIMSHAW (eds), *Standards, Schooling and Education*, Hodder and Stoughton, 1981

statement
The 1981 Education Act provides a legal appeal system for children with **special educational needs**. All **LEAs** have a general duty to identify those children whose special needs call for the authority to determine the special educational provision that should be made for them. The process of identifying and assessing special needs is left to LEAs, who decide on the appropriate provision. This decision taken by an LEA to accept or reject responsibility is known as making a statement. There are procedures for parents to appeal against the local authority's decision. (*See also* **remedial education, school psychological service, special school**.)

ADVISORY CENTRE FOR EDUCATION, *Education Act 1981: The Law on Special Education. A Summary*, 1982

State school
Refers to publicly maintained schools wholly or partly administered by **LEAs**, as distinct from **independent schools**.

statutory instrument
A form of delegated legislation, under an order or regulation by the Queen in Council or one of her ministers, which has the force of an Act of Parliament. Statutory instruments must be laid before Parliament before coming into operation. (*See also* **Parliamentary Papers**.)

streaming
The assigning of pupils to classes on the basis of general ability. The most able pupils are in one stream, the less able in the next and so on. The number of streams depends on the size of the year group. Streamed classes usually stay together for the majority of subjects. It has been shown that streaming affects teachers' judgements of children's abilities and brings about a '**self-fulfilling prophecy**'. NFER surveys found that 50 per cent of large **primary schools** used streaming in

1963 but only 2 per cent employed this form of organization in 1980. There is some evidence that a form of streaming for the basic subjects is becoming more prevalent in primary schools. (*See also* **labelling**, **mixed ability grouping**, **setting**, **unstreaming**.)

J. C. BARKER LUNN, *Streaming in the Primary School*, NFER, 1970

K. POSTLETHWAITE and C. DENTON, *Streams for the Future? The Final Report of the Banbury Enquiry*, Pubansco, Banbury, 1978

student

1. Formerly a term reserved for those pursuing a course of study in an institution of **further** or **higher education**, for example, at a **university** or **college of education**. It is now often used interchangeably in schools with 'pupil'.

2. The non-ecclesiastical equivalent of **Fellow** at Christ Church, Oxford; also for those holding endowed studentships at either Oxford or Cambridge.

Students' Union

A society formed by students of a college or other institution to promote social activities and provide recreational facilities. In many colleges, representatives of the Union serve on official committees which are concerned with academic affairs. At Oxford and Cambridge, the Union is a club with well-known debating societies. (*See also* **National Union of Students**.)

student-teacher

A person undertaking a course of training to become a teacher. The term is also used to indicate the status of such a person whilst undertaking **teaching practice** in an institution. (*See also* **teacher tutor**.)

study leave

A period of leave, usually with pay, made available to teachers in schools or in further education or higher education to attend professional or academic courses. One of the ideas behind **recurrent education** has been the extension of this privilege to the whole population – hence 'paid study leave' as an area of negotiation for trades unions, especially within the **European Economic Community**. (*See also* **sabbatical**.)

study skills

Ways in which students can become more effective in their studies by becoming aware of the learning processes involved. Study skills may be equated with learning examination techniques, though this is a rather narrow interpretation. Courses in study skills should encourage independent learning by presenting to the student information, in a workshop situation and/or by lectures, on some of the following: note-taking, drafting, problem-solving, contributing to group discussion, systematic revision for examinations, and ways of finding out information. Study skills are now being taught in schools and places of further and higher education and are particularly important for those involved in **distance learning**. (*See also* **correspondence course**, **Open University**, **PICKUP**.)

R. TABBENER and J. ALLMAN, *Study Skills at 16+*, NFER Research in Progress, No. 4, NFER, 1981

subculture

Every society has a **culture**. By definition all members of that society will share in some of the aspects of that culture. But within the whole society there may be groups who are identifiable by distinctly different values and beliefs and behaviour patterns. In such cases it would be appropriate to talk of a subculture. In the UK it is possible to identify, for example, a working-class subculture and the subcultures of certain ethnic minorities. It is disputed whether there is an identifiable teenage subculture. (*See also* **minority group**.)

summative evaluation

See **formative evaluation/summative evaluation**.

Sunday School

The Sunday School movement is usually associated with Robert Raikes of Gloucester, who from 1780 established classes for children of the poor who were in employment during the rest of the week. The movement, which saw its task as the inculcation of religion and the elimination of radical ideologies, quickly spread and was eagerly taken up by religious organizations. A century after the movement began over 5¾ million children in England were attending these chools.

M. DICK, 'The Myth of the Working-Class Sunday School', *History of Education*, Vol. 9, No. 1, 1980

T. W. LAQUEUR, *Religion and Respectability, Sunday Schools and Working Class Culture 1780–1850*, Yale University Press, 1976

supply teacher

Teachers employed by an **LEA** to fill vacancies caused by the absence of a regular member of staff. The periods of attachment to a school may vary from one day to longer periods, although some authorities are encouraging half-day employment where possible because of financial constraints.

Swann Report

A committee was set up under the chairmanship of Sir Michael Swann in December 1965 to investigate the shortage of science and engineering graduates. The report published in 1968 showed that the best science and engineering graduates tended to remain at university rather than embarking upon a career in industry. The report was also concerned with the lack of good science graduates entering school teaching. The report recommended some new kinds of postgraduate training, emphasizing links between the academic world and the world of industry. Suggestions were also made about encouraging scientists to make contributions to the work of schools. The report correctly diagnosed at least two major problems, but no solution emerged as a result. (*See also* **Dainton Report, Finniston Report**.)

Working Group on Manpower for Scientific Growth: The Flow into Employment of Scientists, Engineers and Technologists, HMSO, 1968, Cmnd 3760

syllabus

An outline, more or less detailed, of the ground to be covered in a course. The difference between syllabus and **curriculum** is not always clear, but the following distinctions might be helpful. The smallest unit in terms of curriculum planning would be an individual **lesson**; this would be part of a scheme of work covering several lessons (perhaps half a term or a term's work). The scheme would be

related to a syllabus, perhaps a whole year's work.

symbolic
See **enactive, iconic and symbolic**.

T

Tameside case
In 1975, the Metropolitan Borough of Tameside, Lancashire, which had a Labour majority, put forward a plan to the **Secretary of State for Education and Science**, under Section 13 of the 1944 Education Act, for abolishing the borough's five **grammar schools**. This proposal, and the substitution of a **comprehensive school** system, was approved by the Secretary of State in November 1975. At the local elections held in the following May, the preservation of the grammar schools became an issue for the local Conservative Party and they were subsequently returned to power. In June 1976, the Authority informed the **DES** that the 1975 plan was no longer part of the Authority's policy. The five grammar schools were to continue alongside three comprehensives. When the Secretary of State sought a writ of mandamus to compel the Authority to carry out its original plan, the Law Lords concluded that the Secretary had acted beyond his powers in the matter. 'Tameside' thus became associated with local autonomy in education at a time when centralization appeared to be increasing.

K. ALEXANDER, and V. WILLIAMS, 'Judicial Review of Educational Poli-

cy: The Teaching of Tameside', *British Journal of Educational Studies*, Vol. 26, No. 3, 1978

Taunton Report
As a result of the two Royal Commissions, **Newcastle**, on elementary education, and **Clarendon**, on nine leading endowed schools, the Taunton Commission was appointed in 1864 to examine the schools not within the scope of these Commissions. It included amongst its members W. E. Forster, T. D. Acland, Edward Baines, Frederick Temple, then head of Rugby, and Lord Lyttelton. Investigations were carried out into some 800 endowed schools, as well as private and **proprietary schools**. The Commissioners revealed widespread inefficiency and misappropriation of funds. It recommended in its report, published in 1868, that a system of efficient secondary schools corresponding to the three grades of society should be created. The *first grade* should prepare boys for university, with a curriculum of Classics, modern languages, mathematics and natural sciences. The leaving age was 18. The *second grade* was to cater for boys preparing for the professions, business and the Army. Though Latin was included in the curriculum, most of the time was to be devoted to modern subjects as 'the minds of the learners should be perpetually brought back to concrete examples instead of being perpetually exercised

in abstractions'. Boys would leave at about 16 years. The *third grade* was considered the most urgent because of the large numbers of pupils involved, the sons of small tenant farmers, tradesmen and superior artisans. With a leaving age of 14, the schools were recommended to concentrate on the basics of 'very good reading, very good writing, very good arithmetic', as well as some practical subjects. Although provision for **girls' education** was stated to be grossly inadequate, no specific recommendations were made for its extension. Other important recommendations made included the establishment of a 'scholarship ladder' for needy pupils, an independent Examinations Council, inspection of the three grades of schools and the creation of a central authority for secondary education with provincial bodies responsible for curricula. The Endowed Schools Act 1869 omitted many of these recommendations. An **Endowed Schools Commission** was appointed with the task of supervising the re-endowments of the schools' charitable trusts and establishing 'grades' of schools in a given area. (*See also* **Charity Commission**, **grades**, **Woodard schools**.)

R. L. ARCHER, *Secondary Education in the Nineteenth Century*, Cambridge University Press, 1921, reprinted Cass, London, 1966

Report of the Schools Inquiry Commission, P.P. 1867–8, xxviii

taxonomy
Classification, especially in relation to general laws or principles of classification. In education the word is most usually associated with the

work of B. S. Bloom and his *Taxonomy of Educational Objectives*, Longman, 1956

Taylor Report
A Committee of Enquiry under the chairmanship of Mr Tom Taylor was set up in 1975 to review the arrangements for the management and government of **primary** and **secondary schools** in England and Wales. Its report was published in 1977. Of its recommendations, the most striking were that governors should have more involvement in the school curriculum and that governing bodies should consist of four equal elements – **LEA**, teachers, parents and local community representatives. Teachers' union reaction was not favourable; see for example the **National Union of Teachers'** pamphlet *Partnership in Education* (1978). The report still awaits its full implementation, although some recommendations, such as the requirement that schools should have at least two parent governors, were embodied in the 1980 Education Act. (*See also* **parents and education**.)

Report of the Committee of Enquiry: A New Partnership for Our Schools, HMSO, 1977

teachers' associations
Bodies organized on a national scale to safeguard the interests, salaries, working conditions and welfare of their members. They also promote views on educational issues and consult with national and local government and other organizations; they are represented on many bodies concerned with formulating educational policies. There is no one body which speaks for the whole of the

teaching profession in the UK. Schools are represented by the **National Union of Teachers** (NUT), the **National Association of Schoolmasters and the Union of Women Teachers** (NAS/UWT), the **Assistant Masters and Mistresses Association** (AMMA) and the **Professional Association of Teachers** (PAT). Headteachers are separately represented by the **National Association of Headteachers** (NAHT) and the **Secondary Heads Association** (SHA). In further and higher education, there is the **National Association of Teachers in Further and Higher Education** (NATFHE), the **Association of Polytechnic Teachers** (APT) and the **Association of University Teachers** (AUT). (*See also* **Burnham Committee, General Teaching Council, qualified teacher status**.)

R. D. COATES, *Teachers' Unions and Interest Group Politics*, Cambridge University Press, 1972

P. H. J. H. GOSDEN, *The Evolution of a Profession: a study of the contribution of teachers' associations to the development of school teaching as a professional occupation*, Blackwell, Oxford, 1972

teachers' centres

The **McNair Report** (1944) envisaged educational centres within the new **Area Training Organizations** where teachers at all levels could meet to exchange opinions on a range of matters. With the development of the Nuffield Mathematics and Science Project in the 1960s, involving regional trials, pilot centres were set up. The creation of the **Schools Council** at this time provided a stimulus, as their field officers were given as one of their tasks the spread of teachers' centres. Schools Council *Working Paper 2*, issued in 1965, suggested that centres could be started in spare accommodation in existing buildings; two years later, *Working Paper 10* emphasized that their focus should be **curriculum development**. Such centres multiplied rapidly; by the mid 1970s there were more than 500 in England and Wales, though a number have since closed. No one pattern of organization has emerged. Some are based in colleges, schools or independent buildings in an authority and they cater for a variety of purposes: **in-service education** and training, **curriculum development**, as **resource centres**, as information providers and as social centres for teachers.

C. REDKNAP, *Focus on Teachers' Centres*, NFER, 1977

D. WEINDLING, M. I. REID with P. DAVIS, *Teachers' Centres: a Focus for In-Service Education?* Schools Council Working Paper 74, Methuen Educational, 1983

teachers' salaries

LEAs pay the salary scales agreed by the **Burnham Committtee** for teachers in schools and further education institutions. There are five salary scales for school teachers, Scales 1 to 4 and **senior teacher**. New entrants mainly start on Scale 1 with four extra increments for **graduates**. The number of posts available at Scales 2 and 4 and Senior Teacher depends on the number of pupils in the school and their age distribution. The same applies to the salaries of **deputy heads** and **heads**, who are paid on a separate scale. Further education has five salary scales – Lecturer I and II, Senior Lecturer, Principal Lecturer and Reader. **Heads of Departments**' salary scale is determined by the level of work undertaken and that of the Vice-Principal by the numbers attending the institution. Other extra payments are made: for example, where a post carries special responsibility for teachers in **special schools** and for those whose schools attract **London allowance**.

teacher tutor

Some **university departments of education**, **polytechnics** and other institutions concerned with initial teacher training sometimes involve practising teachers in the work of **student–teachers**, especially for professional aspects of the course and school teaching practice. These part-time tutors, often referred to as teacher tutors, are normally senior and experienced members of staff who may receive a small honorarium for their services. (*See also* **tutor**.)

teaching practice

A period of time during a **student-teacher**'s course devoted to gaining classroom experience. Assessment of performance is carried out by supervisors in conjunction with the school. The length of practice varies according to the type of course, either the **PGCE** or **B.Ed**. routes, undertaken by the student.

E. HADLEY (ed.), *Teaching Practice and the Probationary Year*, Arnold, 1982

teaching style

The ways in which teachers differ in presenting materials to their pupils, in particular the kind of social rela-

tionship established within the classroom. Teaching styles may be categorized in a number of different ways: for example, formal, informal; authoritarian, democratic; didactic, enquiry-based; child-centred, subject-centred. (*See also* **ORACLE**.)

team teaching

A method of teaching where a team of teachers work together with a large number of children. This form of organization is often used where a **project** or a **topic** is being pursued, with individual teachers taking responsibility for particular aspects of the work.

J. J. CLOSE et al., *Team Teaching Experiments*, NFER, 1974

technical college

Term covering institutions providing further education courses, often of a vocational character. The impetus for providing this form of education came in the last quarter of the nineteenth century. Reports, particularly those of the **Devonshire** and **Samuelson Commissions**, and legislation – the Technical Instruction Act, 1889, and the Local Taxation (Customs and Excise) Act, 1890 – led to the founding of many polytechnics or technical institutes and **organized science schools**. After 1902, **LEAs** became responsible for most of this work. Qualifications sought by students ranged from **City and Guilds of London** examinations to **external degrees** of London University, mainly on a part-time basis. The 1944 Education Act made LEAs responsible for the development of further education. In the following year, the **Percy Report** recommended important changes in the ways technical colleges could meet post-war demands in this sector. Circular 305 of 1956 classified technical colleges under four headings: **Colleges of Advanced Technology** (CATs), Regional Colleges, Area Colleges and Local Colleges. The **Robbins Report** (1963) was responsible for the transfer of CATs to the university sector. A White Paper in 1966 recommended the creation of 30 **polytechnics** within the non-university sector. A further change arose from the contraction of teacher training from 1972: some **colleges of education** merged with **FE colleges** to form **colleges or institutes of higher education**. The organization of technical colleges is now very complex: it is often more convenient to refer to the type of course offered, being either **AFE** (advanced further education) or **FE** (further education). (*See also* **Percy Report**, **Science and Art Department**.)

A. MATTERSON, *Polytechnics and Colleges*, Longman, 1981

technical high and secondary technical schools

The **Spens Report** (1938) which paid special reference to **grammar** and technical schools, acknowledged that the education of boys and girls beyond the age of 11+ had 'ceased to correspond with the actual structure of modern society and with the economic facts of the situation'. It therefore proposed a new type of higher school of technical character, distinct from the traditional grammar school, offering a broadly based general course combined with specialized studies having a vocational significance. Entrance was to be by means of the selective examination for grammar schools. After the 1944 Education Act, a number of **LEAs** built secondary technical schools, which provided courses of between two and five years' duration. Technical high schools provided courses of from five to seven years' duration. Neither type of school achieved parity with grammar schools (in the eyes of parents) and most of them disappeared with the reorganization of secondary education following the issue of Circular 10/65. (*See also* **'eleven plus' examination**.)

REESE EDWARDS, *The Secondary Technical School*, University of London Press, 1960

Technical Instruction Act (1889)

The decline in British industrial supremacy which was observed at the 1867 Paris Exhibition was attributed to the lack of a good system of industrial education. The report of the **Samuelson Commission** led to the passing of the Technical Instruction Act in 1889. This Act allowed county and county borough councils, established by the Local Government Act of the previous year, to levy a penny rate for **technical education**. Further income became available in 1890 with the so-called 'whisky money', the proceeds of increased duty on beer and spirits. Technical Instruction Committees could be formed by Councils for the purpose of applying the funds. The most powerful example was the London Technical Education Board, which played a leading part in furthering secondary as well as technical education. (*See also* **'eleven plus' examination**.)

P. H. J. H. GOSDEN, 'Technical Instruction Committees', in History of Education Society, *Studies in the Government and Control of Education Since 1860*, Methuen, 1970

Technical Instruction Committees

See **Technical Instruction Act, (1889).**

Technician Education Council (TEC)

Created in 1973 by the **Secretary of State for Education and Science** as a result of the **Haslegrave Report**'s recommendations, the TEC is responsible for the design, validation, examination and provision of programmes below degree level in technician education in England and Wales. (The Scottish equivalent is called SCOTEC.) The numerous awards available before the Council was set up were rationalized. Four qualifications – diploma and higher diploma, and certificate and higher certificate – are now available to students in the fields of engineering, construction and science, and art and design. Validation, assessing and monitoring the awards are in the hands of 20 programme committees. One essential feature of the TEC programmes is a clear statement of **objectives** and each scheme submitted must include, besides a **syllabus**, the proposed **assessment** procedures. 'Complementary Studies', i.e. general and communication studies, form at least 15% of a programme and are assessable. Courses can be followed on a full- or part-time basis. Higher level courses are devised by colleges and validated by **BEC**. There are also some joint BEC/TEC courses. In 1983, TEC joined with BEC to form the Business and Technician Education Council (BTEC). (*See also* **Higher National Certificate, Ordinary National Certificate.**)

technology

Technology may be defined as 'the application of scientific knowledge to the solution of practical problems'. In education the term is used in two very different ways:

1. It is often alleged that schools have the responsibility for teaching the young about technology and its uses in society, but that they often do this in a very incomplete and unsatisfactory way.

2. *Educational technology* often means no more than visual aids, but it should refer to the techniques and understanding of the whole process of learning as well as the 'hardware'. (*See also* **audio visual aids, CAL, CAMOL, new information technology.**)

DES, *Technology in Schools: Developments in Craft, Design and Technology Departments*, HMSO, 1982

term

The **academic year** of schools and colleges in the UK is normally divided into three periods, autumn, spring and summer, though some universities still use older names, e.g. Oxford terms are Michaelmas, Hilary and Trinity. The lengths of both school and college terms vary, though the former are usually of longer duration. (*See also* **half-term, semester, vacation.**)

tertiary college

A college catering for all post 16 education, full- and part-time, in an area. It brings under one roof both the range of courses found in normal **sixth forms** in schools and the vocational and technical courses offered in **further education.** (*See also* **college of further education, Macfarlane Report, sixth form college.**)

A. B. COTTERELL and E. W. HELEY (eds), *Tertiary. A radical approach to post-compulsory education*, Thornes, Cheltenham, 1980

thesis

A treatise, based on research, submitted for an award or qualification, such as an M.A. or Ph.D. It is similar to a **dissertation**, though a thesis may be considered as contributing original knowledge to a **discipline**. (*See also* **graduate, postgraduate, viva.**)

Thompson Report

The Thompson Committee was set up by the Government in January 1981 to review the provision of the **Youth Service** in England and to consider whether existing resources could be employed more effectively. The chairman was Mr Alan Thompson, formerly a **DES** official. The report, issued in October 1982, was critical of the Service, in terms of its unequal availability, lack of co-ordination between the statutory and the voluntary sectors, and unclear objectives. It recommended that a DES minister should co-ordinate all youth affairs, that **LEA**s be given a statutory responsibility to provide facilities for those between 11 and 21 and that the Youth Service be funded at a high level. The report stated that the primary need of people in this age group is social education rather than recreational facilities, and that the Youth Service should co-operate with schools in devising curricula for adolescents. (*See also* **Albemarle Report, McNair Report.**)

Experience and Participation. Report of the Review Group of the Youth Service in England, presented by the Secretary of State for Education and Science, HMSO, 1982, Cmnd 8686

Thomson Report

One of the **Prime Minister's Reports**. The Committee on the position of Natural Science in Great Britain was appointed in August 1916 and reported two years later. The powerful lobbying of the Association of Public School Science Masters, discontented with the low status of science in public schools, had been instrumental in establishing the Committee. Amongst its members were Michael Sadler, Graham Balfour and its chairman, Sir J. J. Thomson. The report recommended that science should be included in the general course of education for all pupils up to the age of 16 and that increasing attention should be given to the teaching of science in girls' schools. Detailed suggestions were made for a balanced **curriculum** for pupils wishing to pursue the subject to 18. Not less than one-half or more than two-thirds of the school week was to be occupied with science and the rest should be spent on literary studies. The report was reissued in 1927. (*See also* **girls' education.**)

The Report of the Committee on the Position of Natural Science in the Educational System of Great Britain: Natural Science in Education, HMSO, 1918, reprinted 1927

three Rs

The Revised Code of 1862 altered the system of Government grants to schools. The money which had been paid to certificated teachers was now given to the **managers**, who paid the teachers according to the average attendance of pupils and their achievements at examinations conducted by **HMI** – hence the title of this system, 'payment by results'. The subjects tested were the three Rs – reading, writing and arithmetic – with plain needlework for girls. This system led to great pressure by teachers on pupils and at the same time led to a narrowing of the curriculum. From 1867 other subjects were allowed to be offered for grant purposes and a liberalizing of the Code continued until the end of the century. (*See also* **basic skills, grants, monitorial system, Newcastle Commission, overpressure in education**.)

P. H. J. H. GOSDEN, *How They Were Taught*, Blackwell, Oxford, 1969

timetabling

Refers to the grouping of pupils, **curriculum** and allocation of teachers in an institution. Traditionally, timetables explained *when* things happened rather than reflected the aims of the organization. A more analytical approach to planning in schools and resource allocation is now favoured which takes into account types of pupil grouping and curriculum philosophy. (*See also* **curriculum: hidden curriculum, flexible grouping, integrated day, staff meeting, syllabus**.)

K. JOHNSON, *Timetabling*, Hutchinson, 1980

R. SIMPER, *A Practical Guide to Timetabling*, Ward Lock Educational, 1980

topic work

A method of teaching, particularly in **primary schools**, which aims at developing children's conceptual development through a study of a particular topic over a period of days or weeks. Some topics may attempt to cover the whole curriculum, but many are confined to subjects such as history, geography and social studies. (*See also* **assignment, project**.)

S. GUNNING, D. GUNNING and J. WILSON, *Topic Teaching in the Primary School*, Croom Helm, 1981

training college

Dating from the nineteenth century, the training college provided courses of training for teachers, mainly for those intending to work in primary schools with some offering courses for secondary school teaching. They were provided either by **LEAs** or voluntary bodies. Courses were of two years' duration up to 1960 when they were increased to three. The **Robbins Report** recommended that their name should be changed to **colleges of education**. This title was adopted in the mid 1960s. (*See also* **Area Training Organization, Committee of the Privy Council on Education, McNair Report, Normal college, Pelham Report, pupil teacher system**.)

D. E. LOMAX (ed.), *The Education of Teachers in Britain*, Wiley, 1973

Training Opportunities Scheme (TOPS)

An adult retraining programme for the unemployed aged 19 or over, organized by the **Manpower Ser-**

vices Commission. TOPS courses provided by **further education colleges** give students skills for a range of occupations, including engineering and secretarial and office work. The programme, which included 75,000 youths in 1980, is likely to be reduced in view of the difficulty of providing employment at the end of courses. These courses are run in skills centres, which also provide some of the industrial training for **YOPs**.

transition from primary to secondary school

In most, but not all, **LEAs** there is a transition at the age of 11 from **primary school** to **secondary school** for the majority of pupils. This can create problems of two kinds. First, there is in many authorities a lack of continuity between the **curriculum** of the primary school and that of the secondary school; second, the régime of the secondary school is likely to be much more formal and puzzling for the 11-year-old than the régime of the primary school, where probably the pupil had only one teacher for all subjects rather than a different teacher for six or seven periods every day. Partly to counteract the difficulties of this transition, **middle schools** were set up by some authorities, and at one stage it was suggested that primary and secondary schools should pay attention to the 'middle years' so that greater continuity would be achieved. The **Schools Council** was associated with this policy in the late 1960s and early 1970s. (*See also* **Great Debate, Plowden Report**.)

M. GALTON and J. WILLCOCKS, *Moving from the Primary Classroom*, Routledge and Kegan Paul, 1983

triangulation

A research technique, particularly associated with the work of John Elliott at the Cambridge Institute of Education, in which **evaluation** is carried out by means of a threefold process. The teacher has a view of what he wants to do (and of how successfully he has achieved it). This may be different from the view or views of pupils; in addition, an independent, neutral observer may have yet further views. The hypothesis is that by open discussion of these three points of view the teachers' performance and competence may be improved. Triangulation in this sense is part of the 'teacher as researcher' model. (*See also* **participant observation**.)

J. ELLIOTT and D. PARTINGTON (eds), *Three Points of View in the Classroom*, Cambridge Ford Teaching Project, 1975

tripartite system

Refers to the threefold classification of secondary schools postulated by the **Spens Report** in 1938, i.e. **grammar, technical** and **modern schools**. Later, in 1943, the **Norwood Report**, basing its findings on psychological evidence, claimed that there were three types of minds corresponding to the schools – the academic, the applied scientific, and those with the ability to handle concrete things rather than ideas. No mention of types of schools was made in the 1944 Education Act; but **LEAs** were allowed to establish various kinds of secondary schools with selection tests determining pupil allocation. (*See also* **'eleven plus' examination, multilateral school**.)

Tripos

An **honours** degree course of study at Cambridge University. The name derived from the three-legged stool on which medieval **undergraduates** used to sit. A student must pass two Tripos examinations to qualify for a B.A. The majority of Triposes are in two parts: it is possible for the student to take both parts of the same Tripos or one Tripos followed by Part 1 or 2 of a different Tripos.

trivium

The three 'arts' of the seven liberal arts – grammar, logic and rhetoric – in the school curriculum of the Middle Ages; the remaining four were called the **quadrivium**. (*See also* **liberal studies**.)

truancy centres

An attempt to deal with the growing problem of truancy in schools. In the **ILEA** alone there are 146 officially sponsored and voluntarily run centres. They are small units with a high staff-pupil ratio, which help children with their learning difficulties so that eventually they can return to their own school. In the case of older pupils, the curriculum is directed towards equipping them for employment.

truant school

From the time of the Industrial Schools Act, 1857, truants could be sent to **industrial schools**, but persistent truants would go to truant schools. These were administered by both lay and denominational bodies. Military drill featured prominently in the curriculum and the régime was deliberately harsh. Children attended these schools for a short period of time and were then returned to their schools. (See also **drill**.)

tutor

1. A person responsible for the supervision of students' academic work either in higher or further education or at school.

2. A private teacher, who is employed to coach an individual usually in order to achieve success in an examination.

3. A member of college or university staff designated as adviser to students.

4. A person, often a form teacher, who acts as counsellor to a group of pupils.

5. College students or older secondary pupils who help young children in schools with their work. (*See also* **counselling**, **house system**, **teacher tutor**, **tutorial**.)

K. BLACKBURN, *The Tutor*, Heinemann Educational, 1975

L. BUTTON, *Group Tutoring for the Form Teacher in the Lower Secondary School*, Hodder and Stoughton, 1981

tutorial

A meeting between a **tutor** and one or more students frequently based on a paper or essay submitted by a student. Such meetings normally take place throughout the student's course. Tutorials are practically universal in institutions of further and higher education. (*See also* **seminar**.)

TVEI

See **New Technical and Vocational Education Initiative**.

U

underachiever

A pupil whose performance at school is measurably or in some other way clearly below what would be expected from his known ability. Underachievers probably fall into at least two main groups: first, individual pupils whose school record does not match their performance on **IQ tests**; second, groups of students (e.g. working-class children or children from ethnic minorities) whose work is generally below average, when there is no reason to believe that their **intelligence** level is below average. (*See also* **intelligence test, multi-cultural or multi-ethnic education, self-concept, self-image**.)

A. O. ROSS, *Learning Disability: the Unrealized Potential*, McGraw-Hill, 1977

undergraduate

A student following a course leading to a **first degree**. (*See also* **graduate, postgraduate, Universities Central Council on Admissions, university entry requirements**.)

UNESCO (United Nations Educational, Social and Cultural Organization)

One of the subdivisions of the United Nations, founded in 1946 to promote international, cultural and educational co-operation. It has its own constitution, member states and budget. Its permanent headquarters are in Paris. It is administered by a Director-General and an international Civil Service of about 800. Member states are required to establish nationally based commissions to advise UNESCO on policy and to encourage participation in activities that flow from UNESCO programmes. UNESCO-sponsored activities can be classified as follows: (1) emergency aid and reconstruction; (2) advancement of knowledge; (3) promotion of human welfare; (4) the encouragement of international understanding.

Unified Vocational Preparation (UVP)

Special courses of broad education and training in practical job skills for young people in which there was no provision for further education and training. The UVP programme, begun in 1976 and sponsored by the DES, was mainly funded by the **Manpower Services Commission**. Courses were organized by employers or colleges. Most of the 6,000 trainees on courses in 1981 were drawn from a fairly narrow range of industries, in particular, retailing. It was superseded by the **Youth Training Scheme** in September 1983. (*See also* **vocational preparation**.)

M. J. WRAY, S. HILL and J. COLLOBEAR, *Employer Involvement in Schemes of Unified Vocational Preparation*, NFER-Nelson, 1982

uniform, school

A survey carried out by the Price Committee in England and Wales in 1977 showed that school uniform was the norm in all **grammar schools**, in 92 per cent of **comprehensive schools** and 80 per cent of other types of secondary schools. It is left to **heads** and **governors** to decide on the design of uniforms and up to what age they should be worn. Some education authorities, notably Humberside, Leicestershire and Sheffield, have abolished compulsory school uniform.

universities: history of

The oldest universities in the UK are Oxford and Cambridge, both founded in the thirteenth century. Scotland established three universities, at Aberdeen, St Andrews and Glasgow, in the fifteenth century and one at Edinburgh a hundred years later. Durham was one of the first of the universities to be built in the nineteenth century (1832), closely following the **Oxbridge** pattern. At almost the same time, in London, a secular institution, University College (1826), was founded with an Anglican rival, King's College (1829), which stressed religious instruction. The University of London was established in 1836 as a degree-awarding body to affiliated colleges in various parts of the kingdom. The provincial **civic universities** of the second half of the century were the result of local benefactors who looked to a science-based curriculum and the **university extension** movement, which created a demand for higher education, for women as well as men. Owens' College, Manchester, was the first, opened in 1851. Between 1874 and 1902, colleges were founded at Birmingham, Bristol, Exeter, Leeds, Liverpool, Nottingham, Reading, Sheffield and Southampton. All were eventually granted full university status. During this period, the University of Wales, a federal body, came into existence. Between the two World Wars, only two new colleges were founded – at Hull and Leicester. After 1945, there was a dramatic expansion of university provision. The University College of North Staffordshire at Keele was the first in 1949, followed in the years 1961–5 by East Anglia, Essex, Kent, Lancaster, Sussex, Warwick and York; in 1963, Newcastle became a university in its own right, formerly being associated with Durham. In Scotland, the University of Stirling was founded and Dundee received its Charter in 1967. The final phase of expansion followed the **Robbins Report**'s recommendation that the nine Colleges of Advanced Technology – Aston, Bath, Bradford, Brunel, Chelsea, City, Loughborough, Salford and Surrey – should become full universities, whilst Strathclyde and Heriot-Watt were founded in Scotland and Cardiff in Wales. Northern Ireland has Queen's, Belfast and the New University of Ulster at Coleraine. The only independent university in the UK is the University of Buckingham. Established in 1976, it offers courses for two-year honours degrees. It has been argued that the post-war expansion, from 17 universities in 1945 to 46 at the present time, was too rapid and that more does not necessarily mean better. Nevertheless, the proportion of the population of the UK who go to university is still small and, at a time when reduction in numbers is being made, the demand for entry remains high. (*See also* **federal university, polyversity, university college, university day training college, university extension, University Grants Committee, validation.**)

W. H. G. ARMYTAGE, *Civic Universities*, Benn, 1953

V. H. H. GREEN, *The Universities*, Penguin, 1969

University Central Council on Admissions (UCCA)

The Council was set up in 1961 to handle all applications for entrance to universities in England (except the **Open University** and Buckingham), Scotland, Wales and Northern Ireland. The Council plays no part in the selection of students but forwards candidates' application forms to universities. Up to five universities can be named on the form. An unsuccessful candidate may take advantage of either the Continuing Applications Procedure which provides for further chances (four more universities may be chosen), or the Clearing Scheme, which operates from September in a final attempt to place candidates. The UCCA scheme does not cover **postgraduate** applicants, who apply direct to universities. (*See also* **clearing house**, **entry qualification**, **open admission**, **Open College**, **undergraduate**, **university entry requirements**.)

university college

A college of university rank which is unable to award its own degrees. Most of the **civic universities** were at one time university colleges, but they have since achieved full university status. (*See also* **federal university**, **universities: history of**.)

university day training college

One of the recommendations of the **Cross Report** was that day training colleges should be established in connection with local universities or **university colleges**. The **Education Department**'s Code for 1890 sanctioned this arrangement for training elementary school teachers and fourteen day training departments were opened; the course was to be of three years' duration. As many of the students were reading for **degrees** they were excused from the examination in academic subjects for the teacher's certificate by 1900. A number of chairs were created, the holders of which advanced the development of the education **disciplines**. (*See also* **university department of education**.)

M. SADLER, 'University Day Training Colleges, Their Origin, Growth and Influence in English Education', in *The Department of Education in the University of Manchester, 1890–1911*, Manchester University Press, 1911

university department of education (UDE)

A university department, specializing in teacher education, normally headed by a **professor**. Courses may range from a one-day **in-service** session to those leading to a **higher degree** qualification. UDEs grew out of **university day training colleges**, which were established in 1890 to enable **student-teachers** to follow a three-year course and take a degree if they wished. They were at first called university training departments (UTD), but after the Second World War most had assumed their present nomenclature. Some are called Schools of Education. The largest department in Britain is in the University of London and has the title of **Institute of Education**. (*See also* **in-service education of teachers**, **McNair Report**, **teacher tutor**.)

university entrance requirements

The minimum requirement is normally the possession of at least two **GCE Advanced levels**, though individual departments to which the candidate applies stipulate more detailed achievements before entry is permitted. (The **Open University** however accepts students who do not possess formal qualifications.) Applications are made in the first instance through the **UCCA** scheme, where five choices may be listed. Entry to Oxford and Cambridge is a more complicated procedure. (*See also* **entry qualification**, **open admission**, **undergraduate**.)

university extension

A movement which began in the second half of the last century, mainly the work of James Stuart, a Fellow at Cambridge, which attempted to set up a 'peripatetic university' in towns where none existed. Following the success of his lectures on gravitation in a number of northern towns in 1867, he persuaded Cambridge to found a range of courses in 1873 in the region surrounding the University. Three years later, London University followed and in 1878 so did Oxford. The success of the movement led to the establishment of **university colleges** such as Sheffield and Nottingham; it also brought into prominence the lack of university education provision for women. Today's **extra-mural departments** of universities are another outcome. (*See also* **universities: history of.**)

P. GORDON and J. WHITE, *Philosophers as Educational Reformers. The influence of idealism on British educational thought and practice*, Routledge and Kegan Paul, 1979

B. ROWBOTHAM, 'The Call to University Extension Teaching, 1873–1900'. *University of Brimingham Historical Journal*, Vol. 12, 1968–70

University Grants Committee (UGC)

Established in 1919, the Committee's main terms of reference were and are to 'enquire into the financial needs of university education in the United Kingdom and to advise the government as to the application of any grants that may be made by Parliament towards meeting them'. Since 1964, on the recommendation of the **Robbins Report**, the UGC has become the responsibility of the **Secretary of State for Education and Science**. Members are appointed by the Secretary of State and serve for five years. Only the chairman is a full-time member. The present Committee consists of 20 members; the majority are academics but there are also **headteachers**, representatives from industry and an education officer. Besides the main committee, there are ten subject sub-committees – business and management, biological sciences, agricultural and veterinary, arts, education, physical sciences and technology, mathematical sciences, dental, medical, social studies – and equipment. Each sub-committee visits university departments to assess their work and to exchange information. At the present time, when universities are facing financial difficulties, the role of the UGC in allocating Government funds has been the subject of much debate. (*See also* **National Advisory Board**, **uni-**

versities: **history of, Vice-Chancellor**.)

R. BERDAHL, *British Universities and the State*, University of California and Cambridge University Press, 1959

university training department

See **university department of education**.

unstreaming

This is the product of a diametrically opposite philosophy to **streaming**. Pupils here are randomly assigned for

teaching purposes without reference to ability, or are deliberately placed in **mixed ability groups**. (*See also* **labelling, setting**.)

upper school

Originally, a term reserved for the top forms of a **public** or **grammar school**, it now more commonly refers to those **comprehensive schools** with feeders from **middle** or **lower schools** which admit pupils at 13, 14 or 15 years of age. The post of head of upper school is often an important one in the organizational hierarchy.

V

vacation

A period of time when an education institution is not in session. The major breaks in the UK are at Easter, summer and at Christmas. Formerly, the term was used mainly in connection with universities. (*See also* **academic year, half-term, semester, term**.)

validation

Universities are empowered by their charters to award degrees; other educational institutions such as **polytechnics, colleges of higher education** and **colleges of education**, do not have such a privilege. In order to run degree courses these institutions have to submit formal plans for their courses either to the **CNAA** or to a university which is prepared to 'validate' their courses. During the 1960s and 1970s, there was a swing away from university

validated courses to courses validated by CNAA. The validation procedure normally consists not only of the formal submission of plans, but also visits by the validating authority to the site for detailed discussions with members of staff about the course being offered. Sometimes validation is approved only on condition that certain criteria are met, either in terms of staffing or buildings, particularly library facilities.

validity

An **intelligence test** or examination rarely measures exactly what it is intended to measure. For example, a test of creativity might give results which are superficially plausible but which, on further investigation, turn out to be no more than a test of intelligence. The validity of many tests of attitudes is often called into question: asking students to say what they would do may not be a valid measure of what they would actually do in real life. For contrast, see **reliability**.

verbal reasoning

One aspect of general intelligence. Verbal reasoning tests (often used in the days of eleven plus selection procedures for grammar schools) focused upon this aspect of intelligence rather than **spatial ability**. It is the aspect of intelligence which is most difficult to separate from environmental factors. (*See also* **intelligence test**.)

vertical age grouping

See **family grouping**.

Vice-Chancellor

The Vice-Chancellor is the chief academic and administrative officer of a university. He is often the chairman of many important university committees and is ex-officio member of all of them. He is involved in the appointment of senior university posts and is the channel of communication with bodies such as the **University Grants Committee** and the **Committee of Vice-Chancellors and Principals**. Vice-Chancellors vary in their style of leadership. It should be noted that in the University of London the Vice-Chancellor is assisted by a **Principal**, who shares the administrative load.

Vice-President of the Committee of Council

A post created in 1856 when the **Education Department** was established. The Vice-President, who was always an MP, acted as spokesman for the Department in the House of Commons, as the **Lord President** did in the House of Lords. The division of functions and responsibilities between the two posts was not clear, but the Vice-President was concerned with the day-to-day running of the Department whilst the Lord President had a variety of responsibilities besides education. Whereas all Lords President were members of the Cabinet, only two of the Vice-Presidents during the period 1856 to 1892 achieved this rank. It is worth noting, however, that the two principal Education Acts of this period, those of 1870 and 1880, are generally associated with the names of the Vice-Presidents who steered them through the Commons – W. E. Forster and A. J. Mundella respectively. The post disappeared in 1900 when it was replaced by the **President of the Board of Education**.

G. SUTHERLAND, *Policy-Making in Elementary Education 1870–1895*, Oxford University Press, 1973

village college

The brainchild of Henry Morris, Secretary of Education for Cambridgeshire from 1922 to 1954, the village college was envisaged as a community centre of a neighbourhood. Its aim was to 'provide for the whole man, and abolish the duality of education and ordinary life'. Thus Morris's first college, opened at Sawston in 1930, contained a school, an adult education centre and a community centre. Morris had hoped that twelve such colleges would be built for the county though in fact only five – at Sawston, Linton, Bottisham, Impington and Bassingbourn – were completed. After the Second World War, this notion was revived in the form of the **community school** or **college**. (*See also* **adult education, community education**.)

H. REÉ, *Educator Extraordinary: The*

Life and Achievement of Henry Morris,
Longman, 1973

viva

Short for 'viva voce'. An **oral examination** most frequently used in connection with the award of **higher degrees**. (*See also* **dissertation, graduate, postgraduate, thesis**.)

vocational guidance

Giving advice to young people and adults about the occupations most suitable to their aptitudes and personality. **Aptitude tests** are extensively used in the diagnosis of special abilities and inclinations. (*See also* **careers guidance, counselling, spatial ability, vocational preparation**.)

L. CLARKE, *The Practice of Vocational Guidance: a critical review of research in the UK,* Department of Employment Careers Service Branch, HMSO, 1980

vocational preparation

The Mansell Report (1979), entitled *A Basis for Choice,* examined the needs of those students wishing to improve their basic skills or to undergo vocational preparation for a full year after the compulsory **school leaving age**. Between 50–60 per cent of the course would be concerned with developing **literacy, numeracy,** social skills and understanding of society: the remainder would provide skills and practices of a particular job. A certificate would be awarded in the form of a **profile**, containing test results and teachers' **assessments**. Unlike the **Certificate of Extended Education** which it was intended to replace, the certificate would not

allow successful students to continue with further academic courses. The report was unclear as to whether courses would take place in schools or colleges of further education. The broader proposals of the **Keohane Report** (1979) for the Certificate of Extended Education possibly provide a more flexible approach. The *Basis for Choice* framework has been incorporated into the **City and Guilds of London** 365 (General) course and has clearly influenced the proposals for the **17+ examination** known as the **Certificate of Pre-Vocational Education** (CPVE) which began to operate from September 1983. (*See also* **New Technical and Vocational Education Initiative, Unified Vocational Preparation, vocational guidance**.)

FURTHER EDUCATION CURRICULUM REVIEW AND DEVELOPMENT UNIT, *A Basis for Choice,* FEU, 1979

voluntary aided school

A type of **voluntary school** where the **governors** control the type of **religious education** given, though parents have the right for their children to be taught according to the **agreed syllabus**. The Church authority concerned appoints two-thirds of its governing body. They are responsible for the capital expenditure on alterations or enlargement of a school, but the **Secretary of State** makes a contribution of 85 per cent towards the expenditure. The **LEA** maintains such schools and pays the salaries of the teachers. Approximately one-half of the total of voluntary schools in England are of this type and some 2,300 of the 5,000 in this category are Church of

England. (*See also* **special agreement school**, **voluntary controlled school**.)

voluntary controlled school

In this type of **voluntary school** the **LEA** is responsible for the total expenditure and maintenance of the building. It appoints one-third of its governing body and the teaching staff, though **governors** are consulted on the appointment of **heads** and on teachers giving denominational religious instruction. Most controlled schools belong to the Church of England. (*See also* **religious education**, **special agreement school**, **voluntary aided school**.)

voluntary school

Originally owned by voluntary bodies, usually religious, but now in receipt of public funds. They may be of three kinds: aided, controlled or **special agreement**, as distinct from those schools which are entirely within the province of an **LEA**. Approximately 30 per cent of **main-** tained schools in England are voluntary schools. (*See also* **religious education**.)

K. BROOKSBANK et al., *County and Voluntary Schools*, 6th edn, Councils and Education Press, 1982

Voluntary Service Overseas (VSO)

An organization established in 1958 and dedicated to assisting development in the world's poor countries. Each year, more than 400 volunteers are sent to work on projects in a number of developing countries. Skilled and/or qualified people such as teachers, doctors, mechanics and engineers between the ages of 20 and 65 and able to spend two years overseas are enlisted. They must be willing to work for local pay only. Not all volunteers necessarily go abroad and some may help to build support for the VSO's work in Britain. The Government provides the majority of the funds for volunteers, supplementing the income raised by VSO.

Waddell Report

In 1970, the **Schools Council** recommended a single system of examining at 16+ and, after some experimenting, repeated its belief in such a system in 1976. Three months later, the new **Secretary of State for Education**, Shirley Williams, agreed that a Steering Committee should be formed to make an intensive study of 'outstanding problems'. The Committee, under the chair-manship of Sir James Waddell, reported in July 1978. Entitled *School Examinations*, the report was published in two parts, the first containing the main recommendations, the second, the reports of two subgroups, the Educational Study Group and the Cost Study Group. The conclusion of the Committee was that a common examination was educationally feasible and could be introduced without causing major difficulties. It recommended that a seven-point grading system should be used, with the first three grades representing the present **O level** pass grades of A, B, and C and the other four representing the present **CSE** grades 2, 3, 4 and 5. An ungraded category was to be included for those who did not gain a certificate. In order to cater for the full range of ability, special papers were recommended in some subjects for pupils of either high or low ability. An important organizational change was that **GCE** and CSE boards were to be regionally grouped, four in England and one in Wales. Schools were not to be limited in their choice of **examining board** by regional considerations. The Waddell Steering Committee recommended an early implementation of these changes, suggesting the first course should start in 1983 with examinations two years later. However, the change of Government shortly afterwards has delayed the proposed starting date. (*See also* **examination boards**, **national criteria**, **sixteen plus examination**.)

Report of the Steering Committee to consider . . . a common system of examining: School Examinations, Part 1, HMSO, 1978

Warnock Report

The Committee of Enquiry into the Education of Handicapped Children and Young People, chaired by Mrs Mary Warnock, was set up in 1973 and reported in 1978. It recommended that the **DES**'s statutory categories should be abolished, that services should be planned on the assumption that one in six children at any time attending schools would need help, and that intellectually impaired children and children with remedial problems should be referred to as children with learning difficul-

ties. Attention was drawn to the need for more parental involvement in children's education and for greater opportunities for young people aged 16–19 years. Special needs were an essential element in initial teacher training and **in-service training** courses. Although the issue of integrating children with special needs into ordinary schools was fundamental to the work of the Warnock Committee, the report did not make specific proposals as to how this should be achieved. A Government White Paper, *Special Needs in Education* (1980), accepted the proposal to abolish categories of handicap as a basis for planning services. This was implemented in the 1981 Education Act, but no concessions were made on the running down of **special schools** or the redistribution of resources to help develop ordinary school-based provision. Special schools were to remain as a bastion of segregated education. (*See also* **integration**, **remedial education**, **special educational needs**.)

L. BARTON and S. TOMLINSON (eds), *Special Education Policy: Practices and Social Issues*, Harper and Row, 1982

T. BOOTH and J. STATHAM (eds), *The Nature of Special Education*, Croom Helm and Open University Press, 1982

Special Educational Needs. Report of the Committee of Enquiry into the Education of Handicapped Children and Young People, HMSO, 1978

Weaver Report

A study group headed by T. R. Weaver, Deputy Secretary at the **DES**, published its report, *The Government of Colleges of Education*, in 1966. The tone is set at the beginning of Chapter 2: 'Our purpose throughout has been to enable the colleges to take full academic responsibility and to exercise it in an atmosphere of freedom, unhindered by unnecessary restrictions' (p. 3). One of its major recommendations was that each college should have an academic board, responsible for academic work, selection of students and other college business. The board was to be responsible for electing members of the teaching staff, other than the Principal, who would serve on the governing body. Legislation was also introduced, requiring **LEAs** to make **instruments of government** for the constitution of college governing bodies; up to this time, many had been sub-committees of LEA committees.

J. D. BROWNE, *Teachers of Teachers. A History of the Association of Teachers in Colleges and Departments of Education*, Hodder and Stoughton, 1979

DES, *Report of the Study Group on The Government of Colleges of Education*, HMSO, 1966

Welsh circulating schools

First established in Wales by the Rev. Griffith Jones in the 1730s, these were free schools for the poor, where both children and adults learnt to read the Bible in the vernacular. They were instructed in the principles of religion through the method of question and answer. Travelling schoolmasters were employed for the purpose, staying at least three months in one place before moving on. They were financed by charitable contributions. (*See also* **free education**.)

M. CLEMENT, 'The Welsh Circulating Schools', in J. L. WILLIAMS and G. R. WILLIAMS (eds), *The History of Education in Wales*, Vol. 1, Christopher Davies, Swansea, 1978

Welsh Office

Up to 1970, the **DES** was responsible for education in Wales. In that year, primary and secondary education was transferred to the Education Department of the Welsh Office, under the Secretary of State for Wales. Eight years later non-university institutions and public libraries in the Principality were also transferred. The Department is headed by an Under Secretary. (*See also* **Department of Education Northern Ireland**, **Gittins Report**, **Scottish Education Department**.)

White Paper

The name given to the majority of Government discussion documents, derived from the colour of the publication. A White Paper describes official policy towards an issue and is often a prelude to legislation, e.g. the White Paper on Educational Reconstruction in 1943 was followed by the 1944 Education Act. (*See also* **Butler Act**, **Parliamentary Papers**.)

William Tyndale School

An Islington, London, primary school which became the subject of an official inquiry by the **ILEA** in July 1975 (*see also* **Auld Report**). This followed the widespread publicity which had been given to the open conflicts between teachers, managers and parents of pupils at the school, arising out of the introduction of a radical change in teaching and organization. The head of the junior department, Mr Terry Ellis, and a number of his staff favoured a less formal teaching system with the children having a large say in what they were taught. The implementation of this system caused divisions both within and outside the school. Several important issues emerged out of the inquiry, not all of which have yet been satisfactorily resolved. These concern the definition of powers and responsibilities of **LEAs** and **governors** and how these should be exercised in a case of conflict over the conduct and **curriculum** of a school, the role of the **DES** in such an affair, the position of local inspectors where the school is in the public eye and the creation of a machinery for inquiry less cumbersome, costly and lengthy than in the Tyndale case. (*See also* **accountability**.)

T. ELLIS et al., *William Tyndale: the Teachers' Story*, Writers and Readers Publishing Co-operative, 1976

J. GRETTON and M. JACKSON, *William Tyndale: collapse of a school – or a system?* Allen and Unwin, 1976

women's studies

Courses at any level of education (**secondary school**, **undergraduate** or **postgraduate**) which are intended to emphasize the contributions made, for example, in history, English literature or philosophy, by women. In this respect, they are similar to **black studies** or working class studies. (*See also* **girls' education**.)

M. RENDEL and D. BARKER, 'Women's Studies' in D. W. PIPER (ed.), *The Changing University*, NFER, 1977

Woodard schools

Founded by the Rev. Nathaniel Woodard in the mid-nineteenth century, the schools were to provide a good, cheap, Christian education for the middle and upper working classes. The money for the schools was raised by private subscription. The first, at Shoreham, Sussex, in 1848, was followed by Hurstpierpoint in 1850 and Lancing in 1857. Woodard anticipated the **Taunton Commission** by creating three grades of schools, according to the social rank of the pupils. (*See also* **grade**, **proprietary school**.)

B. HEENEY, *Mission to the Middle Classes. The Woodard Schools 1848–1891*, SPCK, 1969

workcards

Cards, often devised by the teacher, giving information on a particular subject or topic, with follow-up work arising out of it. Workcards are used as a means of individualizing instruction, as, for example, in a **mixed ability** setting. (*See also* **individual learning**.)

Workers' Educational Association (WEA)

Founded in 1903 by Albert Mansbridge as a means of developing the intellectual capacity of working men, the WEA was an alliance between the universities, trades unions and the Co-operative Society. Up to 1945 the Association provided courses for many thousands of workers and was closely associated with the Labour Party. After the war, the WEA became identified with middle-class leisure pursuits, but many of its activities are now concerned with its original purpose; for example, **day release** courses for shop stewards in aspects of trade unionism run in association with the TUC are offered in the majority of the Association's 21 districts. How far the WEA should cater for a broader spectrum of the working–class population is still being debated within the movement. (*See also* **adult education**.)

M. STOCKS, *The WEA: The First Fifty Years*, Allen and Unwin, 1953

Work Experience Courses (WEC)

Designed to give opportunities for unemployed young people in work experience, these schemes formed part of the **Manpower Services Commission's Youth Opportunities Programme**. The largest was Work Experience on Employer's Premises (WEEP); the others were Project-Based Work Experience, Training Workshops and Community Service.

workhouse school

The first report of the Poor Law Commissioners for 1834 revealed the neglect of the 90,000 children in workhouses. The majority received little or no instruction and lived in a wholly unsuitable environment. Dr Kay (later Sir James Kay-Shuttleworth), then an Assistant Poor Law Commissioner, recommended that small workhouse schools be replaced by large district

schools where children would be taught by a qualified staff outside the workhouse. In 1838, Kay carried out his famous experiment in the institution at Norwood, South London, introducing **pupil teachers** to a liberal curriculum. From 1844, the Poor Law Commissioners provided for the appointment of a paid schoolmaster in workhouses.

F. SMITH, *The Life and Work of Sir James Kay-Shuttleworth*, Murray, 1923

Work Preparation Courses (WPC)

One of the two main schemes under the **Manpower Services Commission's Youth Opportunities Programme** – the other was the **Work Experience Courses** – for assisting unemployed youths of 16–18. These courses, which were skills-based, were of three kinds: Employment Induction, Short Industrial Training and Work Introduction. They were based either in **colleges of further education** or in workplaces.

World Education Fellowship
See **New Education Fellowship**.

Y

Yellow Book

A confidential report on **standards** in education compiled by the **DES** in 1975 for the then Prime Minister, Mr James Callaghan. It voiced many criticisms which were reflected in the Prime Minister's **Ruskin College** speech in the following year and was

the basis for the subsequent **'Great Debate'**.

Youth Opportunities Programme (YOP)

The **Manpower Services Commission** organized a number of schemes under the **Youth Opportunities Programme** for 16- to 19-year-olds who were unemployed. The two main schemes were the **Work Preparation** and **Work Experience**

Courses. Participants could spend up to a year on such courses and receive a training allowance. Approximately a quarter of a million youths took part in this scheme in 1981–2. It was replaced, in September 1983, by the **Youth Training Scheme**.

FURTHER EDUCATION CURRICULUM RE-VIEW AND DEVELOPMENT UNIT, *Supporting YOP*, FEU, 1977

Youth Service

The 1944 Education Act placed responsibility upon **LEAs** to provide adequate facilities for recreation, social and cultural activities for young people. In the same year, the **McNair Report** made recommendations for the supply, recruitment and training of youth leaders. The **Albemarle Report**, *The Youth Service in England and Wales*, published in 1960, made it clear that the Service was in a depressed state and advised the Minister to develop a ten-year plan. Youth Officers are appointed to develop the Service. Local authorities differ in the facilities they provide, but these may consist of a range of premises for youth centres and classes in, for example, arts and crafts, as well as boating centres and discos. Youth Officers are responsible for the employment and training of youth leaders and 'detached' youth workers. LEAs receive advice from local youth committees which include amongst their membership teachers, voluntary organizations, church representatives and local authority members. Grants are also made by local authorities to voluntary youth organizations. The **Thompson Report** (1982), the latest in the line of reports on this subject,

once again pointed out the inadequacies of the present Service.

Youth Training Scheme (YTS)

In December 1981, a Government White Paper entitled *A New Training Initiative: A Programme for Action* was issued. Its main recommendation was that the **Youth Opportunities Programme** should be replaced by a Youth Training Scheme (YTS) representing a different philosophy. Whereas the YOP was concerned with giving youths appropriate skills, the YTS looks to a more radical reform of training as a whole, covering employed as well as unemployed young people. The Government began the programme in September 1983. It guaranteed a year's foundation training for all 16- and 17-year-old school leavers consisting of 39 weeks' industrial experience and 13 weeks' off-the job training or **further education**. Some 460,000 people are catered for by the scheme, which provides for, in addition to work experience, the fostering of basic skills, the provision of occupationally-relevant education and guidance, and **counselling**. The cost of the YTS in 1983–4 is estimated at £1 billion. The **Manpower Services Commission** (MSC) hopes that two-thirds of the places will be offered by industry and voluntary bodies, and the other one-third by colleges, who will make arrangements for work experience. (*See also* **Unified Vocational Preparation**.)

MANPOWER SERVICES COMMISSION, *Past Imperfect, Present Indicative: Youth Training Scheme*, 1983

Z

Z-scores

A form of **standardized** score on a test which is obtained by expressing the raw score (actual score) in terms of the relationship of that score to the mean score (the difference is express-ed in units of the **standard deviation**). For example, a raw score that was above the mean score by one standard deviation would have a Z-score of $+1$; a score which was 2 standard deviations superior would have a Z-score of $+2$; and so on. Raw scores below average would have a minus Z-score, similarly expressed in terms of units of standard deviation.

Educational acronyms

ACACE	Advisory Council for Adult and Continuing Education
ACC	Association of County Councils
ACE	Advisory Centre for Education
ACSET	Advisory Committee on the Supply and Education of Teachers
ACSTT	Advisory Council on the Supply and Training of Teachers
AEC	Association of Education Committees
AEP	Association of Educational Psychologists
AFE	Advanced Further Education
ALBSU	Adult Literacy and Basic Skills Unit
AMA	Association of Metropolitan Authorities
AMMA	Assistant Masters and Mistresses Association
APLET	Association for Programmed Learning and Educational Technology
APR	Age Participation Rate
APT	Association of Polytechnic Teachers
APU	Assessment of Performance Unit
ARELS	Association of Recognized English Language Schools
ASE	Association for Science Education
ATD	Art Teachers Diploma/Certificate
ATO	Area Training Organization
ATSS	Association for the Teaching of the Social Sciences
AUT	Association of University Teachers
AVA	Audio-Visual Aids
BA	Bachelor of Arts
BAAS	British Association for the Advancement of Science
BACIE	British Association for Commercial and Industrial Education
BEC	Business Education Council
BEd	Bachelor of Education
BEI	British Education Index
BEMAS	British Educational Management and Administration Society
BERA	British Educational Research Association
BH	Bachelor of Humanities

BL	British Library
BPS	British Psychological Society
BSC	Bachelor of Science
CACE	Central Advisory Council for Education
CAL	Computer Assisted Learning
CAMOL	Computer Assisted Management of Learning
CAP	Continuing Application Procedure (for university entrance)
CARE	Centre for Applied Research in Education
CASE	Confederation for the Advancement of State Education
CAT	College of Advanced Technology
CBTE	Competency Based Teacher Education
CCETSW	Central Council for Education and Training in Social Work
CCTV	Closed-Circuit Television
CDP	Committee of Directors of Polytechnics
CEE	Certificate of Extended Education
CEO	Chief Education Officer
CERI	Centre for Educational Research and Innovation
Cert Ed	Certificate in Education
CET	Council for Educational Technology
CEWC	Council for Education in World Citizenship
CGLI	City and Guilds of London Institute
CLEA	Council of Local Education Authorities
CNAA	Council for National Academic Awards
CPVE	Certificate of Pre-Vocational Education
CRAC	Careers Research and Advisory Centre
CRE	Commission for Racial Equality
CSE	Certificate of Secondary Education
CSV	Community Service Volunteers
CVCP	Committee of Vice-Chancellors and Principals of the Universities of the United Kingdom
DES	Department of Education and Science
DIpHE	Diploma in Higher Education
DOI	Department of Industry
DSIR	Department of Scientific and Industrial Research
EDU	Educational Disadvantage Unit
EEC	European Economic Community
EFL	English as a Foreign Language
EFVA	Educational Foundation for Visual Aids
EIS	Educational Institute of Scotland
EOC	Equal Opportunities Commission
EPA	Educational Priority Area

EPC	Educational Publishers Council
ERIC	Education Resources Information Centre
ESL	English as a Second Language
ESN	Educationally Subnormal
FE	Further Education
FEU	Further Education Curriculum Review and Development Unit
FTE	Full-time Equivalent
GCE	General Certificate of Education
GCSE	General Certificate of Secondary Education
GPDST	Girls' Public Day School Trust
GRE	Grant Related Expenditure
GTTR	Graduate Teacher Training Registry
GYSL	Geography for the Young School Leaver Project
HCP	Humanities Curriculum Project
HE	Higher Education
HMC	Headmasters' Conference
HMI	Her (His) Majesty's Inspectorate
HMSO	Her (His) Majesty's Stationery Office
HNC	Higher National Certificate
HND	Higher National Diploma
IAPS	Incorporated Association of Preparatory Schools
IB	International Baccalaureate
IBA	Independent Broadcasting Authority
IEA	International Association for the Evaluation of Educational Achievement
IIEP	International Institute for Educational Planning
ILEA	Inner London Education Authority
INSET	In-Service Education of Teachers
INSTEP	In-Service Training and Education Panel
IQ	Intelligence Quotient
ISCO	Independent Schools Careers Organization
ISIS	Independent Schools Information Service
i.t.a.	Initial Teaching Alphabet
ITB	Industrial Training Board
JACT	Joint Association of Classical Teachers
JMB	Joint Matriculation Board
LA	Library Association
LEA	Local Education Authority
MACOS	Man – A Course of Study
MEP	Microelectronics Education Programme
MLA	Modern Language Association
MRC	Medical Research Council

MSC	Manpower Services Commission
MSC	Master of Science
NACAE	National Advisory Council on Adult Education
NACEIC	National Advisory Council on Education for Industry and Commerce
NACGT	National Association of Careers and Guidance Teachers
NACSTT	National Advisory Council on the Supply and Training of Teachers
NAGC	National Association for Gifted Children
NAGM	National Association of Governors and Managers
NAHT	National Association of Head Teachers
NAIEA	National Association of Inspectors and Educational Advisers
NALGO	National and Local Government Officers Association
NAME	National Association for Multiracial Education
NAPCE	National Association for Pastoral Care in Education
NARE	National Association for Remedial Education
NAS/UWT	National Association of Schoolmasters/Union of Women Teachers
NATE	National Association for the Teaching of English
NATFHE	National Association of Teachers in Further and Higher Education
NBL	National Book League
NCAVAE	National Committee on Audio-Visual Aids in Education
NCB	National Children's Bureau
NCDS	National Child Development Study
NCES	National Council for Educational Standards
NCET	National Council for Educational Technology for the United Kingdom
NCPTA	National Confederation of Parent-Teacher Associations
NFER	National Foundation for Educational Research in England and Wales
NIACE	National Institute of Adult Continuing Education
NNEB	National Nursery Examination Board
NTI	New Training Initiative
NUS	National Union of Students
NUSS	National Union of School Students
NUT	National Union of Teachers
ODA	Overseas Development Agency
OECD	Organization for Economic Co-operation and Development
ONC	Ordinary National Certificate
OND	Ordinary National Diploma

ORACLE	Observational Research and Classroom Learning Evaluation
OU	Open University
PAT	Professional Association of Teachers
PGCE	Postgraduate Certificate of Education
PhD	Doctor of Philosophy
PNEU	Parents' National Education Union
PPA	Pre-School Playgroups Association
PRISE	Programme for Reform in Secondary Education
PTA	Parent Teacher Association
PTR	Pupil:Teacher Ratio
QTS	Qualified Teacher Status
QUANGO	Quasi-Autonomous Non-Governmental Organization
RAC	Regional Advisory Council
RSA	Royal Society of Arts
RSG	Rate Support Grant
RSI	Regional Staff Inspector
SAFARI	Success and Failure and Recent Innovation
SAGSET	Society for Academic Gaming and Simulation in Education and Training
SATROS	Science and Technology Regional Organizations
SCE	Scottish Certificate in Education
SCISP	Schools Council Integrated Science Project
SCOTBEC	Scottish Business Education Council
SCOTEC	Scottish Technician Education Council
SCRAC	Standing Conference of Regional Advisory Councils
SCUE	Standing Conference on University Entrance
SED	Scottish Education Department
SEO	Society of Education Officers
SHA	Secondary Heads Association
SLA	School Library Association
SMP	School Mathematics Project
SRC	Science Research Council
SRHE	Society for Research into Higher Education
SSEC	Secondary School Examinations Council
SSR	Staff: Student Ratio
SSRC (ESRC)	Social Science Research Council (now Economic and Social Research Council)
STEP	Science Teacher Education Project
STOPP	•Society of Teachers Opposed to Physical Punishment
TEAC	Teacher Education Advisory Committee
TEC	Technician Education Council
TEFL	Teaching English as a Foreign Language

TOPS	Training Opportunities Scheme
TUC	Trades Union Congress
TVEI (NTVEI)	Technical and Vocational Education Initiative (now New Technical and Vocational Education Initiative)
UCCA	Universities Central Council on Admissions
UCET	Universities Council for the Education of Teachers
UDE	University Department of Education
UGC	University Grants Committee
UKRA	United Kingdom Reading Association
UNESCO	United Nations Educational, Scientific and Cultural Organization
UVP	Unified Vocational Preparation
VOC	Certificate of Vocational Preparation
VSO	Voluntary Service Overseas
WEA	Workers' Educational Association
WEC	Work Experience Courses
WEEP	Work Experience on Employers' Premises
WEF	World Education Fellowship
WPC	Work Preparation Courses
YOP	Youth Opportunities Programme
YTS	Youth Training Scheme

List of useful reference books

I. G. ANDERSON (ed.), *Councils, Committees and Boards. A handbook of advisory, consultative, executive and similar bodies in British public life*, CBD Research, Beckenham, 4th edn, 1980

I. G. ANDERSON (ed.), *Directory of European Associations*, CBD Research, Beckenham, 3rd edn, 1981

M. ARGLES, *British Government Publications in Education During the Nineteenth Century. Guide to Sources in the History of Education, No. 1*, History of Education Society, 1971

M. ARGLES and J. E. VAUGHAN, *British Government Publications Concerning Education During the Twentieth Century. Guide to Sources in the History of Education, No. 7*, History of Education Society, 4th edn, 1982

BRITISH COUNCIL, *British Educational Reference Books*, 3rd edn, 1982

British Qualifications. A comprehensive guide to educational, technical, professional and academic qualifications in Britain, Kogan Page, 13th edn, 1982

J. F. BURNET, *Public and Preparatory Schools Year Book*, A. and C. Black, 1982, 92nd year

CAREERS RESEARCH AND ADVISORY CENTRE, *Degree Course Guides: Guide to first degree courses in the United Kingdom*, Hobsons Press, Cambridge, 1982

CAREERS RESEARCH AND ADVISORY CENTRE, *Directory of Further Education. Guide to courses in United Kingdom polytechnics and colleges*, Hobsons Press, Cambridge, 1982

CENTRAL OFFICE OF INFORMATION, *Education in Britain*, HMSO, 1982

CENTRAL OFFICE OF INFORMATION, *Schools in Britain*, Pamphlet No. 156, HMSO, 1978

CHARTERED INSTITUTE OF PUBLIC FINANCE AND ACCOUNTANCY, Financial Information Service, *Education*, Vol. 20, 1976 and supplements

A. CHRISTOPHERS, *An Index to Nineteenth Century British Educational Biography*, Education Libraries Bulletin 10, University of London Institute of Education Library, 1965

DEPARTMENT OF EDUCATION AND SCIENCE, *The Department of Education and Science: A Brief Guide*, HMSO, 1982

DEPARTMENT OF EDUCATION AND SCIENCE, *The Educational System of England and Wales*, HMSO, 1982

The Education Authorities Directory and Annual, School Government Publishing Company, 1983

The Education Year Book, Longman, 1983

P. and G. FORD, *Select List of British Parliamentary Papers, 1833–99*, Blackwell, 1953

P. and G. FORD, *A Breviate of Parliamentary Papers, 1900–16*, Blackwell, 1957

G. P. HENDERSON and S. P. A. HENDERSON (eds), *Directory of British Associations and Associations in Ireland*, CBD Research, Beckenham, 7th edn, 1982

M. HUMBY, *A Guide to the Literature of Education*, University of London Institute of Education Library, 3rd edn, 1975

S. MACLURE, *Educational Documents, England and Wales 1816 to the present day*, Methuen, 4th edn, 1979

J. V. MARDER (ed.), *Acronyms and Initialisms in England. A Handlist*, Librarians of Institutes and Schools of Education, 1981

J. G. OLLE, *An Introduction to British Government Publications*, Association of Assistant Librarians, 2nd edn, 1973

S. RICHARD (ed.), *British Government Publications. Vol. 1, An index to Chairmen of Committees and Commissions of Inquiry, 1800–99* (1982); *Vol. 2, An index to Chairmen and authors, 1900–40* (1974); *Vol. 3, 1941–88* (1982)

G. TAYLOR and J. B. SAUNDERS, *The Law of Education*, Butterworths, 1976 and supplements

J. E. VAUGHAN and M. ARGLES, *British Government Publications Concerning Education: An Introductory Guide*, University of Liverpool School of Education, 3rd edn, 1969

The World of Learning, 1982–3, Europa Publications, 33rd edn, 1982

Year Book of Adult Education, 1982–83, National Institute of Adult Education, 1982

'Ministers of Education'

Vice-Presidents of the Committee of Council on Education

W. F. Cowper	2 Feb. 1857–5 Apr. 1858
C. B. Adderley	6 Apr. 1858–5 July 1859
Robert Lowe	6 July 1859–25 Apr. 1864
H. A. Bruce	26 Apr. 1864–25 July 1866
T. L. Corry	26 July 1866–18 March 1867
Lord Robert Montagu	19 March 1867–8 Dec. 1868
W. E. Forster	9 Dec. 1868–1 March 1874
Viscount Sandon	2 March 1874–3 Apr. 1878
Lord George Hamilton	4 Apr. 1878–2 May 1880
A. J. Mundella	3 May 1880–23 June 1885
Hon. E. Stanhope	24 June 1885–16 Sep. 1885
Sir Henry Holland	17 Sep. 1885–5 Feb. 1886
Sir Lyon Playfair	6 Feb. 1886–2 Aug. 1886
Sir Henry Holland	3 Aug. 1886–24 Jan. 1887
Sir William Hart Dyke	25 Jan. 1887–17 Aug. 1892
A. H. D. Acland	18 Aug. 1892–3 July 1895
Sir John Gorst	4 July 1895–8 Aug. 1902

Presidents of the Board of Education

Duke of Devonshire	1 Jan. 1900–7 Aug. 1902
Marquess of Londonderry	8 Aug. 1902–9 Dec. 1905
Augustine Birrell	10 Dec. 1905–22 Jan. 1907
Reginald McKenna	23 Jan. 1907–11 Apr. 1908
Walter Runciman	12 Apr. 1908–22 Oct. 1911
Joseph Pease	23 Oct. 1911–24 May 1915
Arthur Henderson	25 May 1915–17 Aug. 1916
Marquess of Crewe	18 Aug. 1916–9 Dec. 1916
Herbert Fisher	10 Dec. 1916–23 Oct. 1922
Edward Wood (later Lord Irwin)	24 Oct. 1922–21 Jan. 1924
C. (later Sir Charles) Trevelyan	22 Jan. 1924–5 Nov. 1924
Lord Eustace Percy	6 Nov. 1924–6 June 1929
Sir Charles Trevelyan	7 June 1929–1 March 1931
Hastings Lees-Smith	2 March 1931–24 Aug. 1931
Sir David Maclean	25 Aug–14 June 1932

Lord Irwin (later Viscount Halifax) 15 June 1932–6 June 1935
Oliver Stanley   7 June 1935–27 May 1937
Earl Stanhope   28 May 1937–26 Oct. 1938
Earl De La Warr   27 Oct. 1938–2 Apr. 1940
Herewald Ramsbotham   3 Apr. 1940–19 July 1941
R. A. Butler   20 July 1941–2 Aug. 1944

Ministers of Education

R. A. Butler   3 Aug. 1944–24 May 1945
Richard Law   25 May 1945–2 Aug. 1945
Ellen Wilkinson   3 Aug. 1945–9 Feb. 1947
George Tomlinson   10 Feb. 1947–1 Nov. 1951
Florence Horsbrugh   2 Nov. 1951–17 Oct. 1954
Sir David Eccles.   18 Oct. 1954–13 Jan. 1957
Viscount Hailsham   14 Jan. 1957–16 Sep. 1957
Geoffrey Lloyd   17 Sep. 1957–13 Oct. 1959
Sir David Eccles   14 Oct. 1959–16 July 1962
Sir Edward Boyle   17 July 1962–31 March 1964

Secretaries of State

Quintin Hogg (Viscount Hailsham) 1 Apr. 1964–16 Oct. 1964
Michael Stewart   19 Oct. 1964–23 Jan. 1965
Anthony Crosland   24 Jan. 1965–30 Aug. 1967
Patrick Gordon-Walker   31 Aug. 1967–5 Apr. 1968
Edward Short   8 Apr. 1968–19 June 1970
Margaret Thatcher   20 June 1970–4 March 1974
Reginald Prentice   5 March 1974–10 June 1975
Frederick Mulley   11 June 1975–10 Sep. 1976
Shirley Williams   11 Sep. 1976–7 May 1979
Mark Carlisle   8 May 1979–13 Sep. 1981
Sir Keith Joseph   14 Sep. 1981–